AGRIBUSINESS MANAGEMENT and ENTREPRENEURSHIP

Third Edition

AGRIBUSINESS
MANAGEMENT

MICHAEL E. NEWMAN

Assistant Professor
Department of Agricultural Education
    and Experimental Statistics
Mississippi State University

AND

ENTREPRENEURSHIP

WALTER J. WILLS

Professor Emeritus
Agribusiness Economics Department
School of Agriculture
Southern Illinois University

Interstate Publishers, Inc.
Danville, Illinois

Cover Photo Credits:

Upper left courtesy of Office of Agricultural Communications, Mississippi State University

Upper right and bottom left courtesy of M. Thomas

Lower Right courtesy of Brendan Marshall, Stock Land FS

Order from

Interstate Publishers, Inc.
510 North Vermilion Street
P.O. Box 50
Danville, IL 61834-0050
Phone: (800)843-4774
FAX: (217)446-9706

Library of Congress Catalog Card No. 93-78223

ISBN 0-8134-2955-2

Preface

As agribusiness has become an integral part of the Agricultural Education curriculum, the need has arisen for an introductory text in the areas of agribusiness management, entrepreneurship, and computer applications. This book has been designed with this purpose in mind.

Agribusiness Management and Entrepreneurship is intended to fill the need for a basic textbook covering the planning, organizing, and managing of an operation; as well as provide a comprehensive source for those who wish to consider a business from the ownership point of view, specifically as it relates to the vast area of agribusiness.

Management and operational information is applicable to both owners and managers of an enterprise. For a unit of study on computer applications, Section III should be used.

Agribusiness Management and Entrepreneurship helps to identify and clarify some of the problems facing managers and/or owners. This book also provides prospective employees with a better understanding of their responsibilities when taking a job. Agribusinesses will find it useful in personal skill development, too.

The principles of business, including supply and demand, planning and organizing, financing, operating, marketing through wholesaling and retailing, distribution, and basic computer applications, are covered. The book is divided into three sections - Business Management, Operations Management, and Computer Applications in Management. Objectives are presented at the beginning of each chapter. Terms to know are italicized within the chapters and defined in a glossary at the end of the book. Chapter review questions follow each chapter.

Topics for discussion, answers to review questions, and other helpful materials are available in the Teacher's Manual. They are important to the effectiveness of this book as a teaching aid. The students should develop answers to the problems and/or carry out the activities described. The work experience they obtain from the businesses in which they are employed will provide them with much resource material. It would be helpful to allocate one or more extra class periods to the discussion of this information.

Acknowledgements

The authors would like to express their grateful appreciation to the professionals who reviewed the material in their areas of expertise and for their many contributions to this text.

Clay Christensen
Specialist, Agricultural Education
Salt Lake City, UT

Joseph Daughhetee, CPA
Illinois Society of CPAs Agribusiness Committee Member
Daughhetee & Associates PC

John Giesemann
Director, Computer Services
Mississippi Cooperative Extension Service

Richard Hawkins
Human Resource Manager
Refrigeration Products Division
Heatcraft, Inc.

Tom Heffernan
Pleasanton HS
Pleasanton, TX

Patrick M. Henderson
Breckinridge HS
Harned, KY

Robert C. Hofmann, Attorney
Dougherty, Hofmann, & Goodwin PC

Tom Hurst
Vicksburg Agriscience
Vicksburg, MI

Brendan Marshall
Certified Crop Specialist
Stock Land FS, Inc.

Elizabeth Morgan
Presque Isle HS
Presque Isle, ME

Patrick J. O'Shaughnessy
Vice President - Commercial Lending
First Midwest Bank

Rodney Pearson
Associate Professor of Information Systems
Mississippi State University

Ed Settle
Biggersville HS
Biggersville, MS

Terry Smith
Certified Insurance Counselor
Life Underwriters Training Council Fellow
Wolford-Cannon Hoecker Insurance

Contents

SECTION III - COMPUTER APPLICATIONS IN MANAGEMENT

Chapter I

BASIC CONCEPTS OF AGRIBUSINESS MANAGEMENT

An individual who is well versed in the basic concepts of business management lays a solid foundation for a successful agribusiness. Mastering these concepts may not be the most exciting part of running a business; however, they are the building blocks upon which the manager can develop further knowledge and abilities. These concepts provide the framework which supports a good management style and philosophy.

OBJECTIVES

1. Describe the recognized organizational structures for business
2. Identify the common characteristics of each of the organizational structures
3. Distinguish between a partnership, limited partnership, and joint venture
4. Identify the advantages and disadvantages of the ways of doing business
5. Distinguish between a regular corporation and a sub-chapter S corporation
6. Compare and contrast how a cooperative differs from a regular corporation
7. Define *management*
8. Discuss the atmosphere in which business activity occurs
9. Describe the five major areas of management
10. Know the types, what's involved, and what must be handled in planning
11. Describe the reasons for business goals and mission statement

THREE WAYS OF DOING BUSINESS

Within the economic system known as *capitalism*, there are three generally recognized organizational structures for business: *sole proprietorship*, *partnership*, and *corporation*. Table 1-1 contains a summary of the differences and similarities of the three ways of doing business.

SOLE PROPRIETORSHIP

In the sole proprietorship an individual decides to go into business; makes the arrangements for *capital*; makes the decisions; and, depending upon the size and nature of the operation, may or may not have other employees. After paying the necessary costs of doing business, any *earnings* that remain may be used as the individual chooses. *Profits* of the business are taxed on the individual's tax return. The *liability* of the business is the responsibility of the individual.

TERMS

accounting	debts	objective
agribusiness	delegation	organizing
Board of Directors	earnings	partnership
capital	economics	patronage
capitalism	economy	planning
cash flow	facilities	preferred stock
Chief Executive Officer	forecasting	profits
Chief Operational Officer	general manager	realistic
	goals	shareholders
common stock	inventory	silent partner
company policy	joint venture	sole proprietorship
consumers	legal compliance	stock
cooperative	liability	stockholder
corporation	limited partnership	structure
criteria	management	

Figure 1-1. A livestock hauling operation and a daily hog and cattle market are the combination of two agribusinesses. (Courtesy, M. Thomas)

PARTNERSHIP

In a partnership two or more individuals agree to carry out certain business activities. It is generally recommended that in a partnership each of the parties involved agrees, in writing, upon what contributions each shall make to the operation, how decisions will be made, and how earnings will be distributed. A partnership is normally dissolved upon the death of a partner. Each partner is responsible for partnership liabilities. A *limited partnership* (*silent partner*) is a special form of partnership where one or more of the partners are only investors, and do not participate in the management of the business. A *joint venture*, which is similar to a partnership, is usually a commingling of capital and management for a single undertaking over a short period of time.

CORPORATION

There are two types of corporations: (1) the investor-oriented corporation and (2) the cooperative corporation. Corporations are chartered under the appropriate state or federal law. Capital is provided by the *shareholders*. These shareholders in turn elect a *board of directors*, who

Figure 1-2. John and Harold formed a partnership and started a new business utilizing skills already attained when the company they worked for went out of business. (Courtesy, M. Thomas)

represent them in making company policy and in hiring and terminating top *management*, usually a *general manager* or *chief executive officer* and *chief operational officer.*

These shareholders provide the risk capital and share the earnings of the corporation, but unlike in the sole proprietorship and the partnership, the corporation *stockholders* have limited liability. That is, they are not individually and personally liable for *debts* of the business.

Corporations may be organized as a regular corporation or as a sub-chapter S corporation. A sub-chapter S corporation is limited to one class of *stock*, may have no more than 35 shareholders, and business profits are taxed on the individual's tax return. Regular corporations may have different classes of stock (usually *common stock* and *preferred stock*), an unlimited number of shareholders, and the business profits are taxed as a single entity with the individual shareholders only taxed on dividends received.

Investor-oriented corporations have few restrictions as to who may own stock. In contrast, the *cooperative* corporation usually limits stock ownership to users of the cooperative, thus, the cooperative shareholders provide the risk capital and are the customers.

There are three cooperative principles:

1. Limited returns on invested capital

2. Democratic control (frequently interpreted as one-person, one-vote)

3. Distribution of earnings to members on the basis of use (*patronage*)

In the U.S., cooperatives have played a major role in providing farm inputs (credit, electricity, feed, seed, fertilizer, petroleum products, etc.) and in marketing and processing farm products (cotton, rice, livestock, milk, feed and food grains, oil crops, fruits, vegetables, poultry, etc.).

For the larger businesses there are certain types of policy matters in which the stockholders make the *company policy* decisions. There are many other types of decisions, particularly those which apply to general policy, that are made by the directors who are elected by the stockholders. It is the responsibility of management and staff to implement these policies within the framework prescribed by the directors.

There are many different levels of management, ranging from the president of a large business, who may have a large number of employees providing information, to two employees together, one of whom is responsible for reporting their activities to the next higher person in the organization.

Figure 1-3. A credit union is a common form of cooperative found in many communities. (Courtesy, M. Thomas)

Table
METHODS OF DOING BUSINESS

Features Compared	Sole Proprietorship	Partnership
1. Who uses the services?	Non-owner customers	Generally non-owner customers
2. Who owns the business?	The individual	The partners
3. Who votes?	None necessary	The partners
4. How is voting done?	None necessary	Usually by partners share in capital
5. Who determines policies?	The individual	The partners
6. Are returns on ownership capital limited?	No	No
7. Who gets the operating proceeds?	The individual	The partners in proportion to interest in business

[1]Source: Cooperatives in Agri-Business, Ed. Cir. 33, FCS, USDA, p. 6.

[2]Basic cooperative principles.

WHAT IS AGRIBUSINESS MANAGEMENT?

Agribusiness is a term used to indicate:

1. Those businesses that sell items to farmers for production, such as feed, seed, fertilizer, machinery, etc.

2. Those businesses that provide services to the agricultural sector of the economy, such as credit, insurance, electricity, etc.

3. Those businesses engaged in marketing, transporting, processing, and distributing agricultural products

Taken as a whole, agribusiness is a major part of the U.S. *economy*. In recent years, farm income from the sale of agricultural products has been over $100 billion. Farmers spent over $75 billion for production supplies. In the food sector of agriculture alone farm income from sales exceeded $55 billion, but *consumers* spent over $160 billion for this food. The data illustrate the importance of the agribusiness sector of the economy and

1-1
UNDER PRIVATE ENTERPRISE[1]

Corporation	
Investor-Oriented	**Cooperative**
Generally non-owner customers	Chiefly the owner-patrons
The stockholders	The member-patrons
Common stockholders	The member-patrons[2]
By shares of common stock	Usually one-member, one vote
Common stockholders and directors	The member-patrons and directors
No	Yes—8% or less (usually less, if any)[2]
The stockholders in proportion to stock held	The patrons on a patronage basis[2]

Figure 1-4. Above is an example of three agribusinesses at a single location.
(Courtesy, M. Thomas)

emphasize that there are many types of agriculturally related job opportunities.

An understanding of some of the basic problems in business management will assist those people who choose agribusiness as a career. Managers must know the technical aspects of agriculture and how technological change at the farm level affects the business. They must also know the factors related to successful business operations, including the importance of organization and working with people. The tools of management also include areas such as *economics, accounting,* production technology, marketing skill, and *legal compliance.*

MANAGEMENT

Different people define management in different ways. The definition of management used in this text combines the most common forms of management definitions currently used.

Management is the responsibility of a person to make decisions, organize resources to implement decisions, monitor the implementation of decisions, and evaluate the effects of decisions on the overall success of a business.

Managers must provide leadership in making decisions that affect the business. This process consists of determining and defining the problem, gathering information regarding the problem, analyzing the alternatives, making the decision, and setting up a means of evaluating the results of the decision.

A very important function of management is placing resources in the best position to accomplish the goals of the business. Managers must efficiently organize the use of people, facilities, capital, and ideas. Relationships with people are very important to ensure that employees are motivated to carry out their duties to the best of their abilities.

Once resources have been committed to a particular operation, they are not available for some other activity. Many resources are so specialized that they have few or no alternative uses. For example, a feed mill has few capabilities other than to grind and mix feed. Once a major decision, such as purchasing a feed mill, is made, the business must use the facility. If too many bad resource commitment decisions are made, the enterprise may no longer be able to continue in business.

A manager is responsible for making sure people carry out assigned tasks and perform at an acceptable level. While the authority for direct supervision of employees is often delegated, the manager still maintains

Figure 1-5. Once resources are committed to a particular specialized operation, they may have few or no alternative uses. (Courtesy, M. Thomas)

Figure 1-6. A manager is responsible for making sure people carry out assigned tasks and perform at an acceptable level. (Courtesy, M. Thomas)

the ultimate responsibility and accountability for making sure decisions are implemented to the extent intended.

Management must also determine whether decisions made have had a positive or negative effect on the business. Employee motivation and productivity, profits, sales, visibility and community goodwill are some examples of factors that will help the manager make his/her determination of whether a decision was good or bad. Good decisions may be implemented in other locations or situations; bad decisions, of course, must be reversed if possible and new decisions made.

THE BUSINESS ATMOSPHERE

The atmosphere in which business activity occurs is constantly changing. Some changes to which management must constantly adjust are:

1. Economic conditions

2. Legal requirements

3. Consumer demands

4. Technology

5. Price relationships

6. Inflationary pressures

7. Tax structures

8. Developments in other countries

9. Availability of resources

10. Environmental concerns

Effective management must look to the future. A review of the past may provide some guidelines for future developments, but a preoccupation with a glorious past frequently results in stagnation of the business.

COMPONENTS OF MANAGEMENT

Thinking in terms of an overall business organization, there are three important components: the stockholders, the directors, and the manager and staff. Relatively few business organizations can neglect their relationships with employees, and no business organization can function without customers for its goods and services. This book is concerned primarily with those aspects of the operation that will improve the relationship between the business and its employees, its customers, and its stockholders.

A commonly used method of discussing management is to look upon this topic as including five major areas (Figure 1-7):

1. Planning

2. Organizing

3. Directing

4. Coordinating

5. Controlling

Figure 1-7
AREAS OF MANAGEMENT

Planning—Think, judge, decide
Organizing ways to implement plan
Directing—Organize out plans and programs
Coordinating—Integrate people and assets
Controlling—Measure success of plan

Planning

The job of determining what is to be done, and where, how, and when it is to be done is *planning* (Figure 1-8). In most business organizations there is day-to-day, year-to-year, and long-range planning.

Figure 1-8
PLANNING IN MANAGEMENT

Types of Planning	What Must Be Planned
Short-term	*Viewpoints*
Intermediate-term	*Objectives*
Long-term	*Goals*
	Policies
	Services
	Staffing
	Work programs
Planning Involves	*Resources*
Thinking	*Facilities*
Deciding	*Improvements*
Judging	*Controls*

Planning requires management to think, decide, and judge or evaluate alternative approaches to activities in which the business will be involved. This means there must be a development of different viewpoints as to the business's goals. Once goals are established, then objectives can be developed to reach these goals. These objectives should be behavioral, that is, capable of measurement. The objective "to provide better service" is vague and difficult to measure; therefore, a set of measurable objectives, like the ones below, should be developed.

1. Increase sales by 20 percent.

2. Increase feed conversion on customer operations by 10 percent.

3. Assist 50 new customers to increase their profitability by $5,000 per year.

These objectives can be measured. If they are *realistic*, they can be important tools in decision making. Once these objectives are established, they are the basis for determining the policies needed to achieve the objectives. Goals and objectives should be in writing. There should be frequent evaluations of results to determine if the business is making progress toward meeting objectives, and if not, to determine what the limiting factors are.

Planning involves an analysis of the services, human resources, capital resources, and *facilities* that are needed to achieve the objectives. If any of these factors must be changed, the type of changes must be analyzed and the necessary steps taken to bring about the change. Planning involves gathering and analyzing information, *forecasting* what will happen, establishing objectives, selecting a course of action, and developing a way to measure progress.

If planning is to be accepted throughout the business, people who will carry out the plan must be involved in making it. A plan developed by management and forced on unwilling employees has only a limited chance of success.

The planning operation quite often calls for a considerable amount of research of varying degrees of complexity, depending upon the nature of the business and the operation involved. Frequently it involves rather extensive analysis of existing facilities, capital, personnel, and other items of this nature. It may require establishing a list of priorities, since few businesses have unlimited resources. Thus, not all proposals can be implemented at any one time.

Planning can be a tedious activity because it demands attention to detail. However, if proper planning is followed, much of the rest of the management of the business organization is greatly simplified. There is a tendency by managers at various levels in a business to minimize the amount of time, effort, and resources they devote to planning because they frequently have little to show for the time spent. This is unfortunate because there are few business activities where the rewards for a particular activity are higher than in careful planning.

Organizing

Organizing is the grouping together of activities, people, and other resources in such a manner as to carry out the plan effectively (Figure 1-9). Frequently this is concerned with the *structure* of the organization and the way in which the efforts of the individuals within that organization are coordinated. Many of the components involved in organization are discussed in more detail in Chapter 2.

Figure 1-9
ORGANIZING IN MANAGEMENT

Develop and keep up-to-date business organization chart
Arrange work flow
Recognize strengths and weaknesses of personnel
Keep organization sensitive to consumer needs
Keep organization flexible

Without proper organization, it is very difficult to carry out a plan. Many different types of organization have been found to work effectively. The procedures used in organizing are closely related to the type of task to be performed and the characteristics of the individuals who will be carrying out the business operation.

Directing

Implementation of the plans within a particular organizational framework is directing (Figure 1-10). This involves diverse categories such as *delegation* of work, communications, and methods of insuring that the business's policy is properly understood.

While management cannot ignore relationships among people when planning and organizing, they may attempt to develop solutions that, in general place emphasis on getting the job done within certain personnel restraints. In contrast, directing is a function that is primarily concerned with employee relationships (see Chapter 9).

Figure 1-10
DIRECTING IN MANAGEMENT

Utilization of people to achieve day-to-day operations
Recognize that each person is different
Treat each person as part of a team
Have good, easily understandable job descriptions
Use established performance standards
Maintain a two-way communication flow
Develop Personnel

Coordinating

Coordinating is concerned primarily with those activities that avoid the development of bottlenecks (Figure 1-11). Some people look upon this activity as being one of achieving a balanced operation. A coordinator is concerned with having sufficient raw materials on hand so that a manufacturing operation will not be held up because of shortages. He/she is also concerned with having sufficient supplies so that salespeople can meet their commitments to customers. By the same token, the coordinator does not want so much money tied up in *inventory* that the operation cannot function, and he/she wants to be sure that there is adequate storage for the available inventories.

Figure 1-11
COORDINATING IN MANAGEMENT

Coordinate activities in business
Coordinate departments in business
Coordinate individual assignments
Coordinate within legal, social, and economic framework
Be timely
Be appropriate
Be understanding

Coordination is often looked upon as an excellent illustration of teamwork in planning the overall operation, individual assignments, and relationships between the business, the economy, and the society within which it functions.

Controlling

Activities that are necessary to insure that the policies of the business are in fact being carried out constitute controlling (Figure 1-12). This includes the preparation of reports to show what has been accomplished, and the evaluation of operations—both to insure that satisfactory results are being achieved and to determine how certain phases of the operation may be improved. In many business operations this phase of management would be greatly improved with a better system of communication between employees and all levels of management. For many managers, controlling represents one of the more distasteful aspects of management because it points up areas of weakness in which corrective action must be taken.

A business needs a system of internal controls that will keep managers and supervisors aware of individual, departmental, and overall performance. Such a control system indicates (1) if policies are being followed; (2) needed policy changes; and (3) performance *criteria* (such as output per employee, output per day, cost per $100 sales) as well as profits, changes in financial position, *cash flow*, and other items of this nature.

Figure 1-12
CONTROLLING IN MANAGEMENT

Measure performance
Require necessary records
Reward success
Take corrective action
Establish control points

In addition to such internal controls, management must recognize the need for external appraisal of the operation, because frequently people working for a business are so much a part of the operation they cannot critically evaluate it. There are two types of external assistance that every business should consider: financial audit and management audit (Chapter 5). Both of these audits can provide an analysis that will further strengthen the management and operating activities of a business.

BUSINESS MISSION AND GOALS

A major aid in carrying out the management functions (planning, organizing, directing, coordinating, and controlling) is a concise statement of business goals and objectives. This begins with a business's mission statement. This statement, in no more than 25 words, should summarize the reason the business exists. "To make a profit" is not in itself a reason for existence. "To sell widgets to customers in a 50 mile radius of my business at a profit" would be an appropriate reason for a business to exist.

If the goals of the business are generally recognized and stated in such a manner they can be helpful in establishing policy, and management is provided some useful guidelines in making decisions. If a business does not have a set of recognized goals, it is rather difficult to design a set of consistent policies that will be helpful in determining the direction in which the business is going. It is easier to understand the seemingly contradictory policies that some businesses make when it is recognized that these businesses do not have a set of goals that provide guidelines for their operations.

Every business, regardless of its organizational structure, should establish a set of goals in concise terms. These goals should be subject to periodic review, as they may change with different economic, political, and social conditions. Without such goals effective management is difficult. Once its goals have been established, a business should define a set of objectives that will help it reach these goals. The objectives must be stated in quantifiable terms because at the end of each year—or other suitable time period—there should be an evaluation of the business's performance against these objectives. Management then is in a position to evaluate operations to determine what progress has been made toward reaching the objectives that support the goals, why more progress has not been made, and what changes will be necessary if the stated objectives are to be met.

When a business has a set of goals and the objectives to meet these goals, the determination of policy can be greatly simplified. Every policy needs to be considered from the standpoint of what it contributes toward the achievement of stated goals and objectives. A realistic set of goals is one of the most important tools in effective management. Many times it is assumed that the goal of a business is to maximize profit, when actually the business may be more concerned with obtaining, or maintaining, a certain share of the market or with providing certain types of services to a specific group of customers. Many businesses might find it interesting to restate their goals and then to look at their objectives and policies to determine the extent to which consistencies or inconsistencies may exist.

CHAPTER QUESTIONS

1. What are the three methods of organizing a business?

2. What is a limited partner?

3. What is a joint venture?

4. What is the management relationship between stockholders, directors, and general manager?

5. What is capital and who provides it?

6. What is a sole proprietorship?

7. What is a corporation?

8. What is the difference between a regular corporation and a sub-chapter S corporation?

9. How does a cooperative differ from an investor-oriented corporation?

10. What are the five components of management?

11. What is a business goal?

12. What is a business's mission statement?

13. What are the three types of planning?

14. What are the six steps in planning?

Chapter 2

ORGANIZING, RESPONSIBILITY, AND APPROACHES TO MANAGEMENT

The history of U.S. industry shows a strong reliance on sole proprietorships. Even with corporate structures, capital and management were tied very closely. The twentieth century has shown a division of capital and management in many businesses. The people who have invested money in a business often are not involved at all in management, thus management may have goals that are different from those of the investors.

Managers of relatively small businesses are often working managers. They are responsible for the overall direction and supervision of the business and also in charge of some phase or phases of the operation. This type of manager must learn to use time wisely, reaching a proper balance between management aspects and operational aspects.

This chapter describes the process of organizing an agribusiness as well as policies and procedures for determining responsibilities and approaches to management.

OBJECTIVES

1. Discuss the basic principles of good business organization.

2. Identify the three separate and distinct functions of management in a business.

3. Describe business organizational charts and lines of reporting.

4. Describe the parent/subsidiary relationship of larger businesses.

5. Identify and define business expansion through vertical or horizontal integration.

6. Discuss the use of objectives as an effective management tool.

7. Discuss profit center management.

8. Discuss the use of strengths, weaknesses, opportunities, and problems as a form of management.

BUSINESS ORGANIZATION

A study of the history of almost any industry would show that there was a heavy dependence on the sole proprietorship, in which one person provided the capital, land, facilities, and much of the labor. It was not until a method was found to separate capital and management that the more complex forms of business organization and operation were developed. In the United States, even though a corporate structure was recognized early as being desirable, capital and management were still very closely tied. During the twentieth century there has been a recognized division of these two functions so that, under present conditions, many people who have capital invested in a business have the primary responsibility of earning a livelihood in some other occupation, or they have capital invested in a number of industries or a number of businesses, getting their income primarily from a return on invested capital.

One of the problems which has developed from this division of labor arises when management has a set of goals that are not the same as those of the investors who have provided the capital. While management is concerned with efficient operation and profitability, stockholders may ques-

TERMS

civic activities	horizontal integration	prudent
conglomerate	image	public relations
credit policy	marketing	regulations
customer relations	net income	retail
depreciation	operating	revenue
dividends	organizational chart	vertical integration
entity	overhead	working conditions
fringe benefits	potential	

tion the company's policies as they relate to the environment, earnings paid on investment, and community affairs. The directors, stockholders, and management must work together to provide suitable solutions for the concerns of all involved in the business. Managers, employees, and those who wish to work in the business are the group to which this book is primarily directed.

The manager of a small business (30 employees or fewer) may be a manager in title and also directly responsible for certain phases of the operation. Therefore, when looking at a situation, the manager sometimes looks at it from the standpoint of operations and sometimes from the standpoint of management. This presents a special problem since management needs to be concerned with a total view of resources as they apply to attaining the goals of the business. A working manager must learn how to use time effectively so that there is a proper balance between attention to the management aspects of the business and the operational aspects for which that manager is responsible. Businesses often fail because the manager did an excellent job of providing a product or service but did not spend enough time and effort on managing the overall business.

PRINCIPLES OF GOOD BUSINESS ORGANIZATION

The organization of a business is very important. It often determines how quickly problems are reported and solutions determined, and provides the framework in which employees perform their jobs. Five principles of good business organization should be followed when organizing an agribusiness.

1. **The organization is simple and levels of authority are easily understood.** This principle provides employees with clear lines of communication and responsibility. The two parts of the principle go hand-in-hand; if the organization is simple, levels of authority will usually be easy to understand.

2. **Resources are available for the business.** The primary resources are land/facilities, labor and equipment, and capital. Since managers are primarily concerned with allocating and utilizing resources so they provide the most benefit to the goals of the business, they must have adequate resources about which to make decisions.

3. **The operation is efficient.** Many managers see this as their primary

responsibility. Once the business is organized and resources allocated, the manager must become concerned with motivating employees to work efficiently and make good use of the resources of the business.

4. **Employee compensation is equitable and provides incentive for productivity.** While the business must be able to provide a product or service for less than the amount that can be charged for it, employee compensation is an area where spending a little more money can result in overall lower costs. Employees who are satisfied work harder and produce more.

5. **Plans are made to initiate business activity and to provide for business growth.** Managers must make an effort to be proactive rather than reactive. This means that they plan ahead for events instead of reacting to events after they occur. Short-term and long-term plans provide the business with a basis for decision making and problem solving.

FUNCTIONS OF MANAGEMENT

In any business organization there are three separate and distinct types of activities in progress: finance, operations, and marketing (Figure 2-1).

Figure 2-1
THREE FUNCTIONS OF MANAGEMENT

MANAGEMENT OF A FIRM		
Finance	Operations	Marketing

FINANCE

Finance refers to the management of all the fiscal transactions within the business. The term fiscal operations refers to the inventory policy and *credit policy* as they affect capital requirements. It encompasses debt capital, cash flow, and other aspects of the operation of the business closely tied to its financial transactions. There are few people who would minimize the importance of sound fiscal management in any business organization.

OPERATIONS

A second area of emphasis in a business is related to operations. The term operations is used to describe those activities which the business engages in to produce the goods and services that are its reasons for existing. For many manufacturing enterprises this is essentially the "engineering" part of the business. In operations a person is particularly concerned with improving production efficiency. This is generally associated with methods of improving output per employee or output per unit of input.

MARKETING

A third major area has to do with *marketing* the goods and services being produced. During the early stages of business development in most industrialized countries, the marketing aspect of the business was minimized. Frequently it consisted of sending out a salesperson or a few product samples, and this would accomplish all that was needed. However, as society became more affluent and complex, progressive managers found they must be more acutely aware of the consumer and what was needed to better service this very important part of their business. They recognized the limitations of a policy that produced goods in the hopes that someone might wish to buy them. Most modern businesses, including agribusiness, are becoming increasingly aware of the need to give more recognition to the requirements of the buyer when determining what they are going to produce and other policies of the business.

In analyzing the operation of the business and in visualizing how it is organized, it is helpful to understand which of the preceding three orientations (finance, operations, marketing) is given major consideration. If fiscal and/or operational approaches are emphasized, with only limited attention being given to the market or buyer orientation, the business has only limited opportunities to grow. It is equally obvious that if any one of these three areas is sufficiently weak, then a business may find itself in financial difficulty. Therefore, it is necessary for a business to have a sufficiently balanced operation so that it can achieve its goals. An extreme example would be one in which an efficient operation has a product or service that no one wants to buy, therefore, there is not much point in producing it.

ORGANIZATION
AND REPORTING

In many businesses, if a person walks into the president's or the manager's office or the board of directors' room, they might see a large chart which shows the organization of the business. This *organizational chart* indicates, at least conceptually, the areas of responsibility of the various people in the organization and the channels of communication. However, in these same businesses it is always interesting to see how a person goes about accomplishing the assigned task. Seldom does the flow of communication and action quite follow the prescribed policy. In order to accomplish many tasks people must work together. Therefore, it is important to know what the real communication channels are to get the job done. Many times it may be as simple as having a relationship with the secretary such that messages will be at the top of the stack when the manager comes in; or it may involve being on sufficiently good terms with someone so that they will put forth that extra effort to complete a particular assignment today rather than tomorrow. Once a person understands this company infrastructure, they are in a position to comprehend how the company is really organized for accomplishing results. Figure 2-2 shows a table of organization. In this particular organization there are very direct flows of communication, channels of responsibility are clearly defined, and these channels of responsibility and communication are fairly short. For many

Figure 2-2
ORGANIZATION OF A SMALL BUSINESS

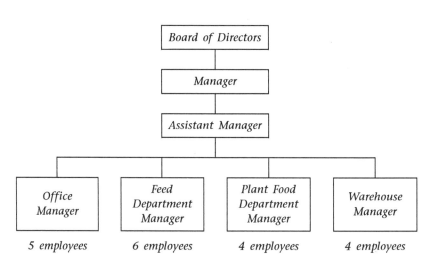

types of operations and for many types of businesses, such a "line" organization has proven highly efficient. In this particular example the staff function, at least at the upper level, has been minimized. To the extent that there are so-called staff functions, these are closely tied in with the operating departments.

In Figure 2-3 a second type of organization is indicated. The staff function is much larger. Under this system, many of the operations must move through the manager unless he or she is highly efficient in delegating authority and responsibility. This highly centralized organization may result in much dissatisfaction because of the difficulty of obtaining prompt answers to problems that arise.

For effective management, there must be a systematic method of making the types of decisions that should not be delayed. The degree of centralized

Figure 2-3
ORGANIZATION OF A SMALL AND POSSIBLY OVER-CENTRALIZED BUSINESS

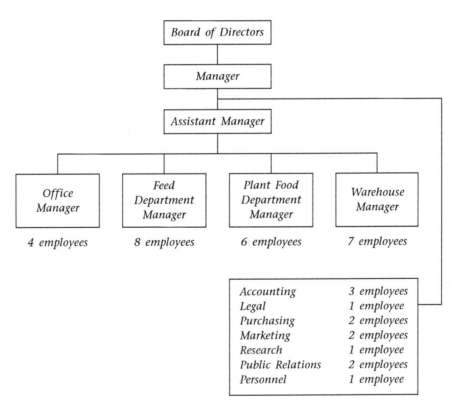

control should be determined by the extent to which employees at every level are willing and able to be held accountable. While there are a large number of people who are unwilling to accept this responsibility, there are also many managers unwilling to empower their employees. In many organizations there is no systematic means by which decisions can be made other than by the general manager. Although the organizational chart may show that there are various assistant positions, the people in these positions have not been delegated the authority to effectively carry out their responsibilities. Many decisions which are fairly routine should be made at a very low level, and in general, the more complex the decision, the higher in the organization a problem must move before the decision is made. Managers should be in a position to continually delegate more and more responsibility to those people with whom they work. This is necessary if they are to meet the continued demands on their time. It also is necessary if the organization is to develop a depth in management personnel at the various levels.

INTEGRATION

There are many ways a business may be organized; one consists of a company headquarters with a number of local organizations. The parent organization determines overall policies and handles certain specialized operations, and grants the local companies a large degree of freedom in determining their *operating* policies (Figure 2-4). Such an organization is generally referred to as a federated type of organization, with the parent company having rather limited but well-defined powers over the operation.

Figure 2-4
RELATIONSHIP BETWEEN LOCAL BUSINESSES AND THE
PARENT COMPANY WITH A FEDERATED ORGANIZATION

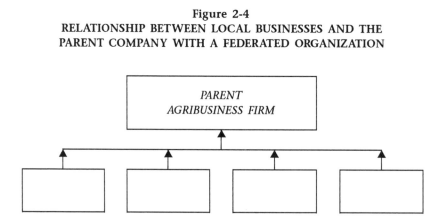

Local affiliated businesses have much autonomy in determining policies and operating procedures.

In other cases the parent company may exert much influence over all of the policies of the operation. This is referred to as a centralized organization (Figure 2-5).

Either a centralized or a federated type of organization can operate effectively. There are many outstanding examples of both types of operations.

Figure 2-5
RELATIONSHIP BETWEEN LOCAL BUSINESSES AND THE
PARENT COMPANY WITH A CENTRALIZED ORGANIZATION

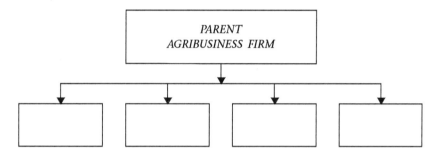

Affiliated businesses have little local autonomy in determining policies and operating procedures.

Vertical Integration

Many times in organizing a business there is the need to expand the operation. The nature of the agriculture industry is such that there are many different farm producing units. Since land is one of the major production items, this frequently means that the units are separated by distance. The size of a particular type of operation is determined by the type of operation involved, the amount of service that is needed, and the cost of transporting the products and/or the services related to them.

Frequently, either to use available facilities and labor more effectively or to service its customers more effectively, a business needs to add new services. *Vertical integration* is the performance of two or more of the marketing functions or steps in the marketing process by one business (Figure 2-6). For example, a company that owns a grain elevator not only purchases and stores grain, but also owns trucks to haul farmers' grain to the elevator, and from the elevator to the next stage in the marketing operation. The elevator enterprise may also process the grain into livestock feed which is sold to other farmers.

Figure 2-6
SCHEMATIC ARRANGEMENT OF A VERTICALLY INTEGRATED BUSINESS

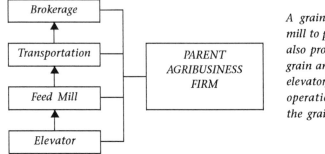

A grain elevator with a feed mill to process part of the grain also provides transportation of grain and feed to and from the elevator, as well as a brokerage operation for merchandising the grain and feed.

There are many elaborate and complex vertically integrated operations. An example would be a hatchery that grows broiler chicks, produces and distributes feed, maintains a broiler processing plant, and transports packaged products to *retail* outlets. There are many reasons for the development of such vertically integrated operations: controlling both quantity and quality from the beginning of the production process until the product is ready for the consumer; coordinating facilities and supplies; and reaching a scale that is sufficiently large to achieve various economies associated with size. Naturally, in such operations a high level of managerial skill is needed.

Horizontal Integration

With *horizontal integration* there are many individual business units involved, each one performing approximately the same type of marketing function over a relatively wide area (Figure 2-7). This is particularly desirable in operations where the production process is such that a single large business establishment would be unable to effectively service the customers in outlying areas. Frequently a business will have a central headquarters with a large number of "branch" plants that carry on operations at the local level. These are horizontally integrated in that there are other facilities that provide additional types of goods and services needed by the local units. Such an operation provides opportunities for the economies associated with size along with some of the more complex types of operations and services needed by the local units.

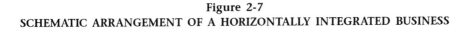

Figure 2-7
SCHEMATIC ARRANGEMENT OF A HORIZONTALLY INTEGRATED BUSINESS

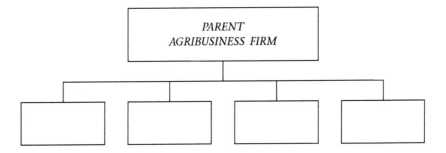

Four processing plants, each buying, processing, and distributing a product under the direction of the parent business.

Figure 2-8. GROWMARK, Inc. has a large number of branch operations that carry on similar types of functions at the local level. (Courtesy, M. Thomas)

Conglomerate Organization

In the *conglomerate* type of business organization, a business may find itself involved in a number of different and frequently unrelated activities as a means of spreading risk and hopefully entering additional markets (Figure 2-9).

Figure 2-9
SCHEMATIC ARRANGEMENT OF A CONGLOMERATE BUSINESS

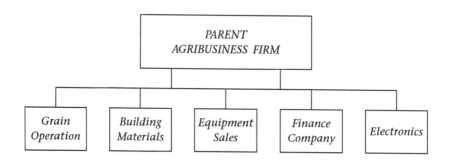

Most businesses will use some combination of vertical integration, horizontal integration, and conglomerate organization. The major objective is to have a combination of activities that will permit them to effectively meet the requirements of their customers. It is not uncommon to find a country elevator that not only buys grain, but also sells fertilizer, feed, herbicides, and coal. This is an attempt by the business to meet the needs of its customers.

The type of business organization is not as important as the ability of the manager to acquire capital and to develop personnel with the overall managerial ability to handle more complex operations. The same may be said for the organizational structure: The important thing is to be sure that the personnel will function in such a way that output per person (or other measure of input) provides efficient and economic service to the customers.

MANAGEMENT RESPONSIBILITY

Management has the primary responsibility of establishing the policy which the company will follow. In many businesses, management is composed of two different groups: (1) the board of directors and (2) the manager and staff.

BOARD OF DIRECTORS

The board of directors is elected by the shareholders. Board members should have a record of sound business judgment, they should be recognized as leaders, and they should have a high degree of loyalty to the organization. The board members have the overall responsibility of determining the policies of the organization. These policies are concerned with diverse activities such as finance, service, pricing, credit, *customer relations*, shareholder relations, *public relations*, employee relations, internal operations, and management development. Many of these activities will be discussed in considerable detail later in this book. In addition to determining the policies of the organization, the directors also have the responsibility of providing sufficient controls in order to assure that the policies are being evaluated and carried out. The evaluation process helps to determine how effectively the business is meeting its goals and points to ways the policies can be change to help meet these objectives.

In many businesses there are "inside" directors. These inside directors determine policy and work either part or full time in carrying out these policies. Many times a director has a specific skill needed in the business, for example, a lawyer or banker. The argument is frequently made that inside directors are not in a position to critically evaluate how policies are being carried out since they are the ones responsible for implementing such policies. There is a growing concern that inside directors may have a conflict of interest. Some government regulatory agencies are taking the position that inside directors have not been as concerned with protecting and representing shareholder rights as *prudent* trusteeship would suggest.

THE MANAGER AND STAFF

It is the responsibility of the manager and staff to carry out the policies established by the board. Frequently the staff members are called upon to assist the board in evaluating existing policies or to make recommendations as to changes in policies.

The relationship between the manager and the board of directors can be a very interesting one. The manager is often the one person in the organization who best understands the interrelationship between the various facets of the business, consequently the board of directors will rely heavily upon the manager's recommendations. This means the manager is placed in the position of assisting the board members in making their policy decisions, as well as assisting them in evaluating the effectiveness of these policy decisions. There is little doubt that the manager and the board of directors must have a close working relationship in which there is mutual trust and respect. One of the challenges that managers and board members must face is that of sufficiently delineating the responsibilities of each group to help them avoid interfering with each other's effectiveness.

Managers should have technical and administrative competence. They need imagination and creativity in order to visualize the future needs of the customers. They should have leadership ability as well as the ability to follow through to insure that the policies are being carried out. Managers must be of high moral character and demonstrate good judgment. In smaller businesses in particular, the manager's major responsibilities include public relations and the coordination of the activities of many other people. A manager must be willing and able to delegate responsibility to those within the organization.

Both the manager and the board are primarily concerned with effective ways to use limited resources to attain the goals of the business. They are constantly seeking information that will permit them to make sound decisions on problems such as: (1) what product or service to provide; (2) where to locate facilities; and (3) how to effectively change with changing times. Making these types of decisions requires the ability to ask the right questions, to know the types of information needed to answer these questions, to critically appraise the data and arguments both for and against the proposal, and to reach a decision from all of this.

Many times managers and directors become so deeply involved with operational details that they do not take the time to look at the broader policy problems that need more careful analysis and consideration. It is usually much easier for them to state an operational problem and develop a workable solution than it is to be concerned with broader policy considerations.

The development of an effective policy can assist in providing guidelines for management. These guidelines should be used by the manager in directing the operation. The failure of the board of directors to develop such a policy is a dereliction of duty. It leads to the manager and the board both trying to do the same thing, with overlapping and frequently conflicting decisions. In addition, the business does not have the needed direction the stockholders have a right to expect.

MANAGER RESPONSIBILITY

The manager has a responsibility to many different groups within an organization. This is true whether that person is the owner, the salaried manager of the entire operation, or the manager of some smaller division or part of the organization. These responsibilities are listed under five headings (Figure 2-10), not necessarily in priority order. The ranking of these general categories will vary according to the specific circumstances and conditions a manager faces.

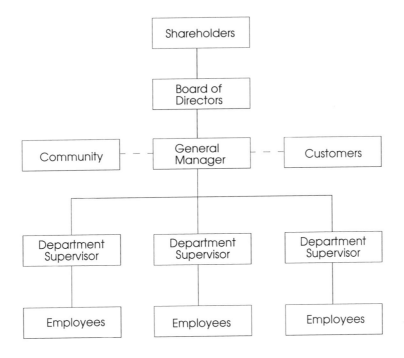

Figure 2-10. The manager has responsibility to many different groups in an organization.

Board of Directors

The manager has a direct responsibility to the board of directors. The manager is charged with carrying out the policies adopted by the board and with reporting to the directors on the success of the operation. In many cases the manager not only has the responsibility for carrying out the policies, but may also be exclusively accountable for the success of the business.

Shareholders

The manager is generally recognized to be a major factor in determining the level of earnings for the business, and as far as the shareholders are concerned, in determining the rate of return they will receive on their investment in the form of *dividends*. As businesses become larger, there probably will be less of a personal relationship between the manager and the shareholders, but in relatively small businesses, this personal relationship may place the manager under considerably more pressure to perform. This relationship may also make it more difficult for a change in management to occur. In many cases there has been a reluctance to change managers even though, on the basis of the usual performance measures, the existing manager was not performing satisfactorily. This raises a very serious question in any management relationship about the extent to which performance criteria should be used to measure the effectiveness of a manager or an employee, and to what extent these objective measures should be tempered by personal acquaintance.

Employees

In most small businesses the manager has a close working relationship with the employees, while at the same time carrying a major responsibility for salary adjustments, including *fringe benefits*. The manager is also generally perceived as being primarily responsible for *working conditions*. The ways in which a manager carries out these responsibilities will probably be a major factor in determining employee output.

These close personal relationships between managers and employees can make for difficult situations, since seldom will a manager have an employee with whom he or she does not at some time have to take a contrary position. The need to maintain a close working relationship, while at the same time recognizing the rights and responsibilities of both the employer and the employee, is essential; but it is difficult to sustain the types of relationships that will result in a smooth running organization.

Customers

A business without customers has little reason for continuing its operations. The manager must be assured that the employees recognize the importance of the customer. The manager needs to check with customers periodically to be sure that they are receiving the good service and treatment that are consistent with the business achieving its desired goals, and provisions must be made to properly evaluate the comments of irate customers. Management that has a tendency to talking to employees in an attempt to develop a measure of customer attitude should try to obtain the same information directly from the customers. Employees tend to minimize the complaints of customers, especially when they feel that the complaints would reflect unfavorably on their own efficiency. Therefore, an employee's report of customer satisfaction may be quite different from the customer's.

Figure 2-11. A good manager recognizes the importance of customers. (Courtesy, M. Thomas)

A good manager recognizes the importance of remaining aware of the customers' attitudes.

Community

Businesses operating in the economy of the next decade cannot overlook their responsibility to society. A number of businesses are re-evaluating their responsibilities to the communities in which they operate, including social costs related to the business which the business is not covering. For example, if the business is contributing to pollution problems or the need for an improved water or sewage system in excess of its contribution to the local economy, a major community relations problem may arise. A company must also examine to what extent it should contribute to community activities. A conflict of opinion about the appropriate level of participation often occurs between management and shareholders and a compromise is sometimes necessary.

Examples of community participation by businesses are many. An enterprise may make financial contributions to agencies such as United Way, Red Cross, Girl Scouts, 4-H Club, and FFA; provide trucks and personnel to support a community activity; give financial assistance for awards to

Figure 2-12. Businesses may participate in community activities by making financial contributions to United Way which provides support to such agencies as the Red Cross. (Courtesy, M. Thomas)

various school and civic organizations; provide facilities for meetings; or fund scholarships. These activities are considered an effort to meet social responsibility. Many shareholders take the position that these funds, if distributed as dividends, could be used to better advantage by the shareholders.

APPROACHES TO MANAGEMENT

There are many ways management may attempt to combine and allocate various resources. Such decisions are made within a framework that prescribes limitations as to the actions that may be taken. For example, there are many legal restrictions that limit what can be done. These may take the form of federal or state laws and *regulations*, or local ordinances. There are restrictions imposed by capital limitations or by availability of personnel. There may be limitations on the amount of risk a business wishes to take. In some cases market *potential* may limit management actions. In other cases competition may provide limitations as to management decisions. It is within these limitations that decisions are made.

MANAGEMENT BY OBJECTIVES

There has been much discussion of the use of objectives as an effective management tool. It is generally recommended that a business have a set of written goals, which are general guidelines as to what the business hopes to accomplish. The firm then develops a set of specific objectives that will permit the business to reach these goals. Such objectives should be measurable so management can determine if they are meeting their objectives. Objectives may take many different forms but usually include market profitability, growth and development, human and physical resources, or products and services. Some examples are:

1. To have 25 percent of the market in our area within five years

2. To increase fertilizer volume 10 percent in the next year

3. To have a net increase of 100 percent in customers served in the next year

4. To have all professional employees participate in at least six days of professional training each year

5. To increase output per employee-hour by 10 percent in the next year

6. To reduce on-the-job-accident hours lost by 20 percent in the next year

7. To increase earnings on net worth to 20 percent within five years

Each of the above objectives can be measured. These objectives will vary depending upon the nature of the business, but they should be high enough to present a challenge. As economic conditions change, management should re-evaluate objectives to ensure they reflect the situation. In most businesses, objectives should be developed each year and monitored throughout that time to measure progress.

Objectives serve as guidelines in making policies. If policies do not contribute to achieving the stated management objectives, then there is cause to explore why the objectives and policies are inconsistent. By using this approach, management is in a position to measure progress. If operating results suggest the business is not making progress toward meeting objectives, there is a need to determine the cause, then corrective action can be taken. The three major reasons that businesses fail to meet objectives are: (1) the objective is unrealistic, (2) the policies will not permit meeting the objectives, and (3) the personnel or other resources are not adaptable to accomplishing the objectives.

The use of this approach to management requires persons who are willing to commit the time and effort to develop objectives and to honestly evaluate the situations that need to be changed in order to accomplish those objectives. In evaluating performance against objectives, individuals should not set objectives too low or be allowed to develop an alibi or excuse for not achieving an objective.

When the development of objectives becomes a combined effort of all persons in the business, there is a greater chance for success because everyone has a vested interest in seeing these objectives accomplished. Each person involved can also make contributions to the policy changes needed to achieve the objectives and also find ways to make the operation function to achieve the objectives.

In many businesses, objectives are developed by the manager and the accountant. After one or two years of using the system they will conclude that management by objectives does not work. What they may have failed to take into account is that such a system must involve those most affected by it to be successful. Management by objectives can make a major contribution to more efficient use of resources and the development of useful policies.

Measurable objectives should be developed at each level of operation within the business, and these objectives should cover specific time periods. Such a breakdown permits a systematic approach to developing working relationships among the different sectors of the operation to achieve a common goal. In developing this approach to management, it should be recognized that there may be conflicts between the objectives of top management and of the shareholders. It should also be recognized that there may be conflicts within the management group. Under such circumstances provisions must be made to resolve such differences. If the objectives are not generally acceptable to the manager, the assistant managers, the department supervisors, and the board of directors, there is little opportunity for them to serve as effective guidelines for more efficient management.

PROFIT CENTER MANAGEMENT

Profit center management is used by many businesses and involves developing certain groups of related activities as a profit center. This organizational *entity* is then operated to show a profit. The manager or supervisor is held responsible for the outcome, and frequently, if the desired outcome does not materialize, either the manager is replaced or the group of activities is discontinued or reallocated to other sectors of the business.

There are two general types of profit center organizations. In some cases profit centers refer to location. For example, a business may have eight different locations and each is designated as a profit center. In other cases, profit centers refer to specific activities, such as feed processing, elevator operations, fertilizer operations, or transportation. In this situation each of these activity groups is a profit center.

There are many businesses successfully using profit center management. As with any specific approach to management, there are also problems that must be solved if the system is to work efficiently. A major consideration is that of allocating business *overhead* costs. Many costs such as labor, utilities, taxes, and *depreciation*, can be easily determined for a particular profit center; however, there are a number of costs associated with the business that are more difficult to allocate. For example, it must be determined how much each profit center should pay toward the general manager's salary or the expenses of the board. A number of head office expenses of this type must be allocated and the need to divide such costs equitably is essential. Some businesses allocate such overhead costs on the basis of percent of total business *revenue* contributed by the profit center, others allocate it on the basis of number of square feet of floor space assigned to the profit center, or on the capital invested in the profit center. There are almost as many different approaches to allocating overhead expenses as there are businesses using profit center management. Some businesses ignore overhead expenses entirely in profit center management, but in that case each profit center must show a higher profit to remain viable.

A second problem that must be worked out has to do with pricing policies for intra-company transfers. The price of corn from the elevator profit center to the feed profit center should not be so high that it makes the elevator a success and the feed mill a failure. A transportation profit center must price its services in such a way as to show a profit while the users of the service are not penalized. It is entirely possible a firm's overall pricing policy will be incompatible with the pricing policy a profit center manager would set. This again suggests profit center management requires developing equitable solutions to mutual problems.

An additional issue every manager must face is whether each activity must show a profit. For example, a fertilizer operation may provide a spreader at no cost or a nominal cost. A profit center orientation may suggest the elimination of this phase of the business, but the manager must examine the net contribution of this activity to the fertilizer business. If the income from the added volume of business is large enough to pay the cost, then the activity may be justified. Many elevators have a feed business that may be making only minor contributions to *net income*, but this service also makes a major contribution to the total elevator business.

Profit center management must make provisions for a number of public relations activities, such as attending and participating in meetings and programs and working with 4-H and FFA groups. These activities involve monetary costs and time. Although it is difficult to show in specific terms how each of these *civic activities* contributes to net income, there is a general belief that such activities make a contribution to net income in the long run (Chapter 14). It should also be recognized that every employee of a business has public relations responsibilities in his or her relationship with customers and the community. Some employees, because of either their characteristics or their jobs, have greater responsibilities or assume more prominent roles in this area than do other employees.

In most businesses there is some minimal critical mass of activities that must be provided to assure an adequate volume of business to attract customers and maintain an acceptable level of income. When management uses the profit center approach, it must recognize the factors contributing to this critical mass, and in an attempt to make every activity show a profit, not eliminate essential contributors to this critical mass. For example, if in a given area customers expect a fertilizer operation to make fertilizer recommendations on the basis of soil tests, this service cannot easily be eliminated.

Profit center management is a system that can assist in identifying the contributions various phases of the business make to net income. It can provide guidelines as to those segments of the business that should be expanded, new activities that should be added, or existing activities that should be phased out. In order to establish acceptable profit levels for the various profit centers, when a particular center is having difficulty or a new profit center is being developed, a specific understanding must be reached as to the length of time the manager has to achieve the established profit level before changes will be made.

SWOP MANAGEMENT

SWOP management is an approach used to develop some businesses. It can be helpful in determining the thrust of a business and then marshalling the resources to make the program effective. In this approach, management:

1. Builds on its **Strengths**

2. Corrects its **Weaknesses**

3. Recognizes and takes advantage of its **Opportunities**

4. Recognizes and minimizes its **Problems**

SWOP management requires time and acceptance by the people involved. It is suggested that the manager and each member of the board of directors list five strengths, five weaknesses, five opportunities, and five problems of the business. They should do this as individuals, without discussion, although hopefully the lists are sufficiently similar to suggest they are all talking about the same business.

As an example, a business might prepare the following list:

Strengths

1. Competent management team

2. Excellent facility

3. Good location to serve customers

4. Favorable *image* among customers

5. Ability to call on regional office for special assistance

Weaknesses

1. Need to train younger staff to assume greater responsibility

2. Poor transportation service for incoming supplies

3. Inadequate training of technical specialists

4. Inventory control

5. Poor coordination between sales staff and warehouse staff

Opportunities

1. Nonaggressive competition

2. Expanded agricultural production with no marketing business to serve it

3. Noncompetitive ag-related businesses willing to work with business

4. Opportunity for an exclusive franchise to provide feed additive

5. Substantially lower costs if volume shipments are handled

Problems

1. Shortage of *working capital*

2. High accounts receivable

3. Poor morale of warehouse employees

4. Potential customers unacquainted with business

5. High cost per dollar of sales

From analysis of these 20 points, management should be able to develop a program that will improve the effectiveness of the business. For the program to function most efficiently, this process should be continued at every level of management.

Essentially, this approach to management requires a critical self-appraisal. It can work only if those involved are willing to take the time to thoughtfully develop the list of strengths, weaknesses, opportunities, and problems. Once this has been done and evaluated, a program can be developed to implement the steps such an analysis dictates. In this way, SWOP management can provide the guidelines that are potentially useful to the business.

SWOT MANAGEMENT

SWOT management is an approach similar to SWOP management except that recognizing and minimizing problems is not considered. The T in SWOT stands for **Threats**. Both internal and external threats are evaluated along with opportunities. From this list, a situation analysis is developed for each area within the business. Then the procedure follows the same pattern as that of SWOP management.

CHAPTER QUESTIONS

1. Name the three distinct activities in progress in any business.

2. What is the purpose of a business organizational chart?

3. What is horizontal integration of a business?

4. What is vertical integration expansion?

5. Name at least three forms objectives may take.

6. What do the initials SWOP represent in this approach to management?

Chapter 3

CAPITALIZATION
OF A BUSINESS

The amount of money a business has available to cover costs of operation often determines its success or failure. This money, called capital, represents the investment of the owners. It is used to buy or rent equipment and facilities, pay employees, purchase inventory and raw materials, and cover other expenses associated with the operation of the business.

This chapter focuses on types of capital, methods of obtaining capital, and factors to consider in the capitalization of an agribusiness.

OBJECTIVES

1. Discuss equity capital and its use.

2. Discuss debt capital and its use.

3. Identify the sources of borrowed funds available to an agribusiness.

4. Discuss fixed and variable rates of interest.

5. Describe the components of the Farm Credit Administration and their purposes.

6. Differentiate between secured and unsecured loans.

7. Identify ways to reduce capital needs.

SOURCES OF CAPITAL

There are two sources of capital for a business: ownership and borrowed. Ownership capital is that *paid-in capital* provided by the owner(s). This is frequently referred to as *equity* or *net worth* in the business. At other times it is referred to as *risk* capital. Net earnings from the business are paid to

Figure 3-1. The farmer may extend credit to the elevator by delivering grain over a period of several weeks or months, not making settlement with the elevator until the end of delivery time. (Courtesy, Office of Agricultural Communications, Mississippi State University)

TERMS

amortized	income and expense summary	pledging
assets		prime interest rate
balance sheet	leverage	profit and loss statement
bond	line of credit	promissory note
cash flow projection	liquidated	retained earnings
collateral	liquidity	risk
credit rating	loan committee	seasonal business
equity	net worth	suppliers
estate	open account	technology
financial accounting	operating loan	variable interest rate
financial statement	paid-in capital	
fixed interest rate	par value	

the owners of this equity, either directly as dividends or indirectly *(retained earnings)* as an increase in the business's net worth. If a business suffers a loss, this loss is reflected in a decreased net worth and frequently in no dividends.

In addition to this equity capital, businesses generally find it necessary (1) to borrow funds from banks or other financial institutions, (2) to have varying amounts of their business financed through accounts payable, and/or (3) to make other financing arrangements with *suppliers* of products they handle.

EQUITY CAPITAL

Investment may be by direct ownership of *assets*, as in the case of a sole proprietorship, it may be investment by the various members of the partnership, or it may be represented by investments through the ownership of stocks. Some authorities do not differentiate between the ownership of stock as an asset and the ownership of debt as evidenced by a note or *bond*. However, from the standpoint of a business organization, stock represents ownership of corporate assets, whereas debt is an obligation that must be repaid. Ownership implies that the stockholder has certain voting rights in determining the policies of the organization.

The sale of stock presents two additional problems. First, it should be decided if stockholders have the right to transfer the stock to someone who is willing to pay whatever the owner may determine this stock is worth. In proprietary corporations this means that if stockholders think the stock is worth more than *par value*, they can sell it at this price, if they can find a buyer willing to pay such a price. In most cooperatives, stocks can be transferred only with the approval of the board of directors and frequently only at par value. This means that if the net assets of the organization are greater than par value, buyers are purchasing an asset (stock) at a net saving. However, if they can sell this asset at par value only, it does not accrue to them as holders of the stock unless the cooperative is *liquidated*. The second problem that must be considered in relation to stock ownership is the extent to which there is a ready market for the stock. For larger corporations this is provided by regulated and readily recognized stock markets, such as the New York Stock Exchange. However, for smaller corporations, there is seldom a ready market for stock so that other means of transferring ownership must be found.

A second source of equity risk capital, and one of the most important, is internally generated funds. This refers to those additions to capital that result from business earnings. Essentially a business has two alternatives for the use of earnings at the end of the year; they may be paid out to investors in the form of dividends on investment or they may be kept in the business to provide added capital. There are some differences in the tax laws for the proprietary forms of business, in contrast with cooperatives, that are not included in this discussion.

A third form of capitalization is the contribution to available capital which arises from sources such as reserves for estimated losses from accounts receivable and income deductions resulting from allowable depreciation. To the extent that these funds are not used in any given year, they may contribute to the availability of funds. However, if the deductions taken are realistic, these funds will be needed to meet the estimated expenditures arising either from the losses due to uncollectible accounts receivable or from the replacement of depreciated items.

DEBT CAPITAL

Most businesses find it impractical to operate only with equity capital. As a result, they must find sources from which to borrow additional funds. These businesses may choose to finance part of their land, buildings, and equipment. There also may be a need for capital to finance inventories, accounts receivable, and other operational items. A business should know the costs for this debt capital in the form of interest along with the contribution this added capital makes to the net returns of the business.

A business is interested in maintaining a *liquidity* position such that, if for some unexpected reason additional funds were needed, it could obtain these funds at a competitive rate. Most studies suggest that interest rate is only one of many factors a business considers when borrowing money. When lenders are considering alternative uses for their available funds, they may place a large amount of emphasis on liquidity as a loan factor. If the business is in a position where the lender cannot expect repayment except over a very long time period, then the lender's *loan committee* may refuse the loan.

A second important factor in debt management has to do with timing—when the money is needed. A business should determine if it will be more advantageous to obtain these funds on a long-term basis with *amortized* payments over a period of time, or to obtain the funds on a short-term basis, renewing for the unpaid balance at maturity. Under certain conditions a business may have a rather broad latitude as to the time when it will need additional capital. For example, management may have the

Figure 3-2. The fertilizer business is an example of seasonal business with strong sales in spring and fall. (Courtesy, Brendan Marshall)

choice of starting a building now, six months from now, or in a year. An analysis of the money market may be an important factor in determining when to make this type of investment.

In some types of business, the policy of having a *fixed interest rate* at the time the loan is made has been followed. More volatile interest rates have fueled a growing trend toward a *variable interest rate* that is tied to a national money market. With a variable rate loan, the interest rate might be 1 percentage point above the cost of prime rate. If the *prime interest rate* is 5 percent, then the business pays 6 percent; if, during the course of the loan, the prime interest rate should increase to 7 percent, then the business pays 8 percent; or, if the prime interest rate should decline to $4\frac{1}{2}$ percent, then the business would pay $5\frac{1}{2}$ percent. This technique has the advantage of permitting interest rates to decline if money markets soften and interest rates are declining. Because it also stipulates that if prime rates go up, then interest rates will follow, it provides a more equitable arrangement between the borrower and the lender.

The importance of managing capital and making the right decisions as to when and how to use borrowed funds cannot be overemphasized when attempting to make maximum use of a business's resources.

SOURCES OF BORROWED FUNDS

There are several different sources of credit available to agribusiness firms. These include (1) banks, (2) the Farm Credit Administration (under certain conditions), (3) insurance companies, (4) government, (5) individuals, and (6) suppliers.

BANKS

In addition to providing a number of services that are important to the operation of the business, the local bank provides a source of both long- and short-term funds, depending upon the situation. Frequently the bank requires the company to maintain a minimum outstanding balance. A local bank has certain restrictions on the maximum amount of money it may loan to any one borrower. These restrictions are imposed by the

Figure 3-3. The local bank provides an opportunity for businesses to borrow funds and provides a number of other services. (Courtesy, M. Thomas)

Figure 3-4. Banks often offer multiple locations as a convenience and service to their customers. (Courtesy, M. Thomas)

federal and state banking authorities. If a business needs more money than the local bank can legally loan, it is customary for the local bank to have an arrangement with another bank, called a participation, whereby the local bank will service the loan and the other bank will fund the "override" (the amount above the amount that can legally be loaned by the local bank). This is a particularly important arrangement for those businesses that have large amounts of *seasonal business*, such as fertilizer dealers with strong spring and fall demands that make short-term inventory financing a major problem.

There are legal restrictions as to the maximum amount of total loans outstanding that a bank may have. These again are established by state and federal banking authorities. Therefore, under certain conditions, even though a small business might wish to borrow money and could meet all the bank's usual criteria for borrowing money, if the bank were "loaned up," it would be unable to finance the operation. However, under these conditons most banks would make every effort to see that a good customer was properly serviced by some other financial institution with which they had a close working relationship.

Interest rates, maturities, and other loan terms will vary with the type of loan, the general cost of money, the strength of the relative credit factors, the loan purpose, and other factors which are discussed later in this chapter.

FARM CREDIT ADMINISTRATION

The Farm Credit Administration is a cooperative credit system that was originally capitalized by the federal government. This original capital has now been repaid. Three units of the farm credit system are (1) Federal Land Banks (FLBs) and the Federal Land Bank associations, which loan money primarily on farm real estate; (2) Federal Intermediate Credit Banks (FICBs) and Production Credit Associations (PCAs), which primarily loan short- and intermediate-term operating credit to farmers; and (3) Banks for Cooperatives, which loan money to qualified agricultural cooperatives. Some mergers

Figure 3-5. A local Farm Credit Services office provides funds for agribusinesses.
(Courtesy, M. Thomas)

within Federal Land Banks and Production Credit Associations in some parts of the country have produced joint operations of FLBs and PCAs operating as "Agri-Banks." All of these farm credit banks receive their funds primarily from the sale of various forms of indebtedness on the money markets.

Those agribusinesses that are qualified cooperatives may use the Banks for Cooperatives as the major source of borrowed funds for both long- and short-term credit needs. This has been a major source of borrowed funds for cooperative agribusiness firms in many parts of the United States.

INSURANCE COMPANIES

One of the major problems facing most insurance companies is that of managing income in such a way as to maximize earnings while at the same time maintaining a reasonable level of liquidity and safety. Insurance companies frequently invest in various types of agribusiness debt financing, particularly in land, facilities, and equipment. They also will frequently have substantial investments in large businesses that are at least partially composed of agribusinesses, and in which the parent company may provide varying amounts of the capital for the local organizations.

GOVERNMENT

For decades the federal government has been much concerned with ways to encourage community development in the non-urban centers. Some state governments—and in some cases local governments—have begun to consider the types of incentives they might provide to encourage dispersion of industries that can function as effectively or more effectively in rural areas than in urban areas. These types of operations frequently are closely related to agriculture. One incentive used is governmental funds, either as grants or at reduced interest rates, which may provide some of the capital needed for community services, such as sewer and water systems. Frequently these funds have been available to help reduce the net cost of the agribusiness firm, for the acquisition of capital, and for the acquisition of land and facilities.

There have been frequent changes in the amounts and types of funds that are available, and the terms under which they could be spent. Not only do these terms vary from year to year, but they also may vary from area to area. It is important for agribusiness firms to know the types of assistance that are available. If management is aware of the alternatives, they are in a better position to make rational decisions that will further the goals of the business. They are also more capable of making a realistic appraisal of what impact the business may have on economic growth and development of the area in which it hopes to operate.

INDIVIDUALS

In many agribusiness operations a large portion of the long-term indebtedness may be in the form of loans from individuals. Individual lenders may provide more flexible loan conditions than the more institutionalized lenders. This results in much less uniformity of loan terms and conditions for those operations that are being financed by individuals. As is true with most other types of financing, the loan is tied very closely to the relationship between the borrower and the individual. It is also heavily dependent upon the life span of the individual. If the lender dies, the loan frequently must be repaid when the *estate* is settled. This somewhat uncertain length of time the loan may be outstanding can be a serious disadvantage to receiving financing from individuals.

SUPPLIERS

Agribusinesses receive varying amounts of credit from their suppliers. This may be as a convenience item for relatively short periods of time (10 or 20 days), or it may be a more highly structured arrangement whereby the agribusiness firm must meet certain criteria in order to obtain credit from the suppliers. Another group of suppliers that helps an agribusiness firm finance its inventories is farmers. Often a farmer will deliver grain to an elevator over a period of several weeks or even months, not making a settlement with the elevator until the end of delivery time. Under such conditions the seller of the grain is, in effect, helping the elevator to finance inventories. Under certain other conditions, buyers of products from agri-

Figure 3-6. Farmers help some businesses finance inventories. (Courtesy, Brendan Marshall)

business firms may take delivery and even make payment for a product some months before it is needed. In effect, they are helping the agribusiness firm finance the inventories related to this agricultural production business. The types of arrangements that are prevalent vary by regions and also change over time.

EVIDENCE OF DEBT

When borrowing money, agribusiness firms may find the lender requires the *pledging* of certain *collateral*, in which case the loan is referred to as a secured loan. Under other conditions no specific collateral is pledged and the debt is referred to as being unsecured. In case of forced liquidation, the secured debt has first claim on those assets which are pledged to protect that particular debt. After the pledge assets have been liquidated to apply on the secured debt, unsecured debts then may come in for their share of the remaining assets. After all debts have been retired, then equity capital shares in the distribution of the remainder of the assets.

Except for so-called *open account* credit, the *promissory note* is probably the most commonly used instrument of debt. Such a note indicates that at some specified future date, or on demand, the borrower agrees to pay to the lender a specified sum of money. The rate of interest is also indicated in this note. Such a note will also indicate if it is unsecured or if certain collateral is pledged to help insure payment of the note.

A second general indication of debt is represented by bonds. The bond also indicates that the borrower will repay a specified sum of money to the lender at a specified time. This bond will carry a stated rate of interest and may or may not be supported with additional collateral or other conditions related to issue. Generally, bonds carry a stated par value, such as $100, $500, or $1,000.

It is necessary for an agribusiness firm to be well acquainted with the tax program, whether it is equity capital or borrowed capital. For example, in most cases interest payments on a debt are deductible expenses for income tax purposes, while dividend payments on equity capital are paid from earnings after taxes.

WAREHOUSE RECEIPTS

The warehouse receipt indicates that an individual or business has a certain amount of products of a specified quality stored at a particular place. If this product is stored in a properly bonded warehouse, the warehouse receipt can then be used in many cases as collateral for a loan. When title to the product changes from one owner to another, or when the product is removed from storage, the loan must be repaid.

This method of financing has been particularly important in the grain business, but many other businesses have also used the warehouse receipt as an efficient method of inventory financing.

TYPES OF INFORMATION
LENDERS WANT

A business preparing to borrow money should recognize that this borrowing process may well be one of the most important selling operations in which the business participates; therefore, it needs to give careful consideration to the types of information required to do a good selling job. Before borrowing, management needs to carefully analyze the various alternatives: those which would reduce its capital requirements, those that would permit it to use its available capital more effectively, and those available for acquiring additional capital. Things to consider include leverage, credit policy, inventory policy, amount and type of services offered, cus-

Figure 3-7. Lenders need specific information when a business prepares to borrow money. (Courtesy, M. Thomas)

tomer characteristics, and supplier characteristics. Once management has carefully analyzed all of these factors, it must then present the results of its findings in as favorable a light as possible to the potential lender. The information the lender wants is the same type of information the borrower should have been studying when making the original decision that dictated the need to borrow money.

The lender needs the following information:

1. How the loan proceeds would be used and what impact the changes would have on the capital position and earnings of the business

2. An analysis of how this business organization is adjusting to the changing *technology* of its customers

3. Characteristics of the business's customers, such as size of operation and shifts in volume of business over the last several years

4. A statement on the availability and stability of the markets to which the business sells its products and from which it buys products

5. The adequacy of facilities to meet the desired goals of the business

6. A projection of capital requirements, earnings, and cash flow during the lifetime of the proposed loan

7. Managerial capacity of the business, which includes information as to the age and experience of those in management positions, the age and experience of the directors, the types of training programs scheduled to keep those in managerial positions current with what is happening in their field, and those programs planned to help provide management depth

8. A list of available collateral to support such a loan

9. Financial strength of the business which is best reflected by a series of audit reports from the past 3 to 5 fiscal years. From this a prospective lender can see changes in earnings, capital position, and applications of earnings in the past. This not only indicates something about financial position but also provide many insights as to the effectiveness of management.

Most lenders are also concerned with other competitive and economic factors that will affect the business organization, both in the short-term and in the long-term. Most lenders would rather finance a loan that will contribute to the income of the borrower than make a safe loan that, in effect, will become an interest-bearing asset but will not contribute to the firm's growth and development.

Naturally it is assumed that the business seeking a loan is a legal entity. The preparation of the necessary documents used by a borrower to make the decision that the use of borrowed funds is desirable requires considerable time and effort. By the same token, this information represents the same type of information and sincerity of analysis that the borrower must have to make a sound decision.

OTHER CONSIDERATIONS

In determining if borrowed capital should be used, as well as the amount and type of such capital, a number of miscellaneous factors need to be considered. These factors vary by type of business, area, and economic conditions. However, the following items are indicative of the types of problems that should concern a borrower.

LEVERAGE

Leverage is a term used to indicate the amount of total capital a business has access to in relation to the amount of equity or risk capital available. For example, if a business has a net worth of $75,000 and total assets of $200,000, it has debts of $125,000. This means that the business is operating to a rather large extent on borrowed funds. So long as a business receives higher returns on borrowed money than it costs to borrow the money, this leverage works to its advantage. However, if the cost of borrowed funds is greater than the added returns from the use of these additional funds, then such an operation works to the business's disadvantage, since the cost of borrowed funds constitutes a fixed expense which must be met the same as taxes or other fixed costs. Excessive borrowing can place the business in a more vulnerable position than would be the case if the business were operating with all equity capital.

One of the major considerations that every business must face is what proportion of borrowed funds to net worth will best permit the company to obtain its objectives. There are relatively few businesses that are in a position to operate without borrowed funds or, from an economic standpoint, can justify operating without borrowed funds.

AVAILABILITY OF CREDIT

Probably one of the most important considerations for many borrowers is whether or not the funds will be available when needed. Most businesses are concerned with building a good reputation in order to establish credit. Once they have proven themselves by repeated performances that are acceptable to reputable lenders, their credit rating will be greatly strengthened. Once credit is established, it will not be necessary to repeat the preliminaries necessary for the first loan for subsequent loans. A good source of credit can be depended upon to adequately meet a business's needs over a period of time.

CREDIT COST

Another item that must always be considered is the cost of the credit. This is generally looked upon as being reflected primarily in interest costs, although other factors associated with obtaining the loan must be figured in when computing interest cost. For example, if there is an additional service charge or if the company is required to submit additional reports that do not contribute to the soundness of the management of the operation but are necessary only to meet the needs of the lender, then these factors would be considered added costs associated with the loan. There are some businesses that have not regularly had an audit or that have not consistently prepared a *financial statement* at the end of each month that feel that the added cost for this type of *financial accounting*, that is an essential part of sound management, should be considered as a cost associated with obtaining money. However, sound business management would dictate that an annual financial audit by an outside auditor and a monthly *balance sheet* and *income and expense summary* (*profit and loss statement*) are an essential part of doing business, and that the cost for these types of reports should not be included as a loan cost.

In addition to interest rate, there are a number of other items that are an essential part of loan cost. For example, the minimum deposit balance that a borrower must maintain in a bank could be an added loan cost, or the fact that certain business transactions would be tied to a particular business even though there were other businesses that would offer a better price is a consideration. The way interest is computed may also be a major factor. For example, is the interest paid only on the outstanding balance? Does the borrower have the opportunity to repay the loan at any time prior to maturity without prepayment penalty with the interest being paid only on the money borrowed for the number of days it was used? Is the interest paid at maturity or is the note discounted at the time the loan is secured?

Another item that frequently is of importance is the amount of elapsed time from the point a business needs money until the time it can receive the money. Many businesses will establish a *line of credit*; then, as they need these funds, they can notify the lender and draw funds from this *operating loan*. In some cases they may need the money on very short notice to meet unexpected demands or take advantage of unexpected opportunities. If they can obtain such funds in a short period of time, they will reduce the amount of the outstanding bank balance that would otherwise be needed.

LENDER MANAGEMENT CONTROL

A factor that both borrower and lender are very much concerned with has to do with the extent to which the lender can exert power over the management of an operation. Most lenders, once they have placed money into an operation, have a primary concern with those management practices that will affect the outcome of their loan. On the other hand, management usually likes to have as much freedom as possible in making decisions. As a result, when management is negotiating for a loan, one of the factors it needs to look at very carefully is the extent to which the lender will want the right to participate in the management's decisions.

A sound credit policy by both the borrower and the lender must include mutual trust. Many times when a loan is in jeopardy, or a lender feels it is in jeopardy, the lender may take steps to more actively participate in the management of the business than was the case when it had more confidence in the operation, particularly as it would affect the performance of the loan.

WAYS TO REDUCE CAPITAL NEEDS

Any business must be concerned with ways to reduce total capital needs. Four methods used by businesses to reduce capital needs are leasing, inventory control, cash operations, and limited operations.

LEASING

In some cases a business may find it is preferable to rent or lease facilities rather than own them. This may be because the business does not have the necessary capital to own such facilities, but the advantages from having the use of them more than offset the extra costs that may be incurred by renting. Another reason a business may wish to lease rather than to own is that, for some operations, technology is changing very rapidly, and the

Figure 3-8. Leasing is one way to reduce capital needs. (Courtesy, M. Thomas)

owners feel it would be more to their advantage to have relatively modern equipment from year to year than to have their limited resources tied up in a capital facility that becomes obsolete before it is worn out. In still other cases, if a business wishes to have access to certain types of equipment, it may find that it is virtually impossible to buy this equipment but that it is available to lease.

INVENTORY CONTROL

Another method that may reduce the amount of capital needed is inventory control. This can reduce the amount of capital tied up in inventory ownership as well as the amount of capital necessary to provide adequate storage for this inventory.

CASH OPERATIONS

A third method of reducing the amount of capital needed is to operate on a cash basis. Credit is not extended to customers; therefore, the business will not have any accounts receivable. If a business extends credit to its customers, then it must have access to the funds that it is, in effect, loaning to these customers.

LIMITED OPERATIONS

Another method of reducing capital requirements is to restrict the nature and scope of the operation, either by limiting the amount and types of services and/or goods that are produced or by restricting the volume of these goods and services.

The methods of financing a business are of prime importance in determining who will have a major role in making the decisions about how the business will operate. The methods of financing and capitalization are also important in determining earnings and how these earnings will be distributed. The art of making management decisions is to build around a proper analysis and interpretation of the financial statement, taking into account the changes that have occurred in this very important decision-making tool in the past year and anticipating the changes that will occur during the years ahead. Operating statements and *cash flow projections* are other financial tools that are important to use in the analysis, which is such a vital part of the management process.

CHAPTER QUESTIONS

1. What are the two sources of capital in business?

2. What is operating capital?

3. What is a prime interest rate?

4. Who makes real estate loans in the Farm Credit Administration?

5. What is collateral?

6. What is a promissory note?

7. List five types of information the business should evaluate when deciding to borrow money.

8. What is meant by the term "cost of credit"?

9. How do businesses handle money needs on a very short notice to meet unexpected demands?

Chapter 4

BUSINESS GROWTH

Many in the business community believe that each year a company should have a larger volume of business, more customers, and larger profits. They also believe in free *enterprise* that is based on the concept of a competitive market. A competitive market is one in which there are enough buyers and sellers in the market so that action by no single buyer or seller can influence the price; the products of competing businesses are enough alike that no buyer or seller prefers one business's product over that of another; that there is relative freedom of entry and exit to the business (relative freedom from legal, institutional, and economic barriers); and both sides of the market have equal access to information and the ability to interpret and to use such information.

Few situations in the economy of the United States exist which sustain such a competitive market. In such a competitive market there would be no true profit. The less efficient businesses would be forced out and there would be a relatively high rate of business failure. Usually there are a limited number of businesses on one or both sides of the market; products are branded, produced under exclusive potential processes, *copyrighted*, *patented*, or there are other barriers to entry, such as lack of capital.

The logical outcome of every business becoming larger each year is that eventually there would be a less than perfect competitive market situation. Except in agricultural production, this is the situation in the U.S. economy.

OBJECTIVES

1. Identify the reasons for business expansion.

2. Understand the methods by which a business may grow.

3. Identify limitations of growth to be considered within the business.

REASONS FOR GROWTH

Many U.S. businesses have operated exclusively within a growing market. Until recent years there was an expanding market because of population growth, real income growth, expanded exports, new production frontiers, and a changing technology with a concurrent expanded production. However, there were some businesses that did not grow unless production adjustments were made to offset technological changes. For example, successful companies making harnesses for work horses in the 1930s found the need for their services to be nearly depleted by 1960.

One of the strong reasons for *business expansion* is that growth is associated with success by many people. However, there are other arguments for growth—a business has more market power to buy and sell if it is larger and transportation costs per unit frequently decrease as the size of the shipment increases. In some cases a buyer may not even consider a particular supply source unless there is assurance of a substantial, dependable volume from that one source. There are also certain economies of operation as size expands up to a point. Beyond this point, per unit cost increases as the size of the business increases. Larger businesses are frequently in a position to develop innovative approaches not available to other businesses.

Many businesses have salary arrangements that provide bonus payments either for growth or for increased earnings. Frequently there is an assumption that growth and increased earnings are synonymous. This is not necessarily the case. There are many examples of businesses growing faster than management or capital. The results have led to severe financial losses.

Prospective employees are often concerned with being a member of a growing business. This is partly because of the "prestige" of being part of a growing organization. In such businesses there is generally a high morale

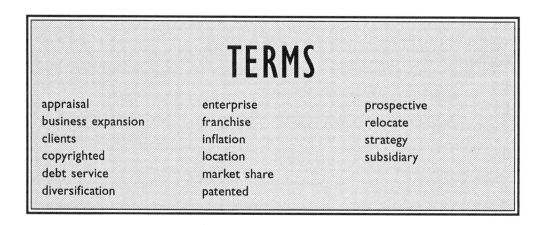

TERMS

appraisal	enterprise	prospective
business expansion	franchise	relocate
clients	inflation	strategy
copyrighted	location	subsidiary
debt service	market share	
diversification	patented	

and opportunities for more rapid promotion. Almost by definition the business must have an aggressive personnel skill development program if sound growth is to occur. This personnel skill development is especially true in a rapidly expanding industry where employees have the opportunity to change employers if they are not moving as fast as they think they should.

METHODS OF GROWTH

A business may take a number of approaches to attain effective growth. Different businesses may take different approaches, depending upon their objectives and the economic situations they face.

One method of growth is to expand the product line to meet customer needs. For example, a business handling fertilizers might expand to include an herbicide line, and another logical expansion would be adding seeds. Additional growth could be achieved by offering a custom spreading and/or spraying service.

A second method of growth is to provide a group of services not directly related to the existing business but used by many of the present customers.

Figure 4-1. A business may grow by expanding its product line to meet customer needs. A business handling fertilizers can expand with herbicides, and then add seeds. Additional growth potential would be provided by a custom spreading service. (Courtesy, Brendan Marshall)

An example of this is when the previously mentioned fertilizer business, located in a farming area with a livestock industry, adds a feed division and/or a custom feed grinding operation.

A third area of growth would be one where the business, in addition to handling farm inputs and related services, would decide to become involved in handling customer marketing; they might expand by operating a grain elevator or livestock auction. Many businesses find it necessary to provide other services in order to expand an existing segment of their business. In some areas, for a company to expand the feed business it must also assure the farmer of a market for the livestock or livestock products. Either the business or a *subsidiary* may provide this market, or the business may develop a working relationship with another business for such a market.

A fourth area of growth is to engage in an activity that attracts a new category of *clients*. This is known as *diversification*. For example, the fertilizer business could add a new line, such as home appliances or a garden store.

A fifth area of growth involves providing additional marketing functions for inputs or outputs. Examples are fertilizer or feed manufacturing, a credit service, a customer record keeping computer service, and other related services needed by customers.

Figure 4-2. A business may grow by becoming involved in handling customer marketing in addition to farm inputs and related services. (Courtesy, M. Thomas)

Figure 4-3. The above business sells a variety of different items including, feed, seed, fertilizer, ethanol, potatoes, lesscare, LP gas, posts, etc. (Courtesy, M. Thomas)

In making analyses of the growth potential alternatives suggested by the above methods, a business needs to carefully analyze factors such as market potential, competition, expected costs and capital needs, net income, and ability to hire and manage employees with the needed skills. Then management can evaluate the alternatives and make a rational decision.

Businesses usually seek a combination of activities that permit them to better serve their customers or *prospective* customers, that permit more effective use of personnel and other resources, and that improve earnings. Many times the activities supplement each other so that any new activity also increases volume and profits for other sectors of the business. Adding a feed business may attract new customers, and these new customers may also transfer their fertilizer business to the firm.

FACTORS INFLUENCING METHODS OF GROWTH

A business may be fortunate enough to be part of a growing market in which there is growth almost in spite of the action taken. Therefore, it is necessary for the management of a business to analyze growth in both an absolute sense and in terms of its *market share*. For example, a business with a 25 percent growth record over a three-year period, measured in physical or monetary terms (corrected for *inflation*), could have reason for a feeling of satisfaction. But if the total market during that same time period grew 50 percent, then its record would look less satisfactory.

A given business has the option of attempting to grow in a given *location*, *relocate* (change its location), or increase the number of locations. The advantage of increasing the number of locations is that it is more convenient for an increased number of customers to do business with the firm. The disadvantage is that there may be a certain amount of duplication of services or an increase in overhead expenses.

One of the problems many businesses encounter in expanding the area served is that they are handling products or services for which they have an exclusive *franchise* for a specific area, and the parent business or supplier firm has similar exclusive franchises with similar local businesses in all contiguous territories. Under such conditions growth must occur within a designated geographic area.

The business may decide to develop in an area in which it would build new facilities and provide a new or a similar product or service. In this case the business is attempting to enter the market and obtain some eco-

Figure 4-4. The owners of this business want its customers to know that there is new management. (Courtesy, M. Thomas)

nomic share of an existing total market. Another option is to buy an existing business, take over its facilities, some or all of the employees, and hopefully most of the customers. Either approach may be used successfully. A business entering a new market rather than taking over an existing business encounters greater expenses relating to awareness of competitors' businesses, brands, products, and services. However, when buying an existing business, there are some potential personnel problems, and there may be some customer relation problems. One who buys a business should always ask: Why is the seller willing to sell?

LIMITATIONS TO GROWTH

Accounts of business growth attempts that fail are many. Many failures can be attributed to an inadequate or inaccurate *appraisal* of growth potential. While the assumption is made that businesses make an adequate appraisal of growth potential, records suggest there are many attempts at growth that are not successful. Therefore, it is appropriate to look at some of the factors associated with lack of growth.

Frequently there are references to the three factors necessary for the successful management of a business (see Chapter 2): finance, operations, and marketing. A successful business that hopes to continue a growth pattern over a period of time needs to maintain strength in each of these areas. In any given business, management may be successful with the existing operation, but growth beyond the business's present scope may be beyond the ability of the existing management. There are many cases of failure that can be attributed to not attracting sufficiently competent personnel.

FINANCE

Many businesses become involved in growth activities at such a rate that they become overextended. Although earnings on invested capital may be high, they are not adequate to meet all operating expenses plus *debt service* needs, including principal payments. Such businesses may have inadequate equity in the business that limits access to additional borrowed funds, or if they have such access, they must pay very high interest rates. This undercapitalization is a signal that there is inadequate risk capital.

Some businesses have been unsuccessful in their growth efforts because they have had inadequate tools to effectively perform the control function

Figure 4-5. It is important for a business to have financing when it is needed.
(Courtesy, M. Thomas)

of management. Growth without control frequently results in chaos that ultimately leads to failure. Businesses must also maintain an adequate financial cushion to absorb short-term losses. Without financial reserves which permit the business to withstand some adversity, the opportunity for successful growth may be limited.

OPERATIONS

Management must be alert to ways to improve input-output efficiency—methods to increase output per unit of input. Growth entails the expansion of volume of existing products and services or the addition of products and services. In either case there is the need for constant review of operations to insure that the necessary efficiency is present. This frequently means management is concerned with changes to increase output per unit of input while employees are often more concerned with maintaining the status quo in operating procedures.

An equally important aspect of operations is preparing for the future. This suggests the need for a research and development program so that the business will be prepared to meet the needs of customers in the next year, the next decade, and the next century. A business must adjust to the constantly changing technology in the industry. Failure to adopt new techniques may place business costs in a noncompetitive range. Failure to adjust product or packaging to future market requirements may result in either product obsolescence or loss of customers.

Businesses that wish to grow provide products and services that meet customer needs. If a business does not adjust to serve customer requirements, customers then shift allegiance to businesses that will. This suggests that if a business is to successfully follow a growth pattern, it must be dynamic in operations, constantly striving to improve operating efficiency and to adjust to a changing technology in the industry, as well as keeping the product-service mix consistent with the customers' needs.

MARKETING

Many companies with efficient production operations have faultered because of failure to market their output. Until the product or service is sold at a profit and payment is received, it is incorrect to assume the operation is a success.

Figure 4-6. Successful business growth can be obtained by proper planning of finance, operations, marketing, and awareness of government regulations as shown by this aerial photo of a successful corn and soybean processing plant. (Courtesy, Lauhoff Grain Company)

In developing a marketing *strategy*, a business must be aware of the competition. Because customers are frequently making comparisons between their alternatives, the business is always at risk of losing customers to the competition. One of the opportunities for business growth is to capture competitors' customers.

A business must develop an effective marketing and distribution program to meet current and potential customers' needs. Growth attempts by many businesses have failed because the business developed such programs without first establishing customer requirements. A successful marketing program must establish a relationship between the business and current and potential customers that inspires confidence in the product, the business, and its employees. Promotional programs should be geared to present the desired message to the desired audience. Many promotional programs fail, either because they do not reach the desired audience, or because the message was offensive or obscure.

Pricing policies cannot be separated from the marketing program. If a business is to continue, it must set prices sufficiently high to meet all costs plus some minimum level of profit, but prices must be competitive and consistent with the value of the products to the potential customers. Timing of payments, credit terms, discounting policies, and other factors of this type all become part of an aggressive pricing program.

GOVERNMENT REGULATIONS

There are government regulations designed to encourage a competitive market, to insure truth in advertising, to prohibit collusion, and to control business growth and business activities related to growth in other ways. Regulations also prohibit businesses from engaging in predatory practices that will work to the disadvantage of competitors.

Government may also adversely affect growth through sudden unexpected shifts in policy that result in changing price relationships, which in turn place facilities out of position, or change areas of production or product mix. For example, a change in the freight rate on corn could change the location of the broiler industry, or a change in freight rates could change market areas.

In any event, the impact of government on business growth and the success potential for such growth must be carefully evaluated. Government production control programs or price supports, including target prices, may be important factors in determining what market functions are performed, where these functions are performed, and who makes the decisions as to where and how market functions are performed. Periodic re-evaluation of the impact of government actions on business success is an essential ingredient of sound management.

CHAPTER QUESTIONS

1. List three reasons for business expansion.

2. List five methods a business may use to grow.

3. What is a franchise?

4. Describe four limitations to growth, include:

    a. one from finance

    b. one from operations

    c. one from marketing

    d. one from government

Chapter 5

MANAGEMENT CONTROLS

In Chapter 1, the five components of management discussed were planning, organizing, directing, coordinating, and controlling. The control function is an essential part of management because it is at this stage that management determines how effective it is in its operations. Management is faced with the necessity of developing and using various measures that permit it to determine how good it is.

This chapter provides some tools the agribusiness manager can use to determine the effectiveness of the business operations.

OBJECTIVES

1. Describe different ways to measure performance of a business.

2. Discuss the need for financial audits in business.

3. Identify and describe the three basic types of financial accounting services.

4. Calculate a break-even point.

5. Discuss the reasons for a management audit.

6. Describe how various financial ratios are useful to management.

PERFORMANCE MEASURES

Management performance can be measured in a number of different ways. Businesses can develop a set of objectives along with quantitative goals that will permit them to measure how well they are performing toward meeting their objectives. Businesses do need goals and objectives, stated in measurable terms; then the results of the business's operations need to be periodically analyzed to determine the extent to which they are meeting their overall objectives. Many businesses, when they take a look at their management results and compare these with objectives, find that they are not being particularly effective in achieving their stated goals. This may mean that either the goals and objectives need to be re-evaluated or the business's *policies* and/or operating procedures need to be changed.

Another method of measuring performance is to compare the outcome of a particular business's operations with that of similar businesses. Such a comparison will permit a business to see where it is operating more efficiently than another business, as well as to see where it is operating less efficiently. From such comparisons management may then be in a position to determine where changes are indicated.

Still another method is to measure performance against some type of preconceived standards. For example, management may decide that it should operate in such a way as to provide a 10 percent rate of return on its investments. If the rate of return is greater than this, management feels it is meeting the goal. If it is less than this, there is need for further improvement.

Another measure of performance is to determine what the particular business contributes to the economy of the community. A review of business developments indicates that in many communities the leaders are becoming more concerned with how each business is contributing to the economic well-being of that community. These leaders may also be concerned with social costs the business is placing on the community that would not otherwise be incurred. There is a growing feeling in many areas that while a business has a responsibility to provide a "reasonable rate of return" to its investors, it also has a major responsibility to contribute to the economic and social development of the community. This is a new concept that many businesses have not devoted much time to analyzing. This contribution

TERMS

account	bookkeeping	production
accounting procedures	break-even analysis	ratio
accounting system	compilation	review
accounts payable	credit	solvency
accounts receivable	fixed costs	turnover
audit	integrity	variable costs
bonding	policies	

may be indicated by factors such as size of local payroll, volume of business in physical terms, and number of customers served. In some cases it may be appropriate to indicate prices from comparable businesses, contributions of a particular business toward a more competitive market, amount of taxes paid, etc.

A combination of the various measures of performance is probably needed to adequately determine management's effectiveness.

FINANCIAL MEASURES

Financial records are an important management tool containing information about the cash position of the business—including cash flow, accounts receivable and accounts payable agings, needed capital requirements in the short-term and in the long-term, and cost ratios—that can provide important guidelines for efficient operation. Such financial records frequently will indicate the extent to which the business is able to engage in

Figure 5-1. Financial records and information are important when measuring performance or making decisions in business. (Courtesy, Illinois Farm Bureau)

new enterprises or to develop a flexibility of operation that permits taking advantage of unexpected opportunities that might arise.

Probably every business manager has an individual set of financial ratios and other information that he or she has found to be particularly valuable in making decisions and measuring performance. These decisions should be made on accrual basis accounting data. Certainly the amount and type of information that is needed for one particular business would not necessarily provide the types of essential answers for some other business. Every manager must determine the types of information needed to make good decisions. Then the necessary arrangements must be made with the accounting department to insure that the *accounting system* will provide the manager with this essential data. It should be recognized that the primary reason for maintaining records is so that they will provide guidelines for rational decision making. In some cases, however, the accounting department is permitted to determine what *accounting procedures* it will follow, and management must adjust its decisions to the types of information that are available. Unless it can receive the amount and type of information it needs, management becomes a tool of the accounting department. This is more likely to be found when trying to adapt to a pre-packaged accounting software computer program.

FINANCIAL AUDIT

Every business should have a complete financial audit, at least on an annual basis. This audit should be made by a qualified, outside, disinterested business. Such an audit will indicate the accuracy of the existing records system, as well as point out such discrepancies as may exist. An audit will indicate the adequacy of insurance coverage, the extent to which there is adequate *bonding* of people who should be bonded, and other items of this nature that are important in sound business analysis. A financial audit is not only an important management tool, but it also provides assurance to management that the financial records of the company are being properly handled, provides assurance to the stockholders that their interests are being maintained, and provides assurance to the lenders as to the financial *integrity* of the business. Many lenders require regular financial audits before they will make a loan and also if they are to continue financing the business. There are three basic types of financial accounting services: (1) *Compilation*, (2) *Review*, and (3) Certified *Audit*. They vary in degree of complexity and thoroughness from a "compilation," which is just an assembly of the *account* information given to the auditor by the *bookkeeping* department into an

Figure 5-2. CPAs offer three basic types of financial accounting services:
compilation, review, and certified audit. (Courtesy, M. Thomas)

acceptable and usable financial statement, to a "certified audit" which actually validates financial transactions, inventories, *accounts payable*, *accounts receivable*, etc. through various work papers, observations, confirmations, and tests.

BREAK-EVEN ANALYSIS

Many businesses use a *break-even analysis* to indicate the level at which they must operate to break even with a given price or to show how price affects the volume necessary to break even for a particular product.

The formula for computing the break-even point is:

$$BE = \frac{FC}{P - VC}$$

Where: BE = volume at which revenue received equals cost of *production*

FC = total *fixed costs* in dollars attributed to the product (fixed costs are those costs that remain constant regardless of volume, such as depreciation, interest, taxes, insurance, etc.)

P = per unit price

VC = per unit *variable costs* (variable costs are those costs that are directly related to production, such as raw materials, labor, utilities, etc.)

Assume that for an operation there were fixed costs of $2,000, the selling price was $1.09, and the per unit variable costs were 84 cents. The business wants to know the volume needed to break even.

$$BE = \frac{2,000}{1.09 - 0.84} = \frac{2,000}{0.25} = 8,000 \text{ units}$$

MANAGEMENT AUDIT

In addition to financial audit, many businesses also make use of a management audit. In a management audit a disinterested outside party comes into the business and carefully analyzes the various operations in order to establish how the business can be operated more effectively using the resources available—including human resources. Such a management audit frequently indicates the extent of duplication of effort and the extent to which activities performed do not contribute to a more efficient operation or to the development of sound management decisions. Quite often these management audits indicate that reports needed at one point in the history of the business's activities are no longer needed; the usefulness of the reports ceases to exist, but the reports continue to be prepared. Management audits may be one of the greatest boons to the elimination of red tape. Certainly, every business needs to take a periodic look at the various activities it is engaged in, at the types of forms that must be completed, and then, in a disinterested manner, determine how each of these activities or forms contributes to more effective and efficient operation and management of the business.

In management controls, which are essentially concerned with ways of measuring management performance, the eventual concern is discovering to what extent sound judgment is tied to effective management. Judgment represents a factor that is not only difficult to measure, it is even difficult to adequately define or describe. It probably can be best defined as the ability to look at a number of alternative solutions to a particular problem and from these alternatives consistently make the kind of decision which permits the business to make satisfactory progress towards achieving its goals and objectives. Sound judgment implies that management does not make many wrong decisions. In many management decisions there is little

Figure 5-3. Many businesses make use of a management audit to analyze the various operations and use of resources. (Courtesy, Office of Agricultural Communications, Mississippi State University)

opportunity to determine what would have been the outcome if some other decision had been made, but it should be recognized that these are only best guesses. A decision, once it has been made, has many ramifications so far as resource use is concerned. As a result, a particular decision will influence a number of other decisions that are made throughout the business. In retrospect, a person could make a guess as to what the outcome would have been if there was an opportunity to make the decision over; however, in most cases one does not have this opportunity. Making a decision today on the basis of the outcome of a decision made a year ago may not necessarily be the wisest choice.

A management-control system should be set up in such a way that a person can continually test the performance of previous decisions to determine how the ability to make good decisions may be improved. If a proposed change in operation is under *consideration*, and this change has been analyzed to show how it will affect cash flow, capital position, and

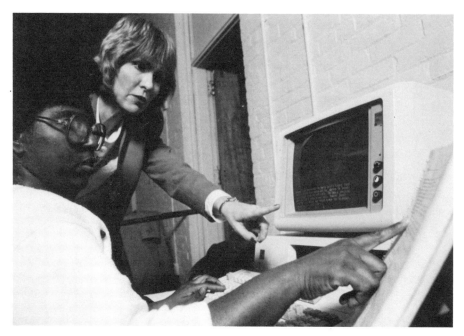

Figure 5-4. Computers are very useful when proposed changes are under consideration. They can be used to help analyze and show the effect of changes upon cash flow, capital position, and income. (Courtesy, DACC)

income; when the change is made, the results of the operation can be used to show in fact how it did affect cash flow, income position, and capital position. This type of data can then be used to help refine the analytical techniques that are involved in making projections for similar types of changes in the future.

EXAMPLES OF
FINANCIAL RATIOS USEFUL
TO MANAGEMENT

There are a number of financial ratios that may be useful to management, although the ratios will vary depending upon the nature of the business. Ratios for a fertilizer company and for a grain elevator could be quite different and still reflect strong businesses.

Ratios for a grain elevator handling corn and soybeans at harvest would be much different than its ratios in June. Management of a business should determine which ratios are most useful in a particular situation. A historical series on a particular *ratio* may be more important than a ratio for only one time period. These ratios are only one management tool that frequently can assist in problem identification.

CURRENT RATIO

Current ratio is the ratio of current assets to current liabilities. It is a measure of *solvency* or liquidity. In many businesses a ratio of 2 to 1 is considered desirable. A ratio of 1 to 1 or less indicates the business may have difficulty meeting its short-term obligations, such as supplier invoices, interest payments, and payroll. Frequently this suggests more of the debt should be transferred to long-term debt, assuming that the short-term problems which created the non-current position have been corrected. This ratio is derived by the formula:

$$\frac{\text{Current Assets}}{\text{Current Liabilities}}$$

Total Liabilities to Net Worth

An additional measure of solvency is the ratio of total liabilities to net worth. In some businesses a ratio of 50 cents to 75 cents of debt to $1 net worth is considered to be in the acceptable range. Many businesses can operate with debt/worth ratios greater than 1 and even up to 4–5 to 1 but that debt must be balanced—spread evenly between short, intermediate, and long-term. The smaller the net worth in relation to the debt, the less financial strength there is for lenders and owners. In many businesses, except in seasonally heavy periods, a rule of thumb suggests liabilities should not exceed net worth. If such a heavy debt load exists, there may be reason to feel the business is undercapitalized. The solution is to increase net worth. The formula for this measure is:

$$\frac{\text{Total Liabilities}}{\text{Net Worth}}$$

Fixed Assets to Net Worth

The ratio of fixed assets to net worth is another measure of solvency. This ratio will measure the degree to which the business's capital has been invested in long-term assets such as plant and equipment. For many agribusinesses fixed assets should be in the range of 65 to 75 percent of net worth. If new assets are not added to a business over time, and the business is operating at a profit, one would expect this ratio to decline. Assets would be reduced by depreciation each year, and net worth would increase by the amount of earnings left in the business each year. The formula for this ratio is:

$$\frac{\text{Fixed Assets}}{\text{Net Worth}}$$

Net Earnings to Net Worth[1]

The rate earned on equity capital is reflected by the ratio of net earnings to net worth. This ratio measures profitability. A wholesale farm supply business should expect 13 to $17\frac{1}{2}$ percent as a good ratio while a retail farm supply business may range from 10 to 32 percent. The formula for this ratio is:

$$\frac{\text{Net Earnings}}{\text{Net Worth}}$$

OPERATING RATIOS[1]

A number of operating ratios may be useful in evaluating performance and liquidity.

Accounts receivable to current assets shows the extent to which current assets are tied up in accounts receivable. Only an analysis of these accounts and their collectability, along with alternative use of funds, can indicate if the ratio is reasonable. The formula is:

$$\frac{\text{Accounts Receivable}}{\text{Current Assets}}$$

The average days in accounts receivable measures liquidity. Two calculations are necessary to determine the average number of days of an accounts receivable. The formulas are:

$$\frac{\text{Total Month Sales}}{\text{No. of Days in Month}} = \text{Average Daily Sale} \qquad \frac{\text{Accounts Receivable}}{\text{Average Daily Sale}} = \text{No. of Days}$$

---

[1]Source: Robert Morris and Associates studies on agribusinesses with sales up to $1,000,000.

Inventory to current assets shows the demand on assets to finance inventory and the importance of inventory on liquidity. A good ratio for a wholesale farm supply business would be 28 to 40 percent. The retail farm supply business usually does not have as much accounts receivable as the wholesaler. Therefore, their total current assets are usually less. A good ratio for the retail farm supply would be 72 to 77 percent. The formula is:

$$\frac{\text{Inventory}}{\text{Current Assets}}$$

Net sales to receivables measures solvency by the extent of sales which are made on *credit* and the extent to which credit sales are making large demands on capital. The higher the ratio, the shorter the time between the sale and collection of cash from the sale. The formula is:

$$\frac{\text{Net Sales}}{\text{Receivables}}$$

Inventory to annual cost of sales reflects a measure of *turnover* and profitability. Many businesses may want a turnover five or six times a year. This varies with the type of business and the time of year when the ratio is computed. The formula is:

$$\frac{\text{Inventory}}{\text{Annual Cost of Sales}}$$

Other operating ratios may be particularly useful to a specific business, such as cost per dollar sales and cost per ton, depending on the type of business.

POLICY AND CONTROL

Management is faced with the need to establish policies that will permit the business to reach its goals and objectives, to see that the policies are carried out, and finally to see how the established policies assist in reaching the business's goals and objectives. This frequently means that management must also be willing to re-examine policies to determine necessary changes to more adequately reach its goals and objectives.

Management needs to be alert to any discrepancies that develop between policy actions and results. At the time a policy decision was made, management would generally have been concerned with how this particular

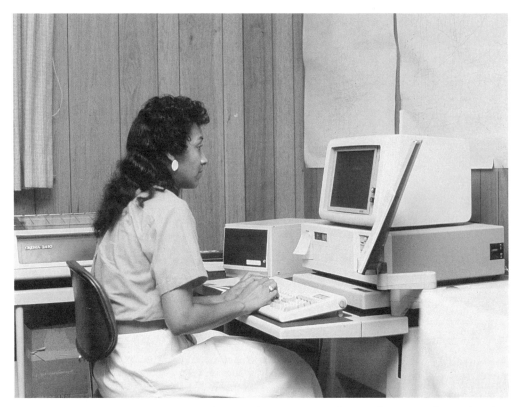

Figure 5-5. Computers are a very useful tool for managers when evaluating ratios and saving historical data for future comparison. (Courtesy, Office of Agricultural Communications, Mississippi State University)

action would affect results. In retrospect, it should then take a look at what actually happened to determine how effective it was in achieving its desired goals.

There is a need for management to continually seek effective ways of measuring performance. When performance is measured, then management is in a position to take corrective measures to improve overall effectiveness.

MANAGEMENT IN RETROSPECT

Throughout this book two aspects of management are emphasized: one has to do with decision making and establishing policy, and the other has to do with carrying out this policy. The discussion has emphasized that management is concerned with five major activities: planning, organizing, directing, coordinating, and controlling.

The discussion has also emphasized the need to define goals and objectives and then set the operation up in such a way that these may be measured. In doing this management can determine how effectively the performance is meeting expectations. It is suggested that attempting to develop a sound management procedure, under conditions where there are inadequate methods of measuring performance, provides a framework in which both managers and employees will have difficulty in receiving the personal satisfaction that should come from a job well done.

Figure 5-6. A successful, well-managed agribusiness in Monmouth, IL. (Courtesy, Brendan Marshall)

This book is an introductory appraisal into agribusiness management. Every effort has been made to minimize the application of abstract concepts to an understanding of management. On more sophisticated levels, management is concerned with the application of many different economic concepts; however, an application of those concepts should come in a subsequent course.

CHAPTER QUESTIONS

1. What are four ways to measure business performance?

2. Where does a manager get financial data for measuring performance?

3. What is a financial audit?

4. What is the purpose of a management audit?

5. What are three basic types of financial accounting services?

6. What is a break-even point?

7. What are two ratios to measure solvency or liquidity of a business?

8. What are the two aspects of management emphasized throughout the first five chapters of this book?

9. What are the five major activities of management?

Chapter 6

THE ENTREPRENEUR AND ENTREPRENEURSHIP

A person who organizes and manages a business, assuming risk for the sake of profit, is known as an *entrepreneur*. *Entrepreneurship* is assuming the risks of owning one's own business. Many young people are entrepreneurs at one time or another. While their amount of risk may be small, they are entrepreneurs in the truest sense. Some examples include the boy or girl with his or her own newspaper route or neighborhood lawn mowing service, a teenager who provides child care, and children with lemonade stands in their front yards on hot summer days.

Today there are many opportunities to take a viable idea and, with an entrepreneurial approach, develop it into a successful business *venture*. This chapter presents the nature and considerations of being an entrepreneur.

OBJECTIVES

1. Define entrepreneur and entrepreneurship.

2. Discuss the advantages and disadvantages of being self-employed.

3. Identify the four types of economic resources used in all economic systems.

4. Identify the personal characteristics of successful entrepreneurs.

5. List the components of a business plan.

6. Explain the purpose of a cash flow statement.

7. Compare buying a business to starting a new business.

8. Identify sources of technical assistance.

NATURE AND CONSIDERATIONS OF ENTREPRENEURSHIP

Individuals are motivated in different ways, but everyone has needs, preferences, and desires. These—coupled with abilities, education, experience, and financial position—cause one to set goals in his or her life that become an individual's driving force.

Not everyone is motivated to be his or her own boss. Some individuals have a need for security and recognition from others. Their personalities may make them excellent employees or managers working for someone else, but they would not consider taking the risk necessary to be entrepreneurs.

Entrepreneurship has both advantages and disadvantages. Entrepreneurs must consider these when evaluating whether or not entrepreneurship is for them. Some advantages and disadvantages are listed below.

Advantages of the entrepreneurial approach:

1. Allows a person to be his or her own boss

2. Provides for increased rewards if the business is successful

3. Capitalizes on creativity

4. Offers increased chances for pride and self-satisfaction

5. Allows an individual to set his or her own work schedule

6. Provides a variety of tasks to perform

Disadvantages of the entrepreneurial approach:

1. Calls for taking risks

2. Requires financial investment

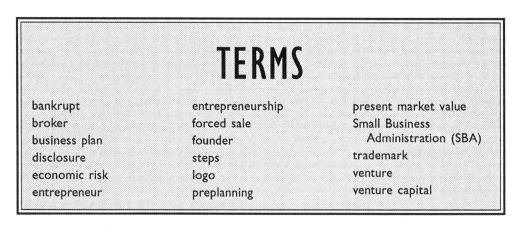

TERMS

bankrupt	entrepreneurship	present market value
broker	forced sale	Small Business
business plan	founder	Administration (SBA)
disclosure	steps	trademark
economic risk	logo	venture
entrepreneur	preplanning	venture capital

Figure 6-1. A franchise gives an entrepreneur larger corporate management
support. (Courtesy, M. Thomas)

3. Provides no guarantee of financial return on investment

4. Often requires more time than other jobs

5. Includes responsibility for compliance with government regulations

TYPES OF ECONOMIC RESOURCES

Four types of economic resources are used in all economic systems to
produce goods or services to satisfy human needs—

1. Natural resources

2. Human resources

3. Capital resources

4. Technological resources

The entrepreneur must determine what resources are needed to operate
his or her business. If these resources are needed for the business to function,
the entrepreneur will have to acquire them.

Natural resources are land or material supplied by land. Human resources are the physical labor needed to produce a product or provide a

Figure 6-2. This is an example of seasonal business limiting the amount of human resources needed. (Courtesy, M. Thomas)

Figure 6-3. For this advertisement the entrepreneur has combined the image of a classic car with the concept of eating buffalo. (Courtesy, M. Thomas)

service. Capital resources are the monies used to purchase buildings, equipment, and supplies that are needed for production. Technological resources are the organizational abilities and administrative expertise needed to manage the business successfully.

PERSONAL POTENTIAL

Successful entrepreneurs seem to exhibit certain personal characteristics which are not present in everyone. While these characteristics are not absolutely essential for success, they do indicate the personality or nature of individuals who are most likely to succeed as entrepreneurs.

Successful entrepreneurs are independent and like to work in unstructured situations. Their actions are of their own choosing; they don't necessarily follow the dictates of others. Entrepreneurs are willing to assume risks and do not restrict their actions to traditional patterns if alternatives have promise for success. They are often creative in thinking of new ways to solve problems. These individuals are self-confident and determined to keep trying until the job is done. They are responsible and accountable for their own actions—willing to assume the blame for failure or problems. Successful entrepreneurs are goal-oriented; they develop plans and execute them to achieve the goals they have set. They use time and resources wisely. They are open minded and willing to listen to new ideas or concepts and are not afraid to ask for advice. Successful entrepreneurs are leaders. These individuals have good interpersonal relationship skills and can get others to follow their direction.

ENTREPRENEURSHIP OPPORTUNITIES

Before the entrepreneur invests *venture capital*, he or she should carefully evaluate the *market niche* of the proposed business. The results of this evaluation, along with other logical steps in the *preplanning* process—including the development of a detailed *business plan*—will dictate if and how one should proceed.

The six most common reasons businesses fail are insufficient sales, mismanagement, inadequate funding or capitalization, bad timing within the economic cycle, bad debts owed to the business, and competition that is more efficient or able to sell a product or service for less. The importance of advance planning in starting a business cannot be overstated. This begins with a precise business plan.

Figure 6-4. A crop duster needs technical expertise and sufficient working capital before entering business. (Courtesy, Office of Agricultural Communications, Mississippi State University)

Components of a Business Plan

The components of a business plan for starting an enterprise include the time, costs, returns, and capital required to achieve success. There are ten steps involved in developing the plan.

1. An idea—What is to be developed or done.

2. Competition—Is anyone else doing it or can it be done better or cheaper?

3. Market—Who will buy the product or service?

4. Resources—What material, human, capital and technological resources are needed to operate the business?

5. Regulations—What are the federal, state and local regulations which will affect this business?

6. Marketing plan—Will it be necessary to advertise? Will sales be seasonal or constant throughout the year?

7. Location—Where will the business be located? How much floor space will be needed? Will space be rented or owned? Will customers come into the business? Will visibility be a factor? Is the possibility of expansion a consideration?

8. Employees—Are additional employees necessary? What qualifications should they have? What will the cost of wages and benefits be?

9. Management—Who will manage the business?

10. Financial plan—Items should include estimated income and expenses for the first year of operation. The components needed include a profit and loss statement, balance sheet containing the assets and liabilities of the business, and a cash flow statement.

Topics covering the various components of a business plan are covered in detail in other chapters of this book. Presented here is a brief description of what information is included in the business plan and why.

Cash Flow Statement

A cash flow statement shows the projected or actual flow of cash into

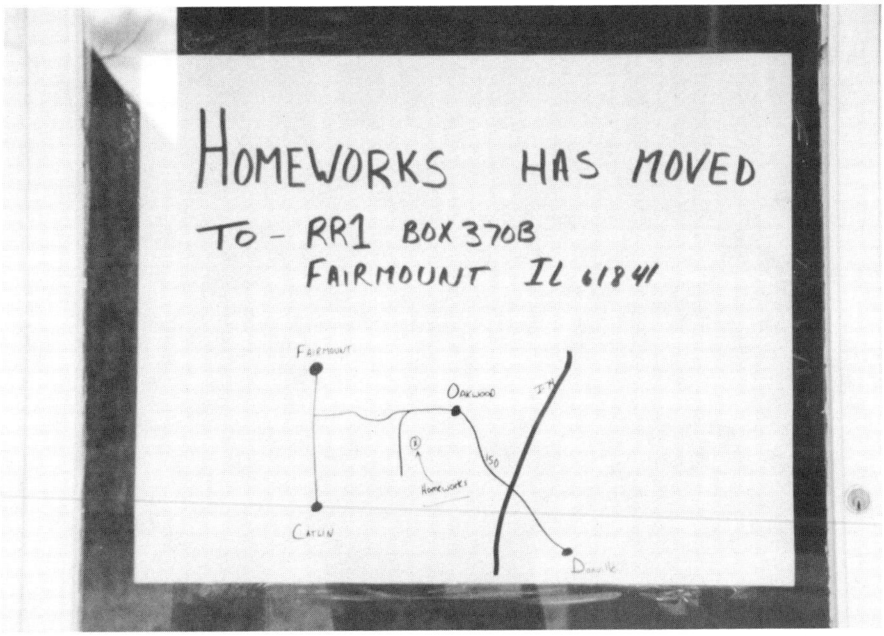

Figure 6-5. This sign is all that remains of a business location that was unsuccessful, causing the owner to relocate. (Courtesy, M. Thomas)

or out of the business for a specific period. A business can be profitable, yet have cash flow problems during certain times of the year. These problems may result from seasonal changes in sales, unexpected expenses, or problems related to credit.

The purpose of the cash flow statement is to alert the entrepreneur to possible cash shortfalls which must be met. By knowing in advance, he or she may plan to get through low cash periods by limiting purchases, getting extended credit terms, concentrating on collecting accounts receivable, or making arrangements for the availability of a line of credit at a financial institution.

When starting a new business, it is very important to have a cash flow statement. Many small businesses fail because the cash available is insufficient to pay expenses. It is not unusual for a new business to have cash flow problems during its first year of operation. More discussion of cash flow will follow in Chapter 15.

Buying or Starting a Business

There isn't a hard and fast rule to determine whether it is better to buy an established, existing business or to start and build a new business.

Figure 6-6. This cooperative business is a converted gas station with a prime location for customer traffic. (Courtesy, M. Thomas)

Figure 6-7. The above sign indicates that there may be a forced sale situation since the business is closed. (Courtesy, M. Thomas)

There are advantages and disadvantages to each. Professional technical assistance will be of great value whether starting or buying a business.

When starting a new business the entrepreneur has the opportunity to create his or her own image. He or she will have full choice of the area of competition, business location, suppliers, facilities, and equipment. It will not be necessary to overcome any prior negative publicity or policies. In this case the entrepreneur is the *founder* of the business.

There are many advantages to purchasing an existing business. However, there can also be a number of pitfalls. The entrepreneur should carefully evaluate the situation before taking the *economic risk* of acquiring the business. A misrepresentation of facts can greatly reduce the chance of the business to prosper. First, one should determine the reason the present owner is selling the business. Is it a *forced sale* or *bankrupt* situation or does the owner wish to retire or change his or her situation? Has the current owner made any *disclosure* of facts that may indicate the possibility of a contingent liability? Is the selling price of the business really the *present market value*? Is the business successful and profitable? Is it well managed? The answers to these kinds of questions are important before the decision is made to consummate the transaction of buying the business.

The advantages of purchasing a going concern are numerous. A business already in operation has an established customer base, sales pattern, and name recognition. The facilities, equipment, and employees—aside from the owner—are in place. Prior history and cash flow are available for analysis. Suppliers already know the business, and a *logo* or *trademark* may already provide immediate recognition. These advantages make it easier for the entrepreneur to perpetuate the business.

Figure 6-8. The entrepreneur will have to decide whether it is better to purchase or lease property. (Courtesy, M. Thomas)

Sources of Technical Assistance

Professional accountants can be very helpful when entering business. They can help develop the business plan, analyze the financial plan, design an accounting system which will be appropriate for the business, and evaluate the financial records of an existing business. They often prepare taxes and audits at the end of the business's fiscal year. They can also assist in preparation of loan documents such as those of *Small Business Administration (SBA)* whose purpose is to promote small business development.

There are a number of reasons to obtain a company lawyer. He or she will be able to handle items for the business such as leases, options and contracts, as well as give advice on the organizational structure of the

Figure 6-9. A business logo provides immediate recognition. (Courtesy, Interstate
            Publishers, Inc.)

business. A detailed comparison of organizational structures appears in
Chapter 1, Table 1-1.

When acquiring property, some businesses use a real estate agent or
broker. That person can be a valuable source in evaluating the options
available to a business for its location. He or she can help ensure that the
location has the proper zoning for the type of business, as well as provide
a number of location options for the entrepreneur to evaluate.

Certain types of businesses have trade associations. Such an organization
can be very helpful to an entrepreneur by providing specific information

Figure 6-10. A company lawyer will be able to handle items such as leases and
             contracts for the entrepreneur. (Courtesy, M. Thomas)

ranging from current regulations that affect the business to price structures for products and services.

The local office of the cooperative extension service is an excellent source of technical information. This office will have publications—based on research at land-grant universities—that cover topics ranging from the production of agricultural products to services for getting a particular type of business started. The telephone directory listing under county government will also provide a source for assistance.

CHAPTER QUESTIONS

1. What is an entrepreneur?

2. What are four advantages of being self-employed?

3. What are the four types of economic resources?

4. What are seven personal characteristics of successful entrepreneurs?

5. What are the six most common reasons businesses fail?

6. What are the ten components of a business plan?

7. What is a cash flow statement?

8. What opportunities are there for the entrepreneur who starts a new business?

9. What are some of the advantages of buying a business already in operation?

10. What are four sources of technical assistance for the entrepreneur?

Chapter 7

BUSINESS RELATED LAWS

The standards of behavior or conduct that society sets and expects of individuals and businesses are defined as ethics. This *ethical* behavior or conduct includes moral standards, ideals, and principles. This chapter provides an overview of the laws that typically affect an agribusiness. It is **not** intended to provide legal advice, but to give the reader an awareness of laws and how they might affect the agribusiness. The agribusiness manager should consult an attorney for advice on compliance with specific laws and regulations.

OBJECTIVES

1. Name the three types of laws.

2. Identify the four general sources of laws.

3. Describe liability and negligence as it relates to business.

4. Describe health and safety regulations regarding agricultural chemicals.

5. Describe common legal requirements of business.

6. Identify common legal documents used in business.

TYPES OF LAWS

Laws are the legal instruments that hold individuals or businesses responsible for their actions. The three types of laws normally affecting a business include: (1) local laws, (2) state laws, and (3) federal laws.

LOCAL LAWS

Local communities, such as cities or counties, establish *ordinances* that

Figure 7-1. Zoning restrictions limit a section or district to a particular use. This business for-sale sign indicates B-2 zoning. (Courtesy, M. Thomas)

regulate certain activities of business. These laws may require a particular permit or *license fee* for specific kinds of businesses. They may be in the form of a *zoning restriction* limiting a section or district in a city to a particular use or a *city zoning ordinance* dividing the city into areas where certain types of businesses may be located. *Building permits*, building codes, and inspection are common in most cities when a facility is constructed or renovated. Other ordinances may also restrict noise, waste, pollution, or

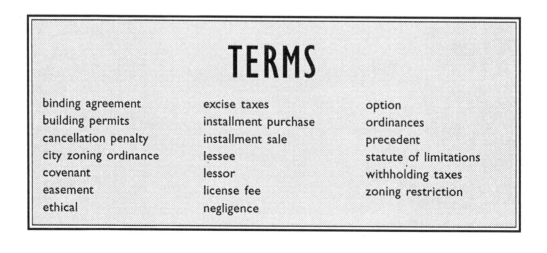

TERMS

binding agreement	excise taxes	option
building permits	installment purchase	ordinances
cancellation penalty	installment sale	precedent
city zoning ordinance	lessee	statute of limitations
covenant	lessor	withholding taxes
easement	license fee	zoning restriction
ethical	negligence	

storage of products or equipment. Local government bodies may also impose local taxes on a business or its products.

STATE LAWS

The state in which a business is located has additional laws affecting the business. Examples of these laws include state income tax, sales or use taxes, licenses, permits, fair labor standards, waste disposal, pollution standards, minimum age of employees, unemployment insurance, and workers' compensation insurance for employees. In addition, certain types of agricultural businesses may have specific laws which affect them, such as regulations on the transportation of fertilizers or chemicals.

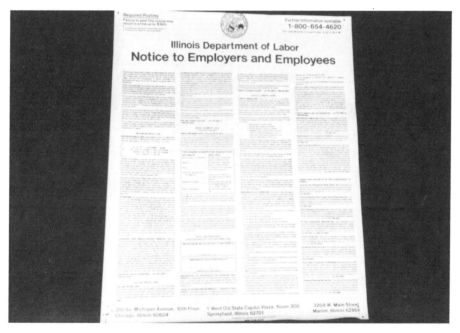

Figure 7-2. Employers are required to display notices to employees in most states. (Courtesy, M. Thomas)

FEDERAL LAWS

Federal laws may be similar to state laws but generally relate to the national population. Examples of federal laws include federal income tax, social security tax on employees and employers, regulation of the handling and storage of hazardous materials, occupational safety and health standards

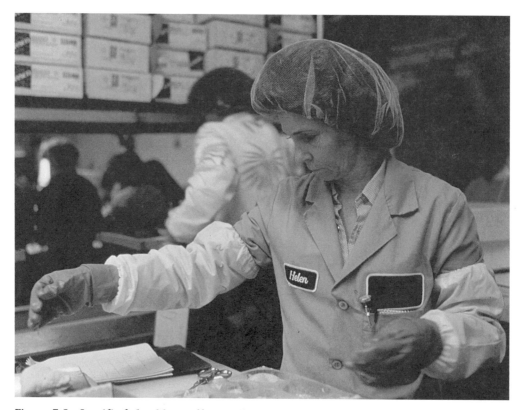

Figure 7-3. Specific federal laws affect agribusinesses, such as those regulating sanitation and storage of food. (Courtesy, Office of Agricultural Communications, Mississippi State University)

with regards to working conditions, federal unemployment insurance, fair trade and antitrust laws, and guidelines for interstate commerce. There may also be specific laws affecting agribusinesses such as those regulating sanitation and storage of food.

Laws are in a constant state of revision or change, with new laws being drafted and/or implemented on a regular basis. A statutory law is a written law as distinguished from unwritten or common law. The *statute of limitations* is a law limiting the period within which a specific legal action may be taken. A major issue being discussed at the federal level which will affect business, if enacted as law, is national health care reform.

SOURCES OF LAWS

Laws may come from many sources but can usually be traced to four basic sources:

1. Custom or common practice

2. Legislative bodies

3. Court decisions and opinions

4. Government regulations

The way people act over an extended period of time often becomes an accepted standard of conduct or common practice. Courts often refer to these customs to settle disputes. Decisions of judges are often referred to in order to settle later claims or disputes of a similar nature. Because a *precedent* has been set by continuing to use these decisions, a common law is established. Local, state, and federal governments are empowered to create, revise, or change laws. These bodies include city councils, county boards, state legislatures, and the U.S. Congress. Government regulatory bodies may pass rules within their power which affect business. Two examples of these bodies are the Environmental Protection Agency (EPA) and the Occupational Safety and Health Administration (OSHA).

LEGAL LIABILITY AND NEGLIGENCE

Of particular importance in law is responsibility or liability for personal injury or property damage. Insurance, as discussed in Chapter 10, is the business's protection against such claims. In most instances the liability must be determined based on *negligence*. It must be proven that harm or injury occurred as the result of an action or lack of action on the part of the business. Businesses may be liable for the negligent actions of their employees. Businesses are also responsible for the safety and well being of their employees. For example, businesses are responsible for providing (1) a safe work place, (2) safe tools and equipment, (3) information and instruction for safe operation of equipment or handling of materials or products, (4) emergency and safety supplies or clothing, and (5) rules and policies for employee conduct while on the job.

AGRICULTURAL CHEMICAL LAWS AND REGULATIONS

Federal regulations require specific care while handling or using chem-

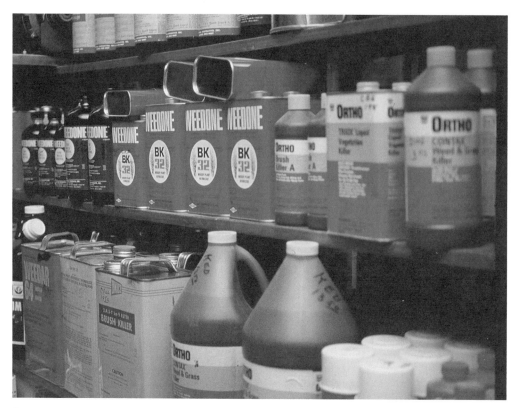

Figure 7-4. Federal regulations require uniform labeling standards for agricultural chemicals. (Courtesy, Office of Agricultural Communications, Mississippi State University)

icals which can kill a living organism. The federal regulations are concerned with:

1. Testing and experimentation

2. Compliance with federal and state laws

3. Uniform labeling standards

State laws vary; however, in most states certification is required before a person may use or handle certain chemicals. A business assumes liability when handling and applying chemicals. Proper care must be exercised.

Regulations affecting the health and safety of employees and the community are an important aspect of the handling and usage of agricultural chemicals. It may be necessary to store chemicals where a spill cannot enter a city's sewer system or an open waterway, or there may need to be some type of protective barrier designed into a facility to contain a spill. In addition, protective clothing and counter-measures may have to be available to those working with chemicals. Caution should always be exercised by checking with regulatory agencies when using agricultural chemicals.

LEGAL REQUIREMENTS AND DOCUMENTS

There are many legal requirements an owner or manager must consider when operating a business. Some requirements are directly affected by the organizational structure as covered in Chapter 1. For example sole proprietorships report business income on their personal income tax returns while for-profit corporations must file an income tax return directly for the business. Other reporting requirements, such as sales tax reporting, are dictated by the governing authority.

Figure 7-5. Regulations affecting health and safety of employees and the community are an aspect of the handling and usage of agricultural chemicals. (Courtesy, Office of Agricultural Communications, Mississippi State University)

COMMON LEGAL REQUIREMENTS

Taxation is the most common legal requirement with which a business must comply. It comes in many forms and varies state by state and community by community. Some forms of taxation include (1) federal, state and local income taxes; (2) federal and state unemployment taxes; (3) real estate taxes; (4) personal property taxes; (5) sales taxes; (6) use or *excise taxes*; (7) social security taxes (employee and employer portions); and (8) *withholding taxes* from employees' wages.

Licenses, identification numbers, permits, and certificates are required by many city, county, state and federal authorities. These may include such items as federal employer identification numbers, state sales tax or reseller's certificates, and identification numbers for withholding taxes. Building permits may be required for construction projects. Work permits may be necessary for employees under legal age in a particular state.

In addition to the various tax returns, a business is responsible for documenting wages to employees and compensation to others. Laws may require periodic reporting to governing authorities, the preparation of annual documents, and providing documents to those to whom compensation was paid in the form of W-2 or 1099 forms.

Figure 7-6. A modern lawyer may use publications and computer data bases when conducting legal research. (Courtesy, M. Thomas)

Other requirements may include workers' compensation, provided through an insurance policy paid for by the business to protect employees in the event of job-related injury or health problems, OSHA standards for a safe work place, and EPA standards to protect the environment.

COMMON LEGAL DOCUMENTS

In the course of business a number of documents or contracts may be necessary. Some common forms are: mortgage, promissory note, security agreement, stock certificate, deed, bill of sale, title, registration, *installment*

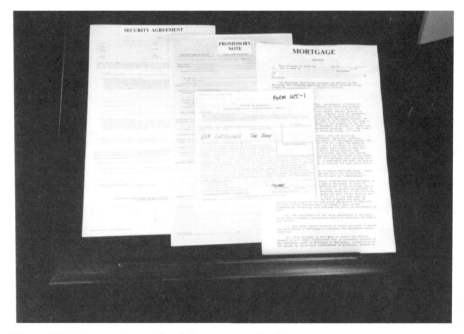

Figure 7-7. Some common legal documents a business owner or manager may work with include a mortgage, promissory note, security agreement, and a Uniform Commercial Code filing. (Courtesy, M. Thomas)

purchase or *installment sale* agreement, and lease. Leases are commonly thought of as an agreement pertaining to land or facilities but today often apply to equipment. Equipment leases may offer the *lessee* an opportunity to purchase the equipment at the end of the lease period from the *lessor* at a fixed price.

The language in a contract, note, or *covenant* is very important. It is too late, after the document is signed, to make a change if there was something in the agreement adversely affecting the business. There may be a *cancellation penalty*, prepayment penalty, or other provision which should be known and understood ahead of time. It is often necessary to have a *binding agreement* reviewed by an attorney in order to determine how the agreement affects the business and its operation.

An *option* may be an important consideration when a business is considering building or expanding its operations. An option may give the business time to consider such a move and yet guarantee the price. Another important consideration in dealing with real property is any *easement* that may exist or may be needed. Easements commonly found involve rights of way for utilities. Easements can also provide access on an exclusive or non-exclusive basis.

CHAPTER QUESTIONS

1. What are the three types of laws?

2. What are the four sources of laws?

3. How does a business protect itself from liability for personal injury or property damage judgments?

4. What are some of the bodies empowered to create, revise, or change laws?

5. What are federal regulations concerned with in the handling or using of chemicals?

6. What is the most common legal requirement with which a business must comply?

7. What are five forms of taxes?

8. What are six common forms of legal documents?

Chapter 8

HUMAN RESOURCE MANAGEMENT

A major element of management is getting things done through people, so the key to successful management is closely related to the ability of the manager to obtain as much productivity per employee as is consistent with good business practices. Employees who are satisfied with their pay, benefits, and working conditions are more productive and loyal to the business. This chapter focuses on processes involved in providing the business with a productive work force.

OBJECTIVES

1. Identify ways of recruiting personnel.

2. Discuss ways of evaluating prospective employees.

3. Define equal employment opportunity.

4. Identify federal laws prohibiting discrimination.

5. Discuss the kinds of information contained in an employee company rules and policies manual.

6. Identify ways to improve employee relations.

7. Discuss the advantages and disadvantages of promoting from within the business.

8. Identify causes of poor employee morale.

PERSONNEL SELECTION

When selecting personnel, management is interested in finding someone who has the technical skills to perform the necessary activities associated with the job, and who meets criteria as to honesty, dependability, and other personal characteristics of this type. In addition, management wants a person who will fit into the organization and be able to work with other people in the business. Finally, a business needs a person who has the potential to develop and assume greater responsibility over the years. In this way, management will be able to develop personnel that will grow with the business.

One technique most businesses find to be helpful in selecting personnel is developing a *job description*, and then hiring someone who meets the criteria they have listed.

SOURCES OF PERSONNEL

When searching for personnel, a business may wish to take many different approaches. Sources of recruiting personnel will vary with areas in the United States and with the particular needed skills or positions. For less skilled jobs, advertising in a local newspaper may be an effective way of recruiting personnel. For other types of jobs a business may check with other businesses in the area or with other businesses in its regional system. Some businesses may be a part of larger systems in which the parent organization has the major responsibility of recruiting personnel for the business. High schools, junior/community colleges, and universities are other sources that may provide helpful leads in locating the right person

TERMS

Age Discrimination in Employment Act (1967)	discrimination	grievances
	employee incentive	job description
Americans with Disabilities Act (1992) and (1994)	Employee Retirement Income Security Act (1974) and (1982)	leave of absence
		nepotism
		probationary period
arbitration	Equal Employment Opportunities	résumés
Civil Rights Act, Title VII (1964) and (1991)		seniority
	Equal Pay Act (1986)	severance pay
commission	Executive Order 11246	sexual harassment
company benefits	Family and Medical Leave Act (1993)	termination
compensation		

Figure 8-1. A job description for a staff employee should include position, reporting authority, and specific duties and responsibilities. These may include technical functions, active participation in sales programs and customer relations.

for the job. The state employment service also may be able to provide prospective applicants. Private employment agencies are often used for a highly-technical skilled position or when recruiting upper management.

In medium-sized or larger businesses there is often a human resource department. The human resource manager has, as one of several duties, the responsibility of recruiting personnel. In smaller businesses this activity is frequently one of the responsibilities of the general manager. Most businesses maintain a file containing inquiries and *résumés* from people who have indicated an interest in working for the business. This file should include a formal application, which indicates the person's previous training and

Figure 8-2. Local newspaper classified ads may be an effective way of recruiting personnel. (Courtesy, M. Thomas)

experience, as well as the names of people from whom business and personal references may be obtained. The prospective employee should advise those people listed as references, so that they will be in a position to indicate their current activities, as well as give their appraisal of the applicant in general. From the employer's viewpoint, these references should contribute to a better understanding of the person's technical potential and personal characteristics, such as honesty, dependability, and diligence. In analyzing references, an employer is soon able to determine those reference sources that consistently evaluate the prospective employee by pointing out strong and weak points, as well as those reference sources that essentially contribute very little to a better appraisal of the person's capabilities. Most employers, in addition to checking with the references that a prospective employee provides, will also make some inquiries of other people who may be able to contribute an additional appraisal of the individual and his or her capabilities.

Another method often used by businesses to determine the capabilities of an applicant is to administer an evaluation test to the prospective employee. Depending upon the nature of the job, many businesses either have developed tests on their own or have arranged to use various types of tests that have been developed by others. In any case, such tests must be approved by the federal government as unbiased and non-discriminatory. These tests may reveal a number of characteristics of the individuals.

The final and most important source of information in evaluating a prospective employee is the personal interview. In the interview, the employer is attempting to discover information about the prospective employee's ability to effectively meet the requirements of the job insofar as technical competency, ability to work with people, and how the applicant would fit into the organization. Then, the employer must evaluate those personal characteristics that are considered important in the job.

Figure 8-3. Some businesses indicate employment opportunities on a sign at their business. (Courtesy, M. Thomas)

The steps a human resource manager uses to evaluate prospective employees are:

1. Evaluating previous training and experience

2. Checking with business and personal references

3. Making additional inquiries of others known by the manager

4. Administering an evaluation test

5. Conducting a personal interview

Hopefully, all of these methods will contribute to the selection of qualified personnel who will contribute to the business's objectives. From the standpoint of conserving the business's resources, it is to the advantage of the business to select personnel in such a manner that the rate of turnover will be held at a minimum. It is generally recognized that the cost of training personnel is very high. During their early training period, most employees do not make a contribution to the business that is equal to the amount of their *compensation*. The length of the training period—the time it takes until a person is thoroughly acquainted with the job and can perform it in an efficient manner—will vary with the capabilities of the individual and with the complexity of the job involved. It is also important from the standpoint of the prospective employee. If he or she does not meet the requirements for the job, this training represents a cost to that individual of being employed in a job that does not offer a future.

Once a person has been employed, it is necessary to have a definite understanding with that individual as to the nature of the job and what is expected of that employee. It should be thoroughly understood what hours he or she is to work each day; who the supervisor is; the organizational line of authority; what the wage scale, *commission* rate, or salary schedule is; the options or *arbitration* procedure for handling *grievances* and misun-

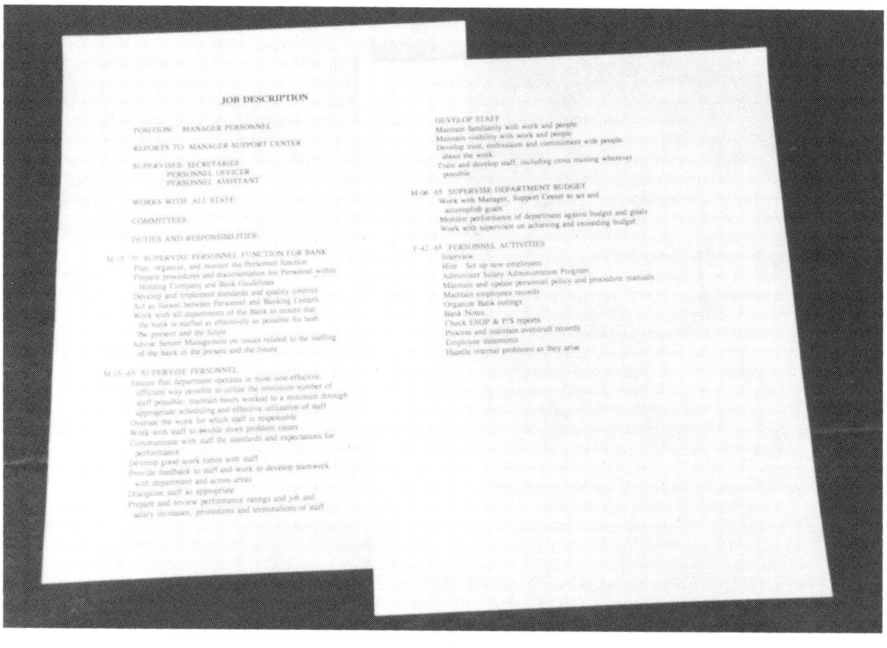

Figure 8-4. A manager's or supervisor's job description includes such items as position, reports to, works with, committee assignments, and duties and responsibilities. (Courtesy, M. Thomas)

derstandings; and what training programs are available. The duties and responsibilities of an employee need to be spelled out specifically, usually in the form of a job description. By the same token, the business should understand what the employee's expectations are so that misunderstandings and frustrations can be kept to a minimum.

The prospective employee should also understand the method of compensation, the deductions from his or her paycheck, and the *company benefits*. Both management and, if applicable, the union, in their relationship to each other and in their relationship with the business's employees, must recognize their joint responsibility to provide efficient, effective service to the business's customers. Very few businesses can afford to ignore customers.

EMPLOYMENT POLICIES AND LAWS

A very important part of human resource management is to ensure that the business's policies and hiring practices are in compliance with federal and state laws. It is the business's responsibility to provide *equal employment opportunities* in personnel activities without prejudicial *discrimination*. These activities include recruitment, hiring, promotion, training, compensation, benefits, working conditions, and termination. Working conditions include both the Occupation and Safety Health Act (OSHA) and the employer's responsibility to eliminate any *sexual harassment* in the work place.

Discrimination against employees cannot be made on the basis of age, race, sex, religion, national origin, physical or mental handicaps, or pay. The following is a partial list of federal laws and orders which support employment opportunities.

1. *Age Discrimination in Employment Act (1967)* prohibits discrimination because of age.

2. *Civil Rights Act, Title VII (1964)* prohibits discrimination based on race, sex, religion or national origin.

3. *Equal Pay Act (1986)* requires equal pay to women who perform the same tasks as men.

4. *Executive Order 11246* prohibits discrimination in employment practices on the basis of race, sex, color, or religion.

5. *Americans with Disabilities Act (1992)* and *(1994)* prohibits discrimination in employment of a qualified individual with a disability based on physical or mental handicaps. A qualified individual with

Figure 8-5. A very important part of human resource management is to ensure that the business's policies and hiring practices are in compliance with federal and state laws. (Courtesy, M. Thomas)

a disability is an individual who satisfies the knowledge, skills, educational experience, personal abilities, and other job related requirements that have been established for a job. That individual can perform the essential job functions with or without reasonable accommodation.

6. *Employee Retirement Income Security Act (1974)* and *(1982)* assures continuation of defined company benefits for employees.

Some additional notices and acts affecting employers and employees include federal and state minimum wage acts, employee polygraph protection act, wage payment and collection act, child labor laws, unemployment insurance act, fair accounting standards board, workers' compensation notice, and *Family and Medical Leave Act (1993)*.

The Family and Medical Leave Act (1993) provides up to 12 weeks of unpaid leave per year for eligible employees of a business with 50 or more employees in the following situations: upon the birth of the employee's child; upon the placement of a child with the employee for adoption or foster care; or to care for a child, spouse, or parent with a serious health condition, or because of the employee's own serious health condition.

Employers also must continue to provide pre-existing health benefits and guarantee that employees will return to equivalent jobs.

A business should develop a set of company rules and policies to inform and guide all employees. This is essential to the efficiency and profitability of the overall business operation and to the service of its customers. These rules and policies should be in written form and supplied to all current and new employees. The information presented includes such items as expected working hours, absentee policy, *leave of absence* policy, tardy policy, telephone policy, compensation policy, employee production requirements, intoxication and drug policy, safety policy and procedures, *seniority* policy, visitor policy, vacation schedule policy, insurance benefit policy, and employee hygiene and housekeeping policy.

SUPERVISION

Unless a business has only one employee, supervision becomes one of the functions of management. The supervisor is the person who allocates the work to the various employees. That person also is the one who determines at the first level how effectively the employee performs assigned tasks. For certain types of activities the employee will have the right to make decisions as to when or how to perform them; for other types of activities the supervisor may have this right; and for still other types of activities someone higher up in the chain of command will be the one who makes the decisions. The supervisor must have the respect of the employees and must be able to determine what techniques can be used to develop an effective working relationship with them. Frequently the supervisor will find that a technique that obtains excellent results with one person does not necessarily obtain the same excellent results with another person.

A supervisor should not become overly friendly with a select few of the employees. If that happens, it may become difficult or embarrassing to take the necessary actions to bring about needed changes in the operation. In addition, it may give rise to charges of partiality in decisions. Both of these factors can lead to difficulties in the efficient management of human resources.

In some businesses *nepotism* may be a factor in supervising personnel. Nepotism is a term used to designate the employment of close relatives of the owner, manager, or other people in managerial or supervisory positions. This practice has two disadvantages. In the first place, other employees working with such a relative may feel, whether justified or not, that this relative is given special consideration in the type of work he or she is requested to do or in the measurement of performance. A second complaint that may develop has to do with the relative's by-passing the normal channels of communication or using his or her influence to bring about so-called needed changes. Either of these situations can be very damaging in small businesses.

In any management arrangement there needs to be a clearly stated policy as to how employees' differences with their supervisors are to be reconciled. These differences may arise from the failure to mutually understand working conditions, job descriptions, or methods of evaluating performance. This system should be thoroughly understood at the time of employment, and it needs to be reviewed at periodic intervals to ensure that it meets the needs of both the personnel and the business.

RECOGNIZING SUPERIOR PERFORMANCE

In personnel supervision some method of recognition for outstanding performance is necessary. The method that is most frequently used is that of merit salary adjustments or bonuses. However, other types of recognition

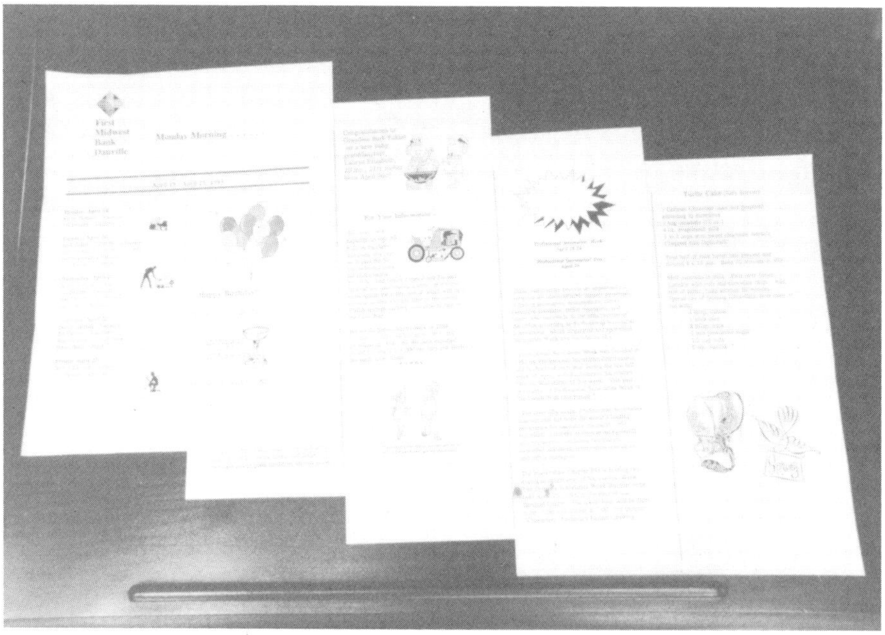

Figure 8-6. Many businesses have found they can improve relations by having an employee newsletter. (Courtesy, M. Thomas)

also have a place. Letters of commendation, special recognition awards at employees' meetings, and other activities of this type may also be used as a means of rewarding exceptional performance. At periodic intervals each employee should participate in a performance review with his or her supervisor. Such reviews provide both the employer and the employee an opportunity to discuss mutual problems. These reviews should provide a means for improving the effectiveness of the employee in meeting the supervisor's expectations and also provide a means for making recommendations to higher authority as to changes in assignments, promotions, and compensation. In such meetings, the supervisor and the employee should periodically review the job description and, where necessary, make changes in the job description in line with the employee's current or prospective duties. These types of meetings make it possible for the employee to know how his or her performance measures against what the business expects and for the business to know how its performance compares to what the employee expects of the company. It is an opportunity to generate *employee incentive* and motivation.

In relationships with employees, the supervisor must be fair and impartial. Under such conditions each employee should feel he or she is given the same treatment as any other employee under the same set of circumstances. An employer must have empathy for the employees and their problems.

EMPLOYEE RELATIONS

Many businesses have found they can improve employee relations by having an employee newsletter and/or by sponsoring various employees' social activities, such as volleyball teams, softball teams, and periodic company parties or picnics. The intent is to help employees identify with the business. Businesses continually need to build employee loyalty. If an employee feels attached to the business and that his or her success is closely tied to that of the business, then this helps create in the employee a desire to do a more effective and efficient job. Each manager needs to determine what actions may be taken to promote this concept among the employees, which in turn becomes a part of business loyalty.

Each employee, regardless of position or responsibility, is either selling the business and its products and services or building up resistance to the business among customers and potential customers. The warehouse employee, the sales person, the truck driver, the janitor, the secretary, and the bookkeeper are all selling their business, not only when they are at work, but also at any time they have contact with someone else. The manager must recognize the importance of this in developing a good employee relations program.

Because the employees are representatives of the business both on and off the job, most businesses are concerned with the extent to which their employees are citizens of the community—taking part in community activities and assuming the many responsibilities of being good citizens of that community.

SUPERVISORS AND PROMOTIONS

Human resource management includes developing a promotion policy. Every business must determine whether to follow the policy of promoting from within the organization or to what extent to go outside the business to obtain managerial replacements. The policy adopted will have much bearing on human resource selection and personnel skill development and education. The major disadvantage of promotion from within is that a co-worker is promoted and the next day is placed in a position of supervising former peers, measuring performance and making decisions that former "co-workers" and "friends" may not like. However, the argument for promoting from within is that it provides a basis for rewarding outstanding performance. Under such conditions, the newly promoted employee, having been properly trained for the position, will not need as much additional training in company policy and other items of this nature as would be the case with a new employee from outside the business. In many small businesses that are part of a larger organization, it may be a better situation to promote an employee from one of the operations to another, instead of from within the same company.

Generally, both those in managerial positions and staff should know what the promotion policy is. The policy should be one that will assure the business of the best management possible within the time and money restrictions that are placed upon the position. Supervisors or managers who are in a position to evaluate personnel play an important part in the early identification of those people showing managerial potential. Such identification is necessary so that these people can be channeled into appropriate education and training programs.

In most businesses there is a *probationary period* during which the employer evaluates the employee's job performance, attitude, and compatibility. In turn, the employee considers the job requirements and working conditions. At the end of this time period, the employee may decide to leave or may be dismissed. If dismissed, in all fairness management should indicate why it felt this was the appropriate action. Generally, at the end of the probationary period the employee will be released only for rather extensive cause. This could involve such characteristics as dishonesty, poor attitude, belligerence, poor workmanship, moral turpitude, or other weaknesses of this nature.

Working with people involves a large number of small things that in total determine the attitude of employees toward their business. While certain guidelines can be developed, many of the items involved are of a subjective nature and are cumulative in effect. The techniques that work for one person will not necessarily work for another. What works under one set of conditions will not necessarily work under another set of conditions, even for the same person.

EXIT INTERVIEWS

An interview with employees who are leaving their position may provide some useful insights into the operation of the business. As a part of the *termination* procedure, human resource managers should develop an exit interview.

Some questions to ask include:

1. Did you receive recognition for contributions to the business?

2. Did management provide sufficient support?

3. Was the work challenging and personally satisfying?

4. Did you feel comfortable and secure in your work?

5. Did the company make use of your qualifications?

6. Were you treated fairly by the company and your supervisors?

7. Were working conditions satisfactory?

Such exit interviews may suggest ways to improve employee training, ways to more effectively hire qualified personnel, and ways to reduce employee turnover. This would also be the appropriate time to distribute *severance pay* if applicable to the particular situation.

MORALE

Poor morale can reduce employee output, can discourage relationships with customers, and in general can be disruptive to an efficient operation. The statement is frequently made that morale problems can be corrected with an increase in compensation. However, observation suggests that when a business has morale problems, management should immediately do some honest, intensive self-evaluation. Management should also talk to an adequate sample of the employees to determine the cause of the problem.

There are many causes for low morale, such as:

1. Favoritism, either real or imagined
2. Poor communication between management and employees
3. Apparent insensitivity of management to employees
4. Unfavorable working conditions, including hours, pressure, parking, or company benefits
5. Failure to recognize performance
6. Inequitable criteria for promotion, salaries, etc.
7. Reluctance to assign responsibilities
8. Failure to respond to employees' requests for information
9. Failure of management to make decisions

This list could be expanded, but it does suggest some of the causes of employee dissatisfaction and poor morale. Management and the supervisory staff have the responsibility to take the necessary steps that are within their power to correct those deficiencies. One of the major factors behind improved morale is better communication between management and employees.

CHAPTER QUESTIONS

1. What are some of the available sources for prospective new employees?

2. How can a human resource manager evaluate prospective new employees?

3. What human resource activities are included in the term "equal employment opportunity"?

4. What are six federal acts or executive orders prohibiting discrimination on the basis of age, race, sex, religion, national origin, physical or mental handicaps, or pay?

5. Why are employee company rules and policies essential to the business?

6. What are some ways a business can improve employee relations?

7. What is the major disadvantage of promoting from within the business?

8. What are at least five factors which may contribute to low employee morale?

Chapter 9

PERSONNEL DEVELOPMENT

A person frequently hears comments about the information explosion. This has many implications for employees who need to keep informed as to what is happening in their particular fields. The amount of published material management personnel must read and understand is often overwhelming. Some experts maintain the life of technical material is five years; however, in some technical areas it is obvious that one-year-old printed material is completely outdated. The one thing that most people will agree on is that there has been a great increase in the amount of new materials coming out in all areas of activity. This is true whether one is concerned with technical product information, new developments, or the latest interpretations of government regulations. Whatever the area of concern, an employee finds an increasing need to remain current with new developments.

One thing that concerns employees in today's economy is the possibility that, within the foreseeable future, they may find themselves or their particular skills obsolete. In the past, people were concerned with technology in relation to obsolescence of the product or obsolescence of machinery and equipment. Now, a factor that may be of even more concern is obsolescence of personnel. A way to reduce obsolescence of personnel is to provide an effective personnel skill development and training program.

OBJECTIVES

1. Discuss the questions that should be answered in choosing a career path.

2. Compare and contrast the positions of manager and general employee.

3. Discuss personal characteristics as they relate to career success.

4. Describe the four general goals of a personnel skill development program.

5. Identify the various types of personnel skill development programs.

6. Discuss personnel skill development program policies a business might have.

7. List and discuss three factors necessary for successful personnel skill development programs.

IDENTIFYING
CAREER OPPORTUNITIES

A prospective employee should ask the following five questions when identifying career opportunities.

1. What are the opportunities for employment and advancement?

2. What are the duties and responsibilities of the job?

3. What businesses have such a position?

4. What is the compensation that can be expected?

5. What characteristics do businesses look for when making hiring decisions?

By answering these questions, a foundation for progress and advancement can be developed. This plan will be a guide for initial educational requirements and personal *skill* development needed to enter and advance in a chosen career.

TERMS

emotional	nonverbal	priorities
empathy	communication	procrastinate
extrovert	optimist	reputation
interpersonal	peer	self-image
relationship	perseverance	skill
introvert	pessimist	work ethic
meticulous	philosophy	

Figure 9-1. A good agriscience or tech prep program provides the basic needs for entry into the work force. (Courtesy, M. Thomas)

CAREER CHOICES: MANAGER vs. GENERAL EMPLOYEE

The general staff employee usually works set regular hours and has specific, often similar, tasks to perform. That employee is responsible for his or her own actions and has freedom in personal behavior away from work. The general staff employee will use minimal communication and *interpersonal relationship* skills depending on that individual's specific job function.

Managers are usually required to work as much as needed—not necessarily specific hours. They are responsible for their own actions and those of employees who report to them. Their job functions may vary as to the type and time required for completion. Managers must be concerned with laws and governmental rules and regulations. They generally need higher level communication and interpersonal relationship skills, as well as public and community relation skills.

There are advantages and disadvantages to both types of employment levels based on the goals of the individual. Because less education and management training is needed for general staff employees, individuals may

Figure 9-2. Managers generally need higher level communication and interpersonal relationship skills, as well as public and community relation skills. (Courtesy, M. Thomas)

enter the work force sooner but may be limited as to the entry level and advancement opportunity. For advancement, this situation would require the employee to work his or her way up through the business, often requiring additional outside education and participation in the business's training programs. The more formal education the individual receives, the better the opportunity may be to enter the work force at the management trainee or management level. College and university programs offer a more formal career and management training program. This may enable the graduate to enter the work force at a higher level and generally receive a higher salary or wage. Any prior employment experience may play an important part in entry level and compensation when hiring a new employee. The entrepreneur in business faces the situation of becoming a manager immediately and being responsible for all aspects of the business. Therefore, entrepreneurs should have sufficient education and background in their market niche before entering business. The entrepreneur takes a high risk with uncertain financial return but, if successful, receives great rewards. The level of education, experience, and job situation determines the entry level and career opportunity of the individual.

PERSONAL ASSESSMENT

Individuals need a positive self-concept, social skills, and a professional image to succeed and advance in business. He or she needs to understand the factors which affect *self-image* and how it relates to productivity and job satisfaction. First, one should perform a self-understanding assessment of personal characteristics and traits. This will provide the basis for improving personal development, as well as understanding one's own *philosophy*. The type of questions an individual should ask in evaluating self-image include:

1. What is the image I have of myself?
2. Am I an *introvert* or an *extrovert?*
3. Are my reactions *emotional*?
4. Do I *procrastinate*?
5. What values do I have?

Figure 9-3. In seasonal agribusiness, it may be necessary for general employees to work extended hours. (Courtesy, Brendan Marshall)

6. What are my *priorities*?

7. Am I *meticulous* in my actions?

8. Am I an *optimist* or *pessimist*?

9. What is my *work ethic*?

10. Is my *perseverance* level high when faced with difficulties?

By honestly answering these questions an individual is able to determine a concept of himself or herself.

In addition to assessing self-image, an individual needs to evaluate his or her social skills in relationship to others. The questions one should ask include:

1. How do others see me?

2. Do I have a good *reputation*?

3. Am I often affected by *peer* pressure?

4. Do I have *empathy* for other's feelings or ideas?

5. Do I communicate well with others?

6. Are my *nonverbal communication* skills positive in relation to others?

7. Do I get along well with others?

One's social skills are not only used to get along with co-workers but also to help provide the desired professional image when dealing with customers and suppliers of the business. A positive self-image and acceptable social skills are essential parts of success.

Communication Skills

In most, if not all, businesses it is necessary for people to communicate with other individuals or groups. This may include written, verbal, and nonverbal communication. One may have to participate in a group discussion, interact at a meeting, listen effectively to obtain information at a presentation, write letters and reports, and/or provide information and answer questions for customers and suppliers. Effective communication skills are an essential part of personal skill development.

BUSINESS TRAINING PROGRAMS

Experts vary in their opinions as to how much time an employee may need to devote to keeping up with new developments. Generally, the more routine the tasks an employee performs, the smaller the need for keeping up with a wide range of activities, unless the supervisor is also attempting to prepare that person for promotion through a personnel training program. However, as the level of sophistication of the employee's position increases, the need for keeping current with recent developments becomes much more critical. Some managers indicate that a minimum of one-fourth to one-third of the time of their higher-level personnel must be spent on educational and skill development activities just so these people can remain current. If they in turn have many employees under their supervision or direction, it becomes necessary to spend another large segment of their time and effort insuring that the pertinent parts of these new developments are passed on to employees in the organization. These comments emphasize the need for effective personnel skill development.

GOALS OF TRAINING PROGRAMS

Most business training programs are concerned with one or more of the following four general areas:

1. Remaining abreast of characteristics of current products and/or services provided by the business

2. Knowing the changes in business policy and the interpretations of these changes and their operational implications

3. Developing additional skills that will permit employees to assume new responsibilities within the business

4. Remaining constantly aware of how new developments may be related to changes in future business policy, particularly for the higher levels of management

Each business, at any given time, must determine what it expects from its training program. This will be largely established by the goals and objectives of the particular business, along with the size and organizational structure of the business. There are some businesses that have a well conceived personnel training program that achieves the goals of providing communication between the employer and the employee and providing the type of information the employees need to do a better job and to grow with the business. Other businesses apparently feel they cannot afford to have a personnel training program. The only realistic approach, however, is to take the view that few, if any, businesses can afford not to have a personnel training program.

In any training program it is necessary to evaluate the program frequently to be sure that it is accomplishing the desired goals. Management must evaluate the extent to which benefits from the program are sufficient to justify the expense. Such an evaluation also considers if there are alternative methods that could be equally or more effective. Therefore, in setting up such a program, it is desirable to indicate the goals that the business hopes to accomplish in carrying out its program. If these goals are designed in such a way that they can be measured, then it is possible to evaluate the personnel skill development program. If the goals cannot be readily measured, then a person might well question the sincerity of management in attempting to set up an effective personnel training program.

Figure 9-4. Colleges and universities offer specialized training programs and seminars on specific procedures or topics. (Courtesy, M. Thomas)

TYPES OF TRAINING PROGRAMS

The type of training program an agribusiness will choose to develop its personnel depends on the size of the enterprise and the requirements of employees. A large business may have someone whose primary job is to plan and implement training programs. Smaller businesses will usually give this job to someone with many other responsibilities. The business will usually need to have a different type of training program for different types of employees. The manager, supervisors, and general employees have different training needs. For example, the feed company's bookkeeper might need little knowledge of livestock feed, but will need to keep up-to-date on accounting practices and tax laws which affect that part of the company. The warehouse employee needs skills in record keeping and advanced storage techniques, while the salesperson needs to know the characteristics of the different feeds and how they relate to the producer's operation.

The three types of training programs used by businesses include routine, specialized, and individualized programs. Whichever type of program is chosen, the underlying focus of the program is to develop employees in areas that contribute to the goals of the business.

Routine programs involve a set meeting time, such as every Monday morning, where employees are updated on changes in policies and procedures. They also allow for an exchange of ideas between employees and management which permits the business to improve the efficiency of operations. A manager or supervisor usually conducts this type of program.

Specialized programs involve training a group of workers with related jobs in a specific procedure or topic. These programs are usually longer than routine programs and are conducted when the employees are able to get away from day-to-day activities to concentrate on the program. These programs may be held in conjunction with other similar businesses in the area. If the program is designed to provide information, a large group setting may be used. If the program is designed to provide hands-on practice or discussion among participants, small groups usually work best.

Individualized programs are usually planned for workers who need training in specific areas that have been identified. Conducting an annual review of employees helps the manager to identify these areas of weakness. If an employee has a weakness, then the supervisor or manager should make arrangements to help the person improve in that area. This may involve sending an employee to another location, such as a research facility or to a meeting held by training consultants.

TRAINING PROGRAM POLICIES

Because the goals of different businesses vary greatly, they often have different policies regarding training programs. The current level of training of the workers and type of business have the most effect on these policies. For example, a business with a high employee turnover will need a more intensive training program to make new employees functional. A business that is in an area with rapid changes in technology or operations also needs an intensive training program to keep employees current.

Depending on the number of employees, trainers may come from the business itself, the parent company, or consulting firms. Employees may also be sent to professional meetings or to a university class or workshop to meet their training needs. An individualized training program may include attending regional workshops on general topics such as writing or communications skills offered by training professionals.

TRAINING TECHNIQUES

As instructional opportunities, training programs should make use of educational techniques to provide interesting and stimulating sessions. Like any good educational program, they should begin at the learners' level and progress to the desired level of comprehension. They should focus on attitudes and knowledge as well as physical skills.

Various educational methods, such as small group discussions, self-paced modules, lectures, and supervised practice are useful in training programs. These methods should be enhanced with visual aids, computers, demonstrations, films, and other media to keep the instruction interesting to the participants. Good information, combined with good methods, improve employee loyalty and morale.

CHAPTER QUESTIONS

1. What questions should a prospective employee ask when identifying a career opportunity?

2. What are determining factors for the entry level and career opportunity of an individual?

3. How can one provide a basis for improving personal development?

4. What communication skills are needed when dealing with other individuals or groups?

5. How can a business reduce personnel obsolescence?

6. What are the four general areas of personnel skill development programs?

7. Why do businesses have different training program policies?

8. What are two effective educational techniques used in training programs?

Chapter 10

RISK MANAGEMENT

Every business and every individual who could suffer financial loss if a certain event should occur is in need of protection against such a loss. *Risk management* refers to developing a plan for reducing the risk or transferring the loss through insurance.

Some people who buy insurance never make a claim so the insurance company is able to retain the entire premium paid in. However, there are valid claims in other cases which are paid out. When one buys insurance he or she is transferring the risk, along with a small premium, anticipating that something bad could happen. The insurance company is betting that it will not have to pay out as much as it receives in premiums from all its policyholders. Even without claims an insurance company has fixed costs of doing business; therefore, the company must operate its business efficiently and invest excess capital wisely to be profitable.

This chapter describes basic concepts related to risk management and insurance. Strategies and factors to consider when developing the insurance program of an agribusiness are discussed.

OBJECTIVES

1. Explain the concept of risk management.

2. Identify some of the characteristics an insurance company evaluates when determining insurability.

3. Discuss the other factors in addition to price which must be considered in selecting insurance.

4. List five things a business can do to provide a safe work place for employees.

5. Identify the two primary categories of insurance.

6. List and explain five specific types of insurance.

7. Discuss the major factors to be considered when selecting an insurance agent and insurance company.

8. List four sources of information which may be helpful when evaluating insurance companies.

9. List the three ways an insurance company uses premium payments received.

10. Describe some guidelines which may be helpful in filing a claim.

RISK MANAGEMENT TECHNIQUES

The concept of insurance was a response to the problems caused by unplanned major losses. One early solution was for a group that shared similar risks to band together and contribute a proportionate amount of money to a general fund. The individual contributions were small compared to the cumulative amount collected from the entire group. Whenever a *catastrophic loss* occurred, the individual suffering the loss could withdraw money from the general fund without having to face the entire burden alone. Out of this type of group came the development of insurance companies.

PRINCIPLES OF INSURANCE

Insurance is the protection by written contract against whole or part

TERMS

agent	conversion privilege	insurance
aggregate	deductible	loss frequency
basic coverage	disability	perils
beneficiary	exclusions	premium
benefits	family living costs	replacement cost
cash settlement	group insurance plan	risk management
catastrophic loss	heir	spouse
claim	independent agents	workers' compensation
coinsurance	inheritance tax	
contingent liability	insurability	

Figure 10-1. The home office of State Farm Insurance, Bloomington, IL. (Courtesy, M. Thomas)

of a financial loss based on the happenings of specific events. Age, sex, physical condition, and medical history all effect an insurance company's calculation of risk for an individual. The unique characteristics of a business such as location, type of business, products handled or services offered, and age and condition of property are some of the many factors an insurance company evaluates when reviewing risk and determining *insurability* of a business. Insurance companies have an extensive amount of data which they use to determine statistically what the probabilities are of a specific event happening and the *loss frequency* in a given time. This data is used in determining the amount of *premium* charged which still permits the insurance company to make a profit.

Insurance costs money, but compared to the potential financial loss or liability the amount may be insignificant. It is important to remember that insurance is designed to protect against major losses or changes in life-style—not for minor occurrences which may only be an inconvenience of minor financial consequence. An evaluation must be made in order to determine what losses can be covered without insurance. This is called retaining the risk or self-insurance. It is important to buy insurance with policy limits high enough to adequately protect against loss but not to buy in excess of needs.

Insurance is not intended to make a profit for the insured. In many states there are very specific laws or rules which strictly forbid the insured from collecting more than once from one or more insurance companies for the same covered loss. However, other insurance company *benefits* can be used to pay amounts not covered by the primary insurance company for the same occurrence. Overinsuring in hope of collecting a profit should a claim occur is illegal. Most insurance laws prevent the insured from collecting in excess of 100 percent of the loss regardless of the number of companies or policies.

A business must be honest with its insurance company. If fraud can be proven, it will result in non-payment of benefits when a claim is filed and in the cancellation of the policy. In some policies there are rules or regulations which usually require that 80 percent of the value of property be insured for the insurance company to pay a *claim* at full *cash settlement* value. If it is proven that the property is underinsured, the benefits payable will be reduced in proportion to the percentage of coverage compared to actual value of the property. Policy limits are the maximum specified amounts an insurance policy will pay the insured under a specific set of circumstances per occurrence or per *aggregate*. Generally, most businesses will insure buildings and equipment at 80 percent of their replacement value, leaving 20 percent to be covered by self-insurance. However, each situation should be evaluated on its own merit. It is possible for an agreement between the insured and insurance company to cover property at less than 80 percent of the value in some circumstances, but this must be spelled out within the policy.

The amount of premium for a particular coverage may be reduced or controlled through the use of a *deductible* or through *coinsurance*. The higher the deductible the purchaser is willing to bear, the lower the premium will be. Another option for lowering premiums is for the insured and the insurer to share the covered loss.

Although price is an important consideration when evaluating insurance, there are other factors that should also be considered.

1. Can the insurance company provide all of the services needed?

2. Is the insurance *agent* familiar enough with the business's particular situation and characteristics to assist in making the right decision?

These are important considerations when evaluating insurance. Similar businesses in the same area and trade associations are often good sources of information about insurance.

Figure 10-2. A burglary and fire alarm system is a risk management technique a business may use. (Courtesy, M. Thomas)

The manager of a business is required to provide a safe business environment for both employees and customers. Anything that can be done to reduce risk means lower premiums which will save money for the business. Some loss control or risk management techniques a business may use include:

1. Good housekeeping

2. Employee safety meetings, training and inspections

3. Providing an easy method for reporting potential hazards

4. Compliance with OSHA and EPA regulations

5. Installing burglar and fire alarm systems

6. Installing and monitoring the condition of safety equipment such as smoke detectors, fire extinguishers, first-aid kits, emergency lighting, and sprinkler systems

7. Developing an emergency evacuation plan with periodic drills

8. Keeping equipment and safe guards for the equipment in a good state of repair

Types of Insurance

The types of insurance available generally fall into two primary categories: (1) life and health and (2) property and casualty.

In business, life and health coverage are employee benefits in addition to wages if the employer pays all or the major portion of the premium. Some common examples of these types of insurance include: group health and life, dental insurance, and disability insurance.

Some examples of property and casualty insurance include vehicle insurance, homeowner's insurance, product or professional liability insurance, and business interruption insurance. Insurance companies commonly offer property and liability package policies as a way to cover most risks. The homeowners policy is usually a package covering all or most of the needs of an individual. The commercial or business package is usually more of a component policy. These policies should be carefully evaluated in order to be sure that all needs are covered. Additions to these types of policies may be made through riders to the basic policy.

Before deciding on the type and amount of property and casualty insurance needed, risks associated with property should be evaluated. This involves taking a physical inventory of all property including buildings, furnishings, equipment, and if applicable, finished goods and raw materials

Figure 10-3. An independent agent represents a number of insurance companies.

inventories. The actual value and replacement cost for each group should be determined. Then consider the different types of *perils* that could cause damage to or loss of this property. This will help determine what type and amount of property insurance is needed.

Risks associated with casualty should also be evaluated. Special consideration must be given to particular types of businesses or unique situations. The insured needs to be aware of any *contingent liability* that may exist. Consider all the different reasons one may be sued, this will help determine the type and amount of liability protection needed.

Business insurance for entrepreneurs operating in the home requires special mention. A homeowner's policy will not cover business associated claims. A separate policy will be needed to cover that portion of the home used for the business and for business liabilities, and should be acknowledged to the homeowner's insurance company.

Another area of insurance that an individual or business may have need for is bonds. A bond is basically a promise that in the event an individual, a business, or a position fails in its duty, the amount or face of the bond will be paid. There are three areas of bonds:

1. Surety—license and permit bonds

2. Contract—performance bonds

3. Fidelity—employee dishonesty, estate guardian, etc.

The underwriting of bonds is dependent on the character and integrity of the person or the personal worth of the business.

Life Insurance. The function of life insurance is to protect the *beneficiary* from the consequences of the insured's death. This may include providing burial and *family living costs* in the case of the individual's death. Businesses also commonly insure key individuals whose temporary or permanent loss would cause the business considerable hardship. Financial institutions may require full or partial collateral assignment of key person life insurance policies when making loans to a business. Similarly, partners may purchase life insurance on one another to settle debts and buy out a partner's share of the business. A corporation may also purchase life insurance on its owners, especially if it is a closely held corporation. This lends a degree of stability to the corporation upon the death of an owner or owners.

Life insurance comes in two basic formats: term and whole life. Term—as the name implies—is purchased for a specific length of time at a fixed rate based on the age and health of the individual. Term policy premiums increase with the age of the insured and length of time covered. The cash settlement value of the policy may be level or decreasing. Term insurance does not have a cash surrender value, but a great deal more insurance for the same or less money can be purchased as compared to whole life. Some term policies may also include a *conversion privilege* that provides an option to convert the policy to whole life.

Whole life, as the name implies, is generally purchased for the entire life of the insured. A fixed premium is guaranteed regardless of changes in health and age. Premiums are paid until the death of the insured or until the policy is paid up. As premiums are paid, the policy builds a cash value which may be borrowed or used as collateral on a loan. Should the insured die before the loan is repaid, the unpaid balance will be subtracted from the death benefit paid out by the insurance company. Dividends can be taken without any loan or interest charges.

Some may choose to purchase term insurance and use the savings in reduced premium as a source for investment capital or just as a way to keep their expenses down. Others may wish to have the security and cash value accumulation of whole life insurance. Insurance companies frequently change policy rates to reflect competitive economic conditions; therefore, it pays to compare the rates of several companies.

The need for life insurance is greater in the earlier stages of life when children are young and the insured is in his or her prime income years. Key person or credit life insurance polices—used to pay off debt in the case of death—may be completely eliminated as the individual or business acquires wealth. In the case of individual life insurance, when the children are all grown and the *spouse* is well provided for as the result of investments and such, the need for life insurance decreases. Life insurance is used many times to create liquidity in wealthy client portfolios to satisfy *inheritance tax* needs. The death benefit provides the *heir* the necessary funds to pay estate taxes.

Health Insurance. The purpose of health insurance is to establish protection that provides payment of benefits for covered sickness or injury of the insured. In business this is generally provided, usually by the employer, on a group of people under a master policy. This master policy is commonly referred to as a *group insurance plan*. With the high cost of health care and the cost of these plans, more and more employers are requiring employees to pay a portion of the cost of these plans. The policy may have different coverage for emergency, out-patient, and in-patient sit-

Figure 10-4. A master policy which may be provided by an employer for employees is referred to as a group policy or plan. (Courtesy, M. Thomas)

uations. It may also have *exclusions* where the policy will not provide benefit payments for certain health problems.

Workers' Compensation. *Workers' compensation* is an insurance system requiring employers to cover employees for job-related injuries. Should a job-related accident or sickness occur, the workers' compensation insurance policy of the business will be the only policy paying for the employee's expenses.

Disability Insurance. *Disability* insurance is protection for the insured if he or she is unable to work because of a disabling injury or illness. It provides income for the insured for a specified period. "Own occupation" riders are available that provide payments for a specified period of time until a worker is capable of resuming his or her own occupation.

Vehicle Insurance. Vehicle insurance is used to provide protection against the costs that may be incurred as the result of an auto accident, especially where the insured is at fault and a lawsuit could result. The *basic coverage* usually provides for liability and property damage to others. Options may include collision and comprehensive coverage on the insured's vehicle.

Property Insurance. Major losses of property would cause a severe economic strain on the owner of a business or, in the case of an individual, a homeowner. Property insurance is designed to provide *replacement cost* or actual cash value for damaged or destroyed real property.

Liability Insurance. Liability insurance is insurance covering anything for which a business or individual may be liable.

Business Interruption Insurance. This insurance is designed to provide protection from loss of business income for a specific period if the business is destroyed and it will take some time to relocate or rebuild. It can also be written on key suppliers to a business to provide protection in case they are destroyed.

Professional Liability Insurance. Professional liability insurance provides protection against claims as a result of providing a service.

Product Liability Insurance. Product liability insurance is the protection against claims arising from use, handling, or consumption of a product that the business creates or was a part of creating.

SELECTING AN INSURANCE AGENT/COMPANY

Careful selection of an insurance agent and insurance company may be more important than selecting the proper coverage. Most individuals aren't aware of the overall options available when buying a policy; therefore, they decide to purchase a policy based only on those options the agent presents to them.

Insurance agents are salespeople. Some are affiliated exclusively with one company, others are *independent agents* who represent a number of insurance companies. It is important to select an agent that has a good understanding of any unique requirements as well as a sincere desire to provide the best possible insurance product to fill the need. When working with an independent agent, the selection of an insurance company should be a mutual decision.

Price should not be the only consideration when comparing different sources of insurance. Other factors, such as service, needs, and financial stability are important, too. Several factors need to be considered when selecting an insurance company:

Figure 10-5. Selecting an insurance agent and an insurance company may be more important than selecting the proper coverage. (Courtesy, M. Thomas)

1. Can the company meet the necessary needs?
2. Is the company sound financially?
3. Does it handle claims in a prompt manner?
4. Are the prices competitive?

SOURCES OF INFORMATION

There are several sources of information that can help a business evaluate insurance companies. The insurance rating guides of A. M. Best and Co.—available at most local libraries— not only provide information on premiums and statistics on the financial viability of all insurers, but also measure service and rates of customer complaints. Many state insurance departments have consumer divisions that help resolve insurance complaints and provide information. Local Better Business Bureaus may also have records on certain insurance companies, particularly if a pattern of complaints has developed. Finally, the most valuable source of information is individuals or businesses already using an insurance company. Most agents are willing to provide a list of other clients. These references are particularly useful in evaluating claims and service.

APPLYING FOR INSURANCE

The effective date of an insurance policy can be very important because this is the date that the policy actually begins. A claim cannot be made before this date, just as a claim cannot be filed after the policy expires.

With some types of insurance, additional requirements may need to be met before the policy can become effective. For example, a life or health insurance policy may require a physical examination. Other types of insurance may exclude certain coverage for a set period of time or permanently. A group health insurance plan may exclude a pre-existing condition for a set period of time, and, therefore, a claim resulting from this illness will be denied any benefits.

When applying for insurance, the effective date and requirements must be understood.

HOW INSURANCE COMPANIES OPERATE

To fully understand insurance one should have a basic knowledge of how insurance companies make and use money. They are in the business of taking on risk for a fee. An insurance policy is purchased as protection against a future risk in exchange for a small premium paid now. This premium is the cost of transferring the risk.

Insurance Company Basics

An insurance company picks and chooses what risks it wants to take. Some companies specialize in life, health, and disability insurance only; other companies insure risks associated with vehicles, real property, and liabilities. The latter are known as property and casualty insurance carriers. An insurance company could sell all kinds of insurance, but few do because a different expertise and way of doing business are required for each area. Insurance companies also select the type of policyholders and the particular environments they want to insure. This is known as underwriting, or managing risk. By doing this an insurance company can operate within certain guidelines that it sets for itself. It then quantifies that risk by setting a premium cost—putting a value on the risk. Then the insurance company is able to sell an insurance policy which meets the guidelines it has set and at the price it has placed on assuming the risk.

Part of the premiums paid goes into a reserve that the company keeps for paying out claims, part goes towards operating expenses, and the remaining portion goes toward investments that the insurance company buys to increase profits. The insurance company hopes that the profits from investment income will offset any losses that may be incurred through claims. Investments alone may determine whether or not the insurance company makes money.

A catastrophic loss affecting a large number of the company's policyholders can have a major impact on profitability and ability to pay claims. In recent years it has cost insurance companies a very significant amount of money to settle policyholder's claims that arose from property damaged during major hurricanes in the southeastern United States. An insurance company usually will choose not to concentrate on a small geographic area because of this exposure to loss; however, reserves are required of insurance companies regardless of their loss ratio.

Insurance companies use statistical mathematicians, called actuaries, to calculate the odds on a specific event happening within a certain period of time. This may range from life expectancy of a particular type of individual to the chances of a particular type of vehicle being involved in a claim. This is usually not as difficult as it may sound because of the amount of statistical data available.

The two areas where an insurance company may get into financial trouble are (1) managing its business and (2) investment of excess capital. Inefficient management combined with the best risk management program will still cause premiums to be increased to cover losses. Investing excess capital is also uncertain business for insurance companies that are very large investors in stocks, bonds, real estate, business loans, etc.

The best insurance companies are successful at operating all three aspects of the business. These are the kinds of companies one should select when transferring risk by insurance.

When a Claim Occurs

When a claim occurs the insurance agent should be contacted immediately in order to ensure that accurate details will be related. A written record should also be made for the business's or individual's records.

Insurance company procedures for filing a claim vary from company to company or by type of coverage. One should become familiar with procedures before it is necessary to file a claim. Most business managers assign responsibility for filing claims to a specific individual. Some helpful guidelines for filing claims follow.

1. Keep a complete record or listing of all property in a separate, safe place. If appropriate, photographs or a video tape of the items may be helpful.

2. Be sure more than one individual is familiar with the insurance policies and knows their location. A safe deposit box is a good place to keep policies and records.

3. If structural damage is involved, take preventive measures to insure no additional damage occurs. This could include boarding up windows, covering unprotected areas, or blocking off access to dangerous or potentially dangerous areas.

4. Notify law enforcement authorities if appropriate.

5. Notify the insurance agent immediately.

6. Should personal injury occur, get medical assistance immediately.

Remember, when a claim occurs, failure to follow proper procedures as specified in the insurance policy could adversely affect the outcome.

CHAPTER QUESTIONS

1. What is risk management?

2. What is the insurance company betting on when it assumes the risk of the insured?

3. Define insurance.

4. What are some of the characteristics an insurance company uses when determining insurability of a business?

5. What are two factors other than price to consider when evaluating insurance companies?

6. What are at least five things the manager of a business can do to provide a safe work place?

7. What are the two primary categories of insurance?

8. Describe five specific types of insurance.

9. What are four factors to consider when selecting an insurance company?

10. What are four sources of information which may help evaluate insurance companies?

11. What three areas does an insurance company use for the premiums it is paid?

12. What would be helpful to have if a property claim should occur and a number of items were missing or destroyed?

Chapter II

WAREHOUSING

The warehousing function of an agribusiness is responsible for the *physical distribution* portion of the business. It provides the facility where the business's products or raw materials are stored and may provide a service to customers as a storage facility for their inputs or outputs. Businesses that provide marketing functions (either purchased inputs or a market for production) must be aware of the importance of warehousing in the business. The seasonal nature of agricultural production makes warehousing necessary for the storage of inputs and also of goods produced. For many products the season is closely related to, and dependent upon, weather conditions. In order to meet the farmers' needs, the business must be in a position to take advantage of these conditions. Because the business cannot know exactly what dates farmers will want delivery of feed or fertilizer or when they will make deliveries of the items they have produced, there is a need for sufficient storage to adequately meet the farmers' requirements.

This chapter provides a description of the various processes involved in planning, building, and operating a warehouse. Product factors affecting warehouse practices are provided as well.

OBJECTIVES

1. Describe the objectives associated with the warehousing function.

2. Identify costs associated with warehousing and storage.

3. Understand how storage affects quality.

4. Identify safety factors for facilities and employees.

5. Identify advantages and disadvantages of handling products in bulk.

6. Identify government regulations affecting warehousing.

WAREHOUSING FUNCTION

The warehousing function has three major objectives:

1. To provide storage when it is needed

2. To keep product losses or damage to a minimum

3. To maintain the *quality* of the materials stored

Meeting these three objectives, while at the same time maximizing use of facilities, is the major difficulty in establishing a sound warehouse policy. Warehousing is an expensive function. There are three major *cost* items involved: building facilities to provide the storage space; operating the facility in terms of labor, equipment, and overhead; and financing the business's inventory.

STORAGE AND QUALITY

Storage needs will vary due to the types of products being handled, the methods of handling, and the extent to which special care is needed in handling the products in order to maintain quality. Some products may require storage where there will not be a chance of freezing. Others may require special containers or shelving. Grain products to be used for food must not become contaminated with chemicals that make them unacceptable for human consumption. In addition, they must be handled in such a way that losses from insect contamination are minimized.

In many cases grains must be artificially dried so they will not spoil. Many times it is necessary to remove excess foreign material so that the grain products can be properly stored. The conditions under which they are stored may determine the types of markets that are available for later use. For example, unless corn is properly dried, the output of starch may be affected by the changes in molecular structure that occur during the

TERMS

cost	physical distribution	resources
OSHA	quality	traffic

drying process. Improper drying may increase losses from "fines" in the handling operation. Many fresh fruits and vegetables must be stored under refrigeration, and frequently under conditions where humidity is also controlled. The percentage of carbon dioxide or oxygen may need to be carefully prescribed. Certain treatments may be needed to control various types of diseases, such as brown rot in peaches. Other storage conditions prevail for dressed poultry and eggs.

These examples indicate the nature and scope of problems involved in warehousing. There is a similar set of problems related to the storage of purchased items, such as fertilizer, petroleum products, and so forth.

Figure 11-1. Signs help identify the business as well as indicate the services provided. (Courtesy, M. Thomas)

One factor that cannot be overlooked is the need to understand the storage characteristics of each of the products that may be involved. It must also be recognized that with any product there is the possibility of cross contamination; for example, when eggs and onions are stored in close proximity, the result may be onion-flavored eggs. Certain chemicals may release gases that are absorbed by feed products. These gases combine with ingredients in the feed and contaminate the feed for the livestock that will use it.

STORAGE AND SAFETY

In any warehousing operation precautions must be taken to avoid explosive or internal combustion conditions. It is essential that flammable materials be stored away from other products, and special precautions must be taken to protect such materials from open flames, sparks, etc. Under other conditions it is necessary to control possibly explosive combinations of dust particles, such as may be generated in certain grain handling or fertilizer operations. Some chemicals require isolation from drains in case of a spill.

A business should make a careful study of materials stored or used in its facilities. The business must be aware of and comply with current federal, state, and local regulations. In addition, *OSHA* regulations should be followed for the safety of employees. This includes special equipment and training in handling hazardous materials, as well as material data sheets supplied by the manufacturer for regulated or hazardous materials.

HORIZONTAL AND VERTICAL STORAGE

Constructing vertical storage space is usually more expensive than

Figure 11-2. Horizontal storage is usually less expensive to construct than vertical storage. (Courtesy, M. Thomas)

Figure 11-3. The type of structure needed is related to the material handling processes that are to be used. (Courtesy, Office of Agricultural Communications, Mississippi State University)

constructing horizontal storage space, but management should not be primarily concerned with constructing the cheapest facility possible. The type of structure to use is, of course, very important in analyzing costs; however, the type of structure is also related to the material handling processes that are to be used. Management should make a decision that will permit the business to minimize its total storage costs, not just the original cost of constructing the storage facilities, taking into consideration the overall costs of constructing, operating, and maintaining the facility.

BULK AND PACKAGED PRODUCTS

Many products may be handled either in bulk or in packaged form. The type of storage facility needed will vary with the characteristics of the product being handled. Generally, if bulk products are being handled, the labor cost of movement into and out of storage on a per unit basis can be

Figure 11-4. The labor cost of movement into and out of the storage facility for bulk products can be greatly reduced by the use of bulk materials handling equipment. (Courtesy, Brendan Marshall)

greatly reduced by the use of equipment made to handle bulk materials. In addition, the cost per unit to the business is less because of volume, as well as not having to pay for packaging. The principal disadvantages of bulk materials are the need for specialized equipment to handle bulk products (suppliers and purchasers of the products, as well as the warehouse facilities, must have handling equipment), losses in transit and storage, and the great amount of care necessary to avoid product contamination.

In recent years the number of businesses delivering bulk feed and bulk fertilizer to the farmer has increased. This has been primarily related to technological changes that minimize the cost of handling products and maximize service to the farmer. In the early history of the grain industry in the United States, much of the grain was packaged (bagged) either at the farm or at the local elevator before being shipped. By the end of World War II, virtually all grain in the United States was moved in bulk. Currently most of the grain exported from the United States is also moved in bulk.

For some products packaging may reduce losses from contamination or normal storage and handling operations. The package may serve as a sales tool, particularly for items being purchased on impulse, but for a large number of the items used in agricultural production, bulk handling permits a lower cost for products than packaging. Certain types of products, however, may be more effectively handled in some type of packaging rather than in bulk. A good example is lumber, which, if moved in individual pieces, is a laborious, high cost operation, whereas, if several pieces are banded together, they can be easily handled with equipment.

Management needs to carefully consider the relative advantages of both bulk and packaged product handling. Whatever method of handling is decided upon, the manager must recognize the types of equipment that are essential for that particular method to be effective. This means that management must carefully consider what functions are to be performed in its particular facilities. For example, in an orchard operation, if management decides that apples are to be graded and packaged in boxes for distribution to retail stores when needed, this dictates a particular type of warehouse and storage facility. On the other hand, if management decides to grade and package the product as needed at the various retail outlets, the apples can be placed in 30-bushel boxes in the orchard, delivered to the cold storage facility, then brought out of cold storage for the packaging operation. This permits the packaging operation to be extended over a longer period of time. This could well mean the packing line would operate for five or six months a year; whereas, in the first case, the packing line might work for only six weeks. If the same volume of apples were to be packed, it is obvious that a longer packing period would necessitate using a smaller facility, which probably would result in a lower per unit packing cost.

If a grain elevator operation only received grain from the farmer and then shipped the grain to a processor, only one type of storage facility would be needed. However, if that same operation were also engaged in drying grain, grinding and mixing feed for sale to livestock producers, and blending grain to meet a specific processor's requirements, then entirely different types of facilities would be needed for performing the various functions.

WAREHOUSE DESIGN

A warehouse needs to be laid out in such a manner that it can efficiently use the *resources* available to perform the functions of the business. This implies there will be a receiving area, required types of storage areas, and a loading area for making shipments. The receiving area should be designed so that the product can move directly from transportation, through the receiving area, to the storage area. If the product is to be weighed, scales should be located at the entrance where their use will not interfere with the flow of *traffic* of other products. It may be necessary to have facilities available for sampling the product and grading it. In many businesses, deliveries to the plant and shipments from the plant are often made in a wide range of shipment sizes. For this reason there is a need for sufficient adaptability of equipment to handle these various shipments.

For example, one transaction over the scales may involve a trailer pulled by a passenger car, the next transaction may be a 750-bushel semitrailer, and the next transaction may be a farm tractor pulling two wagons. For packaged products being loaded in or out, it is necessary to have some type of adjustable loading dock to accommodate the various types of vehicles. Many warehouses are located so that they have not only railroad, but also truck loading and unloading facilities. This provides a flexibility

Figure 11-5. Forklift trucks can do much in speeding the handling of packaged materials that are being warehoused. (Courtesy, Office of Agricultural Communications, Mississippi State University)

of operation that is not available if they are designed to accommodate only one type of transportation.

Forklift trucks can do much in speeding the handling of packaged materials that are being warehoused. This is particularly true with some of the more advanced techniques using pallets. Such storage methods have made it possible to store products easily and safely at greater heights, which has often helped reduce the cost of flat storage.

In storage, care must be taken to be sure that the product moves through the warehouse. For example, the sequence of filling shipment orders must be carried out in such a manner that the oldest product is removed from storage first. This may necessitate some form of date coding of the products. Good warehouse employees are continually looking for ways to regroup products so as to use space and time more effectively. During certain seasons of the year a warehouse will carry large inventories of one product and during other seasons of the year will carry an inventory which is distributed in a different manner. Therefore, the employees continually need to be aware of how to use space in the most efficient manner. They probably will find it advisable to store fast-moving items where they will be readily accessible and the slower-moving items in more remote locations.

Certain items may also seem to disappear; therefore, these items need to be stored where more control can be exerted over them. This is less important with items which, because of size or use, are less likely to be picked up and carried out of the place of business.

Provision needs to be made for adequate parking facilities for customers transacting business or waiting at the warehouse. The parking area should be located where it is reasonably accessible to the customers and where it will not unnecessarily hamper the normal traffic patterns in the community.

Location of the warehouse itself raises questions. For example, locating a business on the south side of town when most of its present and potential business must come from the north indicates that there are strong factors, aside from customer convenience, that influence locating in a particular spot. Many times drainage is a very important issue. Often, prevailing winds are an important factor, in order to minimize public relations problems that may be related to air pollution.

Careful consideration needs to be given as to whether the business office should be located at the same site as the warehouse. From the standpoint of convenience to the customers, this is frequently the case; however, many businesses have found that they can obtain greater efficiency both in the warehousing operation and in office operations if the physical facilities are separated.

Figure 11-6. Careful consideration needs to be given as to whether the business office should be located at the same spot as the warehouse. (Courtesy, Office of Agricultural Communications, Mississippi State University)

Of course, many businesses may have one main office location and also have four, five, or even more warehouse operations at convenient locations throughout their market area, with only minimal office activities being carried out at each warehouse location.

Size of Warehouse Facilities

Customers place a high value on their time, so length of wait becomes a major customer service factor in determining the size and type of facilities considered. The business must weigh what it costs to provide adequate facilities so as to minimize waiting time. A business must also consider the amount and physical size of inventory it needs to have on hand during peak periods. A warehouse location performing a seasonal operation will experience peaks, when demand for all of the business's services will be great at the same time. This may mean that in the future some warehousing operations will be performed on an appointment basis.

Because of the seasonal nature of many warehousing operations, there are often seasonal price movements. Management is faced with the dilemma of trying to accurately predict seasonal price movements, and from this to plan its buying and selling to maximize income, through inventory management, in line with its facilities. This means that warehousing is very closely related to inventory control and management, and the rate of turnover becomes an important management consideration. Management is concerned with how many different products and how many brands or types of a given product it should carry. When deciding how many different types of dairy feed a warehouse should handle, some contributing factors to consider are that each one must be kept separate, and the more different types of products that are stocked, the greater the amount of space per unit of product required. Generally, there is a compromise between the minimum number of products management would prefer to handle and the number of products customers need.

In some businesses it is important that warehousing operations have a

Figure 11-7. A business must consider the amount and physical size of inventory it is necessary to have during peak periods. (Courtesy, Office of Agricultural Communications, Mississippi State University)

minimum quantity or sale size. In other businesses, a separate section of the warehouse is set aside to handle small-lot sales; those customers who want to buy 25 or 50 pounds of many items or a single item would go to one area of the warehouse, and those who wish to buy truck-load lots would go to another. There are warehouses that have certain days on which they will handle only large shipments. This permits them to plan their operation and use facilities and labor in a more efficient manner. It is necessary for the customers to know what the policies of the business are so that both the business and the customers can operate efficiently and effectively.

GOVERNMENT AND WAREHOUSING

There are a number of governmental regulations that must be recognized in warehousing. These regulations may include working conditions as they affect the general safety of the employees (OSHA), storage conditions that maintain the quality of the product, and various types of inspection that insure the integrity of the product when warehouse receipts are involved. They may also include measures that would reduce loss from fire, or provide for inspection of scales and metering devices.

Any business that is engaged in warehousing, either for itself or for others, must ensure that regulations are being followed.

CHAPTER QUESTIONS

1. What are the three objectives of the warehouse function?

2. What are the three major costs of warehousing?

3. How do storage needs differ for different products with regards to quality?

4. What regulations should be followed for safety of employees?

5. What costs are management concerned with when constructing a storage or warehouse facility?

6. What are some advantages and disadvantages of handling products in bulk?

7. What factors should be considered in designing warehouse space?

Chapter 12

INVENTORY CONTROL

The manager of a business should be concerned with the effective management of inventory. He or she strives to maintain sufficient inventory to adequately meet the customers' needs, while keeping the inventory at a level that will minimize costs. The two most readily apparent costs of inventory are (1) the capital investment in the inventory and (2) the investment in space and facilities to store the inventory. In determining the amount of inventory a business should carry, a number of factors need to be considered. In a broad sense, each of these factors represents a cost associated with inventory management.

This chapter provides the manager of an agribusiness with a set of strategies to use when ordering inventory and making storage and valuation decisions.

OBJECTIVES

1. Identify costs associated with maintaining an inventory.
2. Describe the relationship between inventory and lost sales.
3. Discuss the importance of inventory records.
4. Discuss the need for physical inventory.
5. Identify the methods of determining the cost of inventory.

INVENTORY MANAGEMENT

TIME TO REPLENISH STOCK

The amount of *finished goods* a business must have on hand is closely related to the amount of time that lapses between the placing of an order and the delivery of the product. Naturally, the longer the time lapse, the greater the inventory that must be maintained to adequately meet normal business requirements.

A second factor that is closely related to this is the cost of a *back order*. If a company is unable to fill an order, a percentage of its customers will be willing to accept delayed delivery, but others will obtain a similar product elsewhere. Losses due to the business's inability to fill an order (lost sales) occur in three ways: (1) customers cancel the order because they are unwilling to wait for a back order, (2) customers obtain a similar product elsewhere and then refuse or cancel the back order, and (3) customers go elsewhere and permanently transfer all of their business activities to another business (the *competition*). Every business must establish a best *estimate* as to the magnitude of the cost of being unable to provide delivery of a product at the time of customer *demand*. In relation to this estimate, it may be found that there are some rather large differences of opinion between departments within the business, depending partly upon business custom and partly upon the nature of the product involved.

A third cost factor that is closely related to the effective use of space is product obsolescence. There are some products that cannot be carried over from year to year because they lose their usefulness. There are other products that represent a characteristic style for a particular season or year. Many buyers are unwilling to buy an old model when a new model is available. Some products may be legally acceptable one year and not the next year; to carry over an inventory of such products would result in definite losses. With still other products, a rapidly changing technology may make yesterday's product unacceptable to today's buyer. Therefore, an inventory policy should be concerned with handling a product in such a manner as to minimize the possibility of suffering excessive losses because of obsolescence.

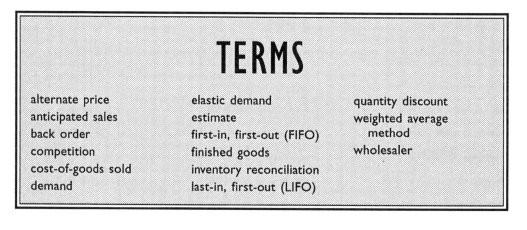

TERMS

alternate price	elastic demand	quantity discount
anticipated sales	estimate	weighted average
back order	first-in, first-out (FIFO)	method
competition	finished goods	wholesaler
cost-of-goods sold	inventory reconciliation	
demand	last-in, first-out (LIFO)	

Figure 12-1. Inventory neatly stored and grouped on pallets in the warehouse makes it easier to locate the goods when a customer places an order. (Courtesy, Office of Agricultural Communications, Mississippi State University)

In looking at inventory, management needs to be concerned with seasonal products, particularly at the impact of weather on product requirements. As was mentioned in the preceding chapter, weather may be a major influence in determining when crops will be planted and therefore determines when fertilizer and other items must be delivered, or when there will be a particularly large demand for petroleum products. Generally, seasonal factors are closely associated with harvest and the time of sale of many products. Unusual weather conditions may place particularly heavy demands on inventory management. For example, a farm supply business in a deciduous fruit area may order and accept delivery of large quantities of packaging materials normally needed by its customers during the year, only to have a freeze or a hailstorm occur which destroys the crop. The business's inventory items now are not needed for another year. These types of problems further point up the need for careful inventory management analysis.

Figure 12-2. Management needs to be concerned with seasonal products when looking at inventory. (Courtesy, Brendan Marshall)

HOW MUCH INVENTORY TO ORDER

Management and the marketing and sales staff may argue about the size of the inventory. The sales staff would prefer an inventory sufficiently large and diverse to meet any customer needs. Management wants to keep lower levels to hold down investment in space and inventory.

The amount of inventory needed can be determined by the time it takes from the date of placing an order until the date the order will be received at the warehouse after factoring in *anticipated sales*. The longer this time span, the larger the inventory needs to be. In some cases, certain price advantages exist for volume purchases, and transportation costs per unit are often lower. Other factors related to inventory management are (1) out-of-stock costs and (2) economic order quantity.

Out-of-stock costs are related to the inconvenience to the customer caused by the business's inability to provide a product when needed. Even more important than the loss of business from this sale may be that the customer who goes to a competitor is, in some cases, lost permanently.

Economic order quantity is determined by the following formula:

$$EOQ = \sqrt{\frac{2 \times A \times C}{P \times I}}$$

Where: EOQ = economic order quantity
          A = units of item needed during period
          C = cost of processing an order
          P = price per unit of product purchased
          I = annual inventory carrying charge as
                percent of annual inventory value

Assume a business estimates quantity at 7,200 units, cost of processing a requisition at \$10, purchase price at \$3 per unit, and annual inventory carrying charge as a percent of annual inventory value at 0.2%. Substituting these figures in the formula would give:

$$\sqrt{\frac{2 \times 7,200 \times 10}{3 \times 0.2}} = \sqrt{\frac{144,000}{0.6}} = 489^+ \text{ or } 490 \text{ units}$$

If the product was used at a relatively uniform rate, this would suggest ordering about 15 times a year: 7,200 ÷ 490 = 14.7. Management must then evaluate the supplier's pricing schedule to determine if further economies could be obtained by reducing the number of orders and increasing the quantity per order to receive a *quantity discount*. In addition, because of the occasional uncertainty concerning the availability of a product or delays in transportation, many businesses have found it necessary to carry a larger inventory of a product. This has increased their costs because of added investment in warehouse facilities and inventory on-hand.

PRICING POLICIES AND INVENTORIES

In many cases it is an established principle that one of the ways to use space more efficiently is to have a pricing policy that encourages the efficient use of space. For example, there are many businesses that follow the policy of selling a product which has *elastic demand* for advance delivery at a lower *alternate price* than they charge for the same product when purchased as needed. They can justify such a policy on the basis that it costs less to handle the former transaction than it would to handle a transaction in which they are carrying the inventory for the buyer. In many cases, where forward delivery is involved, a *wholesaler* or someone else has the responsibility and assumes the cost of carrying the inventory. Many times, at the end of the season, it may be more economical to reduce the price of a product and move it than to attempt to store it for several months until it is needed. If a person assumes there is a relationship between the price of a marketing service and the cost of performing this service, then the fewer services that are performed, the lower the cost of performing such services. When this is projected to price, one can understand why or how pricing can be used as a technique for permitting efficient use of space.

INVENTORY RECORDS

In a business it is necessary to maintain adequate inventory records to permit sound inventory control decisions. For all products these records

Figure 12-3. Maintaining quality and preserving product integrity are important parts of inventory management. (Courtesy, Office of Agricultural Communications, Mississippi State University)

should include the "cost price," quantity of product, and its location. Cost price refers to the actual cost to the business of manufacturing or purchasing the items in its inventory. For some products it may be necessary, because of quality considerations, to have further information indicating the source of the product, since there are certain sources that are more dependable or there are certain buyers willing to pay higher prices for products from designated sources.

If a business handles a very small number of products, the inventory control and management system may be very unsophisticated. As the number of products increases, the need for a more complex system becomes more evident. In many businesses inventory records are maintained on a computer so that relatively fast answers are available. The need for timely, accurate inventory records cannot be overstated. It should be recognized that if a product cannot be found, it makes little difference whether the business has the product on hand or not, from the standpoint of meeting the customers' needs.

Another problem that affects the cost of maintaining inventory has to do with the extent to which products from different sources may be mixed. If products may be mixed, then this permits a much more efficient use of storage space than would be possible under other conditions. For example, it is generally an accepted practice that regular gasoline from two different deliveries may be mixed without any particularly adverse effects.

PRODUCT INTEGRITY

A related problem in inventory management has to do with maintaining the integrity of a product. For example, once a product is placed in storage, the warehouse has the responsibility to maintain the quality or integrity of that product. If a business has soybeans with 21 percent oil, and these beans are sold on the basis of 21 percent oil, it would be unfortunate if they were blended with some having only 16 or 17 percent oil. As an increasing amount of buying and selling activities becomes a part of specification marketing, where various quality characteristics of the products are spelled out in definite terms, the need for a storage and inventory control system that permits the preservation of product integrity becomes more important.

Physical Inventory

In any inventory system it is imperative that a physical inventory count

Figure 12-4. A physical inventory count of all products on hand needs to be carried out at periodic intervals. (Courtesy, Office of Agricultural Communications, Mississippi State University)

of all products on hand be carried out at periodic intervals. Some businesses have found that such a complete count on an annual basis is adequate. Other businesses have found that, during certain seasons of the year, a monthly physical inventory permits them to have adequate control, while at other times a weekly physical inventory may be desirable. This frequency of physical inventory is dictated by several factors, such as:

1. The characteristics of the product

2. The rate of turnover of the product

3. The rate of turnover of personnel

4. The frequency with which non-employees have access to the storage area

A physical inventory of items which frequently disappear, such as candy or screws in small packages, would probably be more necessary than a physical inventory of small gas engines. Seldom will a physical inventory of all products reflect identical figures to those shown on the inventory record. There are many reasons for this, but for many products there is a certain amount of inventory shrinkage due to pilfering. Once a business has recognized the nature and extent of loss from this source, it is in a better position to take the necessary corrective measures to reduce this as a potential loss source.

A second source of storage losses is waste or damage, which may occur because of poor warehousing practices such as bags of feed or fertilizer broken due to improper use of equipment or during loading and unloading operations. In any event, the nature of these losses needs to be identified and steps taken to control them as much as possible.

A third type of shrinkage has to do with losses related to storage and/or conversion factors. An example of this would be the storage of 20 percent moisture corn which, during the storage process, is reduced to 14 percent moisture and the inventory system has no method of adjusting volume to recognize this moisture loss as also a volume loss. Certainly, in *inventory reconciliation*, every effort should be made to see that the records are adjusted to adequately reflect the quantity of a product on hand. At the same time, an effort should be made to determine the principal factors relative to the various types of losses occurring so that corrective action may be taken to reduce such future inventory discrepancies. Many times the adequate control of such discrepancies is closely related to an on-going personnel training program within the business. Different types of businesses, and even departments within businesses, have different types of inventory loss experience. Every business should establish what it will accept as a normal loss, then take the necessary steps to control the storage or warehouse operations so that these losses do not affect the normal efficient operation of the business.

INVENTORY VALUATION

In making the necessary financial entries related to inventory, there is the problem of what to maintain as the unit cost price of a product. The cost price of a product, depending upon the overall economic conditions, can have a major effect on the short-term profitability of an operation. This is reflected on the business's financial statement through *cost-of-goods sold*. When a business buys a product or raw material the cost price of the item may be different than those already on hand. Some businesses follow a policy of inventory valuation according to the cost of the product when it was purchased, *first-in, first-out (FIFO)*. Others follow the policy of using a replacement cost for the product, *last-in, first-out (LIFO)*. Still others adopt the policy that costs should be charged against revenue on the basis of an average, taking into consideration the number of units acquired at each price and determining the average (*Weighted Average Method*). These three different methods for determining the cost of inventory are applied to earnings and tax analyses. In the long-term it probably makes relatively little difference whether a business uses a weighted average, last-in, first-out (LIFO), or a first-in, first-out (FIFO) method of inventory valuation, but in the short-term it may make a big difference. In either case inventory records should be kept on a consistent, comparable basis year after year so as to avoid the types of discrepancies that occur when the method of pricing inventory records is constantly being changed.

CHAPTER QUESTIONS

1. What are the two readily apparent costs of inventory?

2. What are possible losses due to a business's inability to fill an order?

3. What should be considered in determining the amount of inventory to order?

4. What is the economic order quality in the following situation?

     units needed = 5,000
     price per unit = $3.00
     inventory carrying charge = .5%
     cost of processing order = $5.00

5. What are the three methods for determining the cost of inventory?

6. What is a physical inventory?

7. What are four factors that affect the frequency of a physical inventory?

Chapter 13

MARKETING AND SALES MANAGEMENT

Marketing includes everything that occurs between the time a product is produced and when it is used. It is closely related to economics, the social science that studies the production, distribution, and consumption of goods and services. Our *market economy* is based on private ownership of property and free enterprise principles rather than that of a *command economy* where most of the means of production and distribution are regulated or controlled by a centralized decision-making structure. In a free enterprise system, there must be an ongoing series of sales transactions for a business to exist and operate. These sales transactions consist of the exchange of a product or service for monetary value. This is why marketing and sales are so important to the business and to management; without it, a business cannot exist.

This chapter focuses on the idea that a business should have a marketing plan to move its products or services. Advertising, sales and customer relations strategies are discussed as they relate to the overall marketing function of the agribusiness.

OBJECTIVES

1. Describe the purpose of the sales transaction in a free enterprise system.

2. Identify what goes into the development of a marketing plan.

3. Describe the purpose of advertising and what various methods are available.

4. Identify sources of information used in market research.

5. Identify the three essential elements of any sales transaction.

6. Discuss how the cost-price relationship affects customers and competition.

7. Discuss how quality affects products or services.

8. Identify the types of services provided to customers.

9. Identify ways of measuring sales performance.

10. Describe the responsibilities of the sales staff in working with customers.

ADVERTISING

Advertising and sales are a vital part of a market economy operating under the free enterprise system. They provide the means by which a business makes a profit and they fill a need, derived or conceived, that a consumer has for a product or service, or they improve the quality of life. The product may (1) save time, (2) save money, (3) provide greater convenience, (4) increase knowledge, (5) satisfy a basic need, (6) provide for better health or safety, (7) increase recreational time, or (8) improve a skill or operation.

In order for a business to continue in operation there must be an ongoing series of sales transactions. These transactions are planned for and carried out by the marketing and sales department of the business. In a

TERMS

advertise	economist	markup
advertising agency	loss leader pricing	price
advertising campaign	lower margin	qualifying
advertising copy	margin	sales forecast
business referral	markdown	sales manager
command economy	market areas	supply
competitive pricing	market economy	surveys
contact person	marketing plan	target market
cost benefit	market penetration	trade association
demographics	market pricing	trade discount
direct mail	market research	warranty
discount	market segments	

Figure 13-1. One purpose of sales in a market economy is to satisfy a basic need of a consumer. (Courtesy, Office of Agricultural Communications, Mississippi State University)

small business or sole proprietorship it may be the responsibility of the owner or manager, whereas in a medium-size or larger business there may be many people involved in carrying out this function.

For each of the *market segments* where a business intends to *advertise* its products or services there must be a *marketing plan* developed to help the business achieve its *sales forecast*. Some businesses have a very formal process and others may plan on a more informal basis. *Market research* will provide helpful information on the needs and wants of consumers in the *target market*. With this data, management is able to analyze how its products or services can fill the needs of consumers. It may also provide information indicating a need for a new product or service not available to the consumer, creating an opportunity for business growth. Internal marketing plan elements include: sales history, inventory *supply*, financial statement, and budget available to carry out the marketing program. Additionally, external elements important to market research are the *demographics* of the target market,

Figure 13-2. A sign may make potential customers aware of products or services available, as well as identify the business location. (Courtesy, M. Thomas)

statistics available from a *trade association* for certain businesses, census data, government agency reports, voter registration lists, a professional analysis prepared by an *economist*, and the results of customer *surveys*. Based on this information, management is able to make a sales forecast, develop a marketing plan, and carry out the *advertising campaign*.

Advertising supports the business by transforming consumer needs into a decision to buy a product or service. Effective advertising will:

1. Make potential customers aware of products or services

2. Assist in sales efforts of staff

3. Increase perceived value or worth

4. Motivate customers to look for a specific brand

5. Remind consumers of availability

6. Help consumers receive greater quality or utility from products or services

7. Strengthen buying decision

METHODS USED IN ADVERTISING

Businesses advertise in a variety of ways and locations, including newspaper, radio, television, brochures or catalogs, "yellow pages," handbills, letters, and word-of-mouth. Many public relations activities (see Chapter 14) are also methods of indirect advertising. Advertising campaigns may be handled within the marketing and sales department of the business or, in some cases, professional assistance can be obtained through an *advertising agency*. Dealers may find that manufacturers of materials are willing to supply aids to assist in preparing a local advertising program.

The methods used in advertising are directly affected by the marketing and sales promotion budget. Professional advertising agencies can aid in developing any or all parts of an advertising program. However, they can be expensive so their assistance may be limited by budget constraints. The method used, along with the *advertising copy*, is a very important part of the business's advertising campaign.

Sales Promotions

In addition to the methods of advertising that are thought of as media

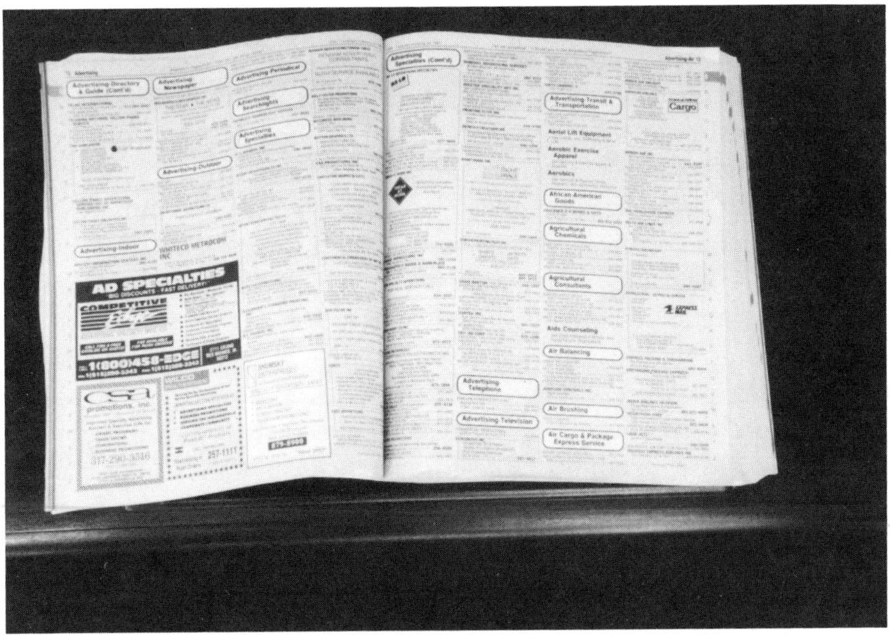

Figure 13-3. Buying space in the telephone book "yellow pages" is one of the most common forms of advertising. (Courtesy, M. Thomas)

advertising, there are many other ways in which a business can effectively promote its products or services. A "sale" or "special introductory offer" where a *markdown* to the regular selling price is applied or a *discount* is offered to first-time customers is a common promotion. Another type is the use of *loss leader pricing* to attract customers into the business. Sales promotions are effective tools for certain businesses; they can attract new customers to the business, reinforce the current customer base, or help reduce seasonal or out-of-date inventory items.

SALES ELEMENTS

In any marketing and sales program there are three essential elements: *price*, quality, and service. These elements cannot be too strongly emphasized. They apply to a large corporation like General Motors the same as they do to a small entrepreneur who has a lawn mowing business. All three of these factors are examined when a sale is being considered and must be consistent with the consumers' needs. Many managers feel that two elements must be equal to or better than that of the competition for most sales transactions to take place.

By definition, the customers of an agribusiness, on at least one side of the market, are farmers. As was mentioned in Chapter 1, agriculture is essentially a manufacturing process in which the farmer combines various purchased inputs with land, labor, and capital to produce agricultural products. Although it is recognized from many standpoints that farming operations are quite similar to other manufacturing business when it comes to selling them goods and services or buying a product from them, there may be a tendency by some agribusinesses to treat the farmer as any other user of "consumer goods"; that is, they assume the farmer has little knowledge of product specifications, technical product requirements, competitors' products, prices, etc. However, recent changes in agriculture have led to different types of relationships between agribusinesses and their customers. Large agriculture producers buy more of their inputs on bids and sell more of their product on contract or bids meeting certain specifications. This practice has led to a decline of the importance of brands and advertising for these customers. Agribusinesses have had to change their approach to serving these customers, relying on more competitive pricing and services to sell the product.

Timeliness is an essential part of many agricultural operations. This timeliness often is closely tied to weather conditions. The production process on the farm is such that if a serious error in production is made, the operation cannot be discarded and started all over until the next production season. This is why agricultural producers put such high value on dependability, honesty, integrity, and other such characteristics in the people who provide them with their goods and services and the people who buy their products.

In many local *market areas* one may find that customers favor doing business with a particular salesperson. If the sales rep moves to another business, the customers move their business with them. Their reason for doing this is that they have confidence in the salesperson's honesty, the integrity of the products, and the dependability of service. The agricultural industry is one in which large volumes of business are done throughout the industry on the basis of seemingly informal arrangements, where the two parties make the transaction by a handshake, a statement indicating yes or no, or a nod of the head. This again points up the heavy dependence upon the personal characteristics of the salesperson working with them.

Many studies indicate that sales representatives are a major source of product information that farmers consult before making decisions concerning agricultural practices, when and where to market, and other major areas of concern. This emphasizes the need for people who work with farmers to have a high level of technical information. Salespeople must know how their products or services can meet the farmer's production requirements. This implies that the business representative, in addition to knowing the product, must also have a general knowledge of agricultural technology and agricultural practices that may be helpful to customers. Furthermore, they must be able to disseminate this information to their customers in such a manner that the producer can understand how to use it in making sound decisions.

PRICE-COST RELATIONSHIPS

In pricing a product or service, it should be recognized that there is a relationship between the cost of providing the service and the price at which the service is provided—*cost benefit*. If the *margin* is too great between the price charged and the cost of providing the product or service, then an existing business may find new businesses entering the area, providing the product or service at a *lower margin*, and acquiring its customers because of price. In another situation, a business may have priced a service with too much *markup*, thus it becomes more profitable for customers to do it themselves. Once a customer has adopted a different method of doing business, it becomes much more difficult to regain the lost opportunity.

For example, in one study it was found that the cost of having corn dried at an elevator was high enough to justify installing facilities to dry corn on individual farms. Once this had been done, it became very difficult for the elevator to regain this lost business opportunity. Therefore, in pricing a product, a business must be aware of the various alternatives that may be available to their customers and use *competitive pricing*.

Farmer-Dealer Competition

Some farmers have such a large volume of business that they are recognized as dealers. This means they receive a *trade discount* and pay dealer prices rather than retail prices for products. Frequently the larger farmers handle more products during a year than some of the smaller dealers within their area. This has particularly important implications for those businesses that have an exclusive franchise for a product within a particular market area but may provide little or no service to some of their largest potential customers.

One of the problems that is facing many of the businesses now engaged in providing goods and services to agriculture is how to service the large commercial agricultural operations, while at the same time protect the integrity of the local franchised dealer. This problem is of special importance when considering sales policy within the area, as it will be related to pricing policy, services, and other items of this nature.

Appearance and Price

An important sales tool for many businesses is appearance. This encompasses the physical appearance of personnel, products, and facilities. Customers want to do business with those who meet their concept of how the business should appear. For example you would not find a bank operating out of an old warehouse. To the agribusiness, this means the facility and staff should be clean and neat. Customers want a product that is easy to handle and that, in their opinion, is displayed in good taste. Packaging is an important part of the product design and a marketing function. It may not add to the need, utility, or quality of a particular item, but in can be the initial factor which causes a customer to examine the product further. If a product does not look like it is worth $10, a customer would probably not pay $10 for it.

Figure 13-4. The sign on this landscaping business's truck implies quality. (Courtesy, M. Thomas)

QUALITY

Quality is the degree of excellence a product or service possesses. Some products or services are designed to be of lesser quality, others may be of high quality. Often terms like *warranty* or "money back guarantee" are indicators of higher quality. Utility is also an indicator of quality. Some products are used once and then disposed of while others are able to be reused. The quality during the first usage may be equal; however, after that the reusable product is of higher quality due strictly to product life. Quality and product life are additional factors in the pricing equation.

SERVICE

Management must know the amount and type of services that their customers need and their willingness to pay for these services. Services cost money. There is a close relationship between the amount of services provided and the *market pricing* policy for products. There are three general service areas. One of these has to do with the handling of the product or service, such as supply or availability, delivery time, and/or storage service. A second is the extent to which the business may be helping to finance through

Figure 13-5. This professional agribusiness's advertisement indicates a high level of service. (Courtesy, M. Thomas)

extension of credit. Third is the extent to which the business may be providing technical and management information. There are many businesses using one or more of these services as an important selling tool.

In the process of pricing products there is a general tendency for various competing businesses to charge approximately the same prices, competitive pricing. However, it should be recognized that it is very difficult to make price comparisons without knowing what services are included. As the size of agricultural production operations has increased, so have the many factors which may cause a series of prices to be in effect, depending upon location, services, and volume. In commercial agriculture during the next decade, it will be much more difficult to accurately establish the prevalent prices for agricultural input and output from competing businesses.

Due to the new, highly competitive conditions that exist, particularly where there may be surplus capacity at least during parts of the year, most businesses have adopted the policy of competing using services. It becomes much more difficult to measure the quality of service, since this is a subjective factor that must be very specifically tailored to the requirements of each individual customer, and such services are often identified with a particular person. The extent of price competition is difficult to measure, since businesses frequently have an understanding with the customer that they will not disclose to others what their price is.

MEASURING PERFORMANCE

There are two common techniques for measuring sales performance of businesses or individual salespeople: (1) market share and (2) percent of increase over a past period, usually over the previous month or the same period from the prior year.

From an agricultural census or other data, it is possible to develop information indicating the trend of the total market area and from this to make estimates as to the share of this market that a particular business has. The business is then in a position to measure performance on the basis of whether its *market penetration* is increasing or decreasing. From some standpoints this measure may be more helpful in indicating performance than changes in volume, as it indicates what is happening insofar as the business's percentage of the total is concerned. For example, sales could be increasing in volume each year but, at the same time, be a reduced share of the total market; or the business could be in an area where agriculture is declining and, in effect, be increasing its market share at the same time the total volume is decreasing. An increase in volume over some past period, such as the previous year or for each of the past five years, is a measure that would indicate performance. This measure, however, could be more closely tied to income positions than share of market, since there is some relationship between volume and earnings.

In some cases it may only be possible to increase volume or increase market share with excessive cost. Therefore, a third measure of performance that might be considered is sales cost per dollar of sales. If additional business can be obtained only at an excessive cost, it may well be that the additional revenue costs more than it contributes to income.

In most businesses, a sales forecast is developed by management in consultation with the *sales manager.* Such estimates of expected performance are necessary ingredients for planning storage, inventory, capital, and other essential parts of the business operation. Sales functions must be coordinated with the total operation. A method of evaluating the effectiveness of advertising campaigns or sales promotions, as well as the sales forecast, which provides for feedback and revision must be developed. Frequently businesses set quotas as to the number of contacts the sales staff are expected to make with prospective customers and with existing customers. Many companies follow a policy of awarding bonuses for additional volume in excess of the quota. The objective is to encourage personnel to put forth a greater effort and to increase sales volume, and then to provide some means of recognition for those who achieve outstanding performance.

The individual salesperson needs to develop a prospect list. Many companies feel that a prospect list built from *business referral* by satisfied customers is one of the better sources of new customers; other businesses follow the policy of building such a list from answers to inquiries made in an advertising campaign. Once such a list has been made, salespeople need to develop, in a consistent manner, a knowledge of the products each customer needs and how the business can provide the goods and services needed to make each prospective customer's operation more nearly meet their personal goals. This awareness of the potential to assist the prospective customers in meeting their objectives may be developed through personal letters, *direct mail* materials, and personal contact. Most successful sales staffs have developed a combination of methods to assemble a good prospect list and then use several related approaches to develop these prospects.

WORKING WITH
THE CUSTOMER

A good sales staff must continually work at keeping their existing customers satisfied with the products and services they have to offer. At the same time they must also work at *qualifying* and developing new customers. They need to know the types of goods and services customers want and need, and the extent to which their business can provide them. There are cases where good customers have never purchased certain products or services because no one had ever told them that the business was able to provide such goods or services.

People skills are basic to success in sales. Each customer is an individual, and the sales staff must know which products and services meet a particular customer's requirements. The *contact person* must be in a position to develop a sales approach that will motivate a particular customer to respond as the salesperson wishes. This means the salesperson should also be able to evaluate the characteristics of the customer. Expectations vary greatly among individual customers—some customers may want to see the salesperson once a month and other customers may want to see the salesperson once a year. It is important that the salesperson know what each customer wants and then, insofar as possible, meet these requirements. There are some customers who, when they are busy, do not want to see a salesperson; then, when they are not busy, expect the salesperson to stop by for a visit on a regular basis. Tailoring the sales approach to each customer on the basis of that individual's specific needs and requirements becomes an important part of the sales strategy.

Much selling is done by personal contact. While it is recognized that this particular type of selling is relatively expensive, most businesses also recognize that the personal relationship involved in such an approach is generally more effective than other methods of selling. At the same time the salesperson is selling products, he or she is also providing many other types of information that will help the potential buyer make a decision. The salesperson is also able, through these contacts, to help develop a more favorable image for the business.

Direct mail is another approach that is used to develop early contacts and, for some businesses, comprises a major part of their total selling effort. Many sales staffs effectively use a systematic direct mail approach to keep their customers informed of new developments or to remind them that the company and the sales staff is always interested in their operation and ways that they may better serve them. However, in most farming operations, where either farm inputs or purchasing of farm production is the major

Figure 13-6. Sales brochures and catalogs are common forms of direct mail advertising. (Courtesy, Interstate Publishers, Inc.)

Figure 13-7. For many types of agricultural operations one of the most effective long-range selling tools is a customer education program. (Courtesy, Brendan Marshall)

focus of the business, the final sales effort must be on an individualized, personalized basis.

For many types of agricultural operations one of the most effective long-range selling tools is a customer education program. In many agricultural communities the business, either on its own or in cooperation with the Agricultural Extension Service or the local school's Agricultural Education Department, sponsors field days or demonstrations. Under such conditions the customers and prospective customers have an opportunity to see particular products. For example, plots may show the results from applications of different fertilizers or from the use of different herbicides for specific crops. Many businesses also hold meetings where they discuss technical information helpful to their customers; at the same time these customers have an opportunity to discuss results with other users or potential users of the product. This exchange of ideas and experiences with customers is a valuable sales approach.

In addition to holding field days and meetings, many businesses provide a publication which is sent to customers and potential customers. This publication not only carries information about particular products but also frequently provides timely information that will help the readers to more effectively carry out their operations. These types of customer education programs are helpful in developing a better relationship between the business and customers. This in turn is generally thought to be related to better sales. It is important for the customers to know and understand what products and services are available from the business. It is also important for them to know how the business functions, what its general policies are, and how it can contribute to a more efficient operation.

In some businesses, the sales staff's responsibility extends beyond sales; the sales personnel are also responsible for making deliveries. Many salespeople are concerned about whether or not they have sufficient time to perform their sales function. One often hears comments to the effect that devoting so much of their time to delivering products does not permit sufficient time to make the contacts necessary for their sales function.

In all other sales programs the salesperson must have a close working relationship with the people who are making the deliveries. If a salesperson promises delivery on a particular date, then that individual must be sure the product will be delivered at that time. The sales rep also must be sure that the person making the delivery is acquainted with the particular preferences and dislikes of the buyer. The coordination of sales activities and the warehousing function cannot be overemphasized.

The salesperson also needs to know how sales activities are interrelated with warehousing operations. A salesperson who has a good working relationship with the warehouse manager often is able to provide much better service to his or her customers than a member of the sales staff who does not recognize the interdependence of the two operations.

In some companies sales personnel are responsible for collecting money from their customers. In other businesses the collection and/or credit department is an entirely separate operation from sales. The argument for the first method of operation is that when sales representatives know they are also going to be responsible for collecting for the sales, they will tend to concentrate most of their efforts primarily on those customers that present a minimum of collection problems. This may mean that they are not as anxious to expand sales as would be the case if someone else were responsible for collection. If the sales function and the collection function are separated, sales staffs may become primarily concerned with volume without giving any consideration as to how the buyer may pay for the product or service.

Generally, those characteristics which are typical in a good salesperson are not necessarily the same set of characteristics one would require in a good credit and collection employee. By nature the salesperson must be an optimistic person who sees the great potential their product has to help customers and potential customers increase their earning ability. Conversely, a good credit and collection person must by nature assume that not everyone is honest and that most people are overly optimistic concerning their ability to repay. The relationship between sales and collections is one that must be developed by each individual business to meet its particular requirements.

CHAPTER QUESTIONS

1. What is the difference between a market economy and a command economy?

2. What are some of the ways a product or service can fill a consumer need?

3. What are some of the internal elements used in developing a marketing plan?

4. What are some of the external elements which may be important to market research?

5. What are the three essential elements present when any sale occurs?

6. What is meant by the term "quality" in relationship to a product or service?

7. What are the three general "service areas" in business?

8. What must a good sales staff know when working with existing customers or potential customers?

Chapter 14

PUBLIC RELATIONS

The function of a public relations program is to build goodwill in the community. The program does not generally promote a particular product, but tries to build community support for the agribusiness in general. Some people view the idea of a public relations program as a way for a business to indicate a social consciousness, building good feelings toward the business from employees, customers and potential customers.

A public relations program can be very important to the success of an agribusiness, but the techniques for measuring its effect are very complex. A business manager often does not know exactly how much a change in community involvement is related to the profit and loss of a business. Experts generally agree, however, that businesses that are well thought of in a community (or region) are more successful than competitors who are not held in as high regard. The basic idea is that, other factors being similar, consumers will want to do business with a company they like and respect.

This chapter describes some public relations concepts and gives the agribusiness manager some strategies to use when implementing a public relations program.

OBJECTIVES

1. Understand the purpose of public relations as a part of business.

2. Identify activities associated with public relations.

3. Understand how to develop relationships and work with mass media.

4. Understand the purpose of advisory committees and how they work.

PURPOSE OF A PUBLIC RELATIONS PROGRAM

The purpose of a business's public relations program is to gain acceptance of the business and its products or services by the community. Most businesses try to develop a public relations program in such a way that people will recognize the business and what it contributes to the community. In addition, it is hoped the *publicity* will also appeal to prospective customers and thus contribute to an increased *sales volume.*

Frequently there is a difference between the information established customers need compared with that needed by new customers. Public relations is an attempt to make an appeal to these various audiences in such a manner that they will all respond in the desired fashion.

Most managers would agree that no amount of public relations effort can adequately offset an unsatisfactory product or a service that does not adequately meet the customers' needs. A history of satisfied customers is one of the best public relations tools that a business can hope to have.

Every employee is a public relations representative for his or her business. In most rural communities this is true not only when the employee is on the job but also when away from work. The physical appearance of the facilities is important in developing a satisfactory image for the business. The quality of service is still another public relations tool that is available to the business.

PUBLIC RELATIONS ACTIVITIES

There are a number of different activities that may also be important in developing a favorable image for the business and the goods and services

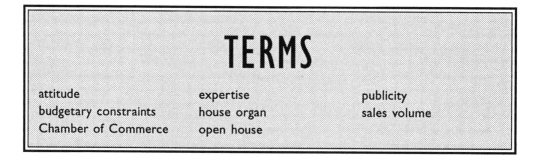

TERMS

attitude   expertise   publicity
budgetary constraints   house organ   sales volume
Chamber of Commerce   open house

Figure 14-1. This billboard indicates support for a number of agriculture related organizations. (Courtesy, M. Thomas)

it provides. These various activities are not necessarily listed in the order of their importance. It should be recognized that some activities may be more important in trying to reach certain groups, and some may be more important at one time than others, but they all represent activities that help determine the community's *attitude* toward the business.

COMMUNITY PARTICIPATION

As a public relations effort, many businesses encourage their personnel to participate in community affairs. This indicates to the community that the business recognizes its responsibility to be part of the community and to participate in these necessary activities. This also provides the business with a means of identifying problem areas, either where the business activities are not properly understood or where they have been at fault. In addition, if personnel know the nature of the adverse comments that exist, they are in a position to correct misinformation and alert the appropriate people in management to areas where the business needs to more actively engage in presenting its side of the story.

Some of the types of activities that fall into the category of community participation include providing leadership and financial support for the

Chamber of Commerce, United Way, scouting, and local planning commissions. Additionally, a business may use an *open house* as a way to attract members of the community to the business.

An agribusiness should encourage its employees to serve on the advisory committees of local vocational education programs. This involvement builds goodwill while at the same time helps the business ensure that it will have a quality pool of potential employees to meet personnel needs.

Figure 14-2. Businesses may become a member of the area Chamber of Commerce. This indicates to the community that the business recognizes responsibility to the area and provides a means for businesses to work together with common goals. (Courtesy, M. Thomas)

MEETING PLACE FACILITIES

Many businesses, when building new facilities, have made provisions for a meeting room or community room that can be used for public meetings when properly requested. In many small rural communities this facility contributes much to maintaining the community as a viable social and economic unit.

Figure 14-3. Businesses can use educational tours to bring about a better understanding of their business or products. (Courtesy, Brendan Marshall)

EDUCATIONAL TOURS

High school and elementary students need to better understand the world in which they live. Businesses have an excellent opportunity to provide facilities for educational tours so these students can obtain a better understanding of the business world, as well as seeing how the food and fiber they use every day is produced. Businesses can serve a very useful purpose by providing teachers with real-life examples to use in their classroom instructional programs. Such cooperation with teachers can help make courses more interesting to the students and at the same time bring about a better understanding of the methods used by business. Business will see more involvement in this tech prep orientation to education.

YOUTH ACTIVITIES

Many businesses provide awards and sponsor contests for organizations such as FFA and 4-H clubs, as well as recognizing outstanding performance on athletic teams, debate teams, and other activities. They also provide various certificates and awards to encourage excellence in education. Many businesses sponsor teams in youth athletic programs such as little league baseball.

WORKING WITH MASS MEDIA

There are a number of activities a business is involved in that may become newsworthy events, at which time the business is in a position to provide news stories and pictures. The person in charge of working with the media needs to know what local editors or writers consider news material, how they want the information prepared, and when they would like to receive the materials. Most editors are looking for good, dependable sources of local news items, provided the material presented is news and not primarily advertising for the business's particular products or services. If material is furnished to the local newspaper in the form of a press release, it should be a computer printed or typed original copy; it should arrive at a time that makes it convenient for the local editor to review it before the paper's publication deadline.

A business should have someone who is primarily responsible for working with newspapers, radio, and television stations. That person should develop a relationship with the local reporters so that he or she can notify them of any good news stories, even though these stories may have nothing to do with that individual's particular business. This helps convey to the leaders of the community the overall interest of the business in the community and what is happening in it.

A local business may produce or sponsor informational programs that better acquaint interested people in the community with the nature and activity of the business. Some of these informational programs may be highly technical in nature and of interest to very limited audiences while others may be of much broader interest. For example, the business handling farm chemicals may have one program which would be of primary interest only to those people who are buying and using farm chemicals; while another program, aimed at chemicals and environmental problems, would emphasize a much broader area of interest as far as the community as a whole is concerned.

PUBLIC SPEAKING

Some businesses provide speakers on a variety of topics in their areas of *expertise* to civic groups, business clubs, social clubs, or churches. In some areas the speakers have been most beneficial in bringing about a better understanding of agriculture and its problems, as well as those of agribusinesses that are directly tied to production agriculture.

PERIODICALS

Many businesses either publish their own *house organ* or subscribe to a newsletter that allows for a certain amount of personalization and localization of information. These periodicals may provide many types of information to appeal to the many types of audiences that a public relations program is designed to reach. Such publications may contain pages devoted to employee advancement or relations, business development and growth, technical developments, economic developments, and special aspects or problems of the particular business, industry, or area being represented.

ADVISORY COMMITTEES

In many areas businesses have used local advisory committees to strengthen their public relations programs. An advisory committee is generally composed of a group of people from the community. People who differ in age and occupational backgrounds, who come from various areas of the community, and have different educational backgrounds, make this committee a true cross section of the community. Another type of advisory committee could be comprised of various customers of the business. This committee is used as (1) a sounding board for developing new ideas, (2) a method of identifying or developing alternative solutions for operational problems, (3) a means of determining reaction to policy changes and of measuring the effectiveness of explanations for changes in policy, and (4) a method of disseminating information on what the business is doing or proposes to do.

Much skill is required if such a group is to make a maximum contribution to a better understanding of the business, its problems, possible solutions, and what it may do to develop more efficient working relationships with its customers. Where an advisory committee has been properly selected and used, it can make some major contributions to a more efficient operation. If an advisory committee is not used as a source of help and is not properly organized, it can be a liability rather than an asset.

There are two common problems concerning advisory committees.

1. The committee forgets that it is only advisory. It should be pointed out, however, that if such a committee is formed and management

consistently chooses to ignore suggestions that the committee makes, then the members will soon lose interest in serving on such a committee.

2. Management uses advisory committee meetings as a place to do all the talking which, in effect, attempts to force the committee to give its approval to management's preconceived conclusion. Under such conditions the committee does not function in an advisory capacity. The members of the committee will realize that they are not being used as they should be, and the effectiveness of the committee is destroyed.

RESPONSIBILITY FOR PROGRAM

In many businesses the development of the public relations program becomes a primary responsibility of the general manager. This activity is in addition to his or her other duties. That individual frequently becomes so involved with the day-to-day operational problems of the business that there is inadequate time available to develop a long-range public relations program that provides a unity of purpose with a central theme. Under such conditions the public relations program frequently becomes a disjointed activity that contributes little to achieving the objectives of a well thought out, continuous program.

In other businesses one frequently finds the newest employee being assigned the task of public relations in addition to other duties. This approach is frequently self-defeating, as the person responsible for the program often has limited information about the business and its products or services. That individual is so busy trying to develop sufficient skills and learn the duties of a new job that he or she has little time to devote to working on the overall public relations program for the business.

The public relations program for a business must be appropriate for the audience that the business wishes to reach. It must be recognized that many of the activities suggested will involve competition with activities of other businesses, various community and social activities, and all forms of entertainment for the audience's time. In a society where time is a very valuable commodity, it must be recognized that the public relations program, if it is to reach the audience and be effective, must be well-planned and appealing.

Management must decide what it wants a public relations program to accomplish. Using the best information available, management must also determine the cost of such a program, then readjust the broad objectives of the program to a level consistent with its *budgetary constraints*. Once a decision is made concerning the nature and extent of the public relations program, the business needs to develop a means of measuring the extent to which the program is achieving the stated objectives. Management must appoint someone to implement the program, monitor its progress, and determine what changes are needed to enable it to be more effective.

CHAPTER QUESTIONS

1. What are the goals of a business's public relations program?

2. What are eight types of public relations activities?

3. How can a business use advisory committees?

4. What are two common problems in using advisory committees?

5. How can management make the public relations program more effective?

Chapter 15

FINANCIAL RECORDS AS MANAGEMENT TOOLS

Like any business manager, the agribusiness manager must keep accurate and complete financial records. These records are used to analyze the performance of the business and make the necessary management decisions. Also, the owners/directors of the business use these records to assess the effectiveness of management.

This chapter discusses the most common business financial records and strategies managers use to analyze these records. Several terms will be introduced in order to increase the readers knowledge of financial record keeping. Definitions for terms presented in italics are in this book's glossary. For further information on accounting principles and procedures it is suggested that the reader obtain a book on the subject from the library.

OBJECTIVES

1. Identify ways management can measure performance.

2. Describe general accounting principles.

3. Classify financial accounts and sub-groups.

4. Describe the basic flow for processing business transactions in financial record keeping.

5. Define the terms commonly used in accounting.

6. Describe what is contained in and how to use a financial statement.

7. Identify sources and uses of funds in the business and how they affect financial accounts.

8. Describe what is contained in, and how to use, a profit and loss statement.

201

9. Describe how to use a cash flow statement.

10. Discuss the purpose and method of using budget projections.

11. Discuss the purpose of and how to use production control records.

12. Describe ways to evaluate investment alternatives considering rate of return, pay-back period, and discounted future earnings.

MEASURING BUSINESS PERFORMANCE

In the business community, management must be concerned with having sufficient funds available to meet *expenses*. Employees must be paid, *vendors* must be paid, and investors expect a return on their investments; therefore, management must be concerned with *earnings* and cash management. There are four major financial *records* that can assist in management decisions: Balance Sheet, Profit and Loss Statement (Income and Expense Summary), Cash Flow Statement, and *Budget* Projections.

TERMS

accountant	debentures	posting
accrual basis	down payment	preservation
accumulated	earnings	price sensitivity
administrative expenses	economic downturn	procedures
auditors	expenses	profitability
audit trail	factory overhead	property tax
bad debts	financial restrictions	purchase order
balancing	fiscal year	raw materials
budget	funded	records
business transaction	general ledger	remitting
business venture	good will	reserve
cash basis	inelastic demand	taxation
cash disbursement	interest expense	transactions
cash discount	invoice	valuation
cash flow problem	journal	vendors
cash payment	long-term liabilities	work in process
cash receipts	obsolete equipment	
chart of accounts	petty cash	

Management is subject to evaluation by owners, by the board of directors and/or shareholders, as well as by suppliers and bankers who appraise the financial soundness of a business and weigh the risks involved before extending credit or granting loans. Government agencies are concerned with financial activities for purposes of *taxation* and regulation. A business may also use its financial records as a way to measure management's performance.

The two most commonly used criteria for measuring performance are: (1) against the performance of the business in previous years and (2) against performance as revealed by an average of a number of businesses in the same industry. Some of the comparisons that may be useful are discussed later. Two other measures of performance are: (1) against objectives (see Chapter 2 for discussion on development of measurable objectives) and (2) projected performance as reflected in the budget projections for the year.

Each of the four approaches mentioned above can assist management in determining its strong and weak points. This should then suggest approaches to strengthen the overall operation. Such an analysis will indicate the types of problems management should consider when making changes in policies and *procedures* so performance can be improved.

FINANCIAL PRINCIPLES AND ORGANIZATION

Financial records within the business are controlled by the *accountant*, bookkeeper, or vice president of finance. That individual is concerned with the recording of *transactions* for the business and the preparation of financial statements or reports from these records. He or she may also provide management with historical or estimated data to assist with operations evaluation or planning. In some operations that person may also be responsible for preparation of tax returns, budgets, and government reports.

Property owned by a business is referred to as assets. Rights or claims to the properties are referred to as equities. In accounting: Assets = Equities. Equities are subdivided into two principal types: (1) Liabilities—debts of the business and (2) Capital—equity of the owners. Therefore, the accounting equation is expressed as: Assets = Liabilities + Capital. All business transactions can be stated in terms of their effect on these three elements of the accounting equation. When a business generates revenues and has expenses through the activity of business that effect must be incorporated into the equation also. This is expressed: Assets = Liabilities + Capital (+ Revenues − Expenses).

Although the transactions completed by a business can be recorded in terms of their effect upon this equation, such a format is not practical. The transactions may effect increases and decreases in many different asset, liability, capital, revenue, and expense items; therefore, it is necessary to maintain a record for each type of item. A business must have one account devoted to recording increases or decreases to cash, another account devoted to equipment, another devoted to office supplies, etc. All financial accounts maintained by a business are listed in the business's *chart of accounts*.

Figure 15-1. In many businesses financial transactions are recorded directly into a computer. (Courtesy, M. Thomas)

Accounts within the major categories of the equation are further classified into related sub-groupings. An example of classification of accounts with sub-groupings and appropriate accounts for a business's Balance Sheet is illustrated in Figure 15-2. (A number of new terms are introduced in this chapter. The reader should use the extensive glossary in the back of the book to become familiar with these terms. This should lead to a basic understanding of the process.)

Figure 15-2
CLASSIFICATION OF ACCOUNTS WITH SUB-GROUPINGS
FOR A BALANCE SHEET

ASSETS

Current Assets
cash
notes receivable
accounts receivable
reserve for *bad debts*
raw materials inventory
work in process
finished goods inventory
supplies
prepaid expenses

Fixed or Plant Assets
land
buildings
equipment
accumulated depreciation

Other Assets
good will
cash surrender value life insurance

LIABILITIES

Current Liabilities
accounts payable
notes payable (current portion)
mortgage payable (current portion)
taxes payable
Long-term Liabilities
notes payable (long-term portion)
mortgage payable (long-term portion)

CAPITAL

Equity
capital stock
retained earnings

An example of classification with sub-groupings of a business's Profit and Loss Statement (Income and Expense Summary) is illustrated in Figure 15-3. The illustrations presented are only examples and will vary from business to business. For instance, a manufacturing operation would have additional sub-groupings.

Figure 15-3
CLASSIFICATION OF ACCOUNTS FOR A CORPORATION
WITH SUB-GROUPINGS FOR A PROFIT AND LOSS STATEMENT
OF A WHOLESALE OR RETAIL OPERATION

REVENUE
> Sales
> Less returns and allowances
>> Net Sales

COST OF SALES
> Inventory—beginning of period
> Purchases
>> Total Available for Sale
> Inventory—end of period
>> Total Cost of Sales

GROSS PROFIT

OPERATING EXPENSES (*Factory Overhead*)
> Salaries, wages
> Payroll taxes
> Rent
> Utilities
> Insurance
> Depreciation
>> Total Operating Expenses

NET INCOME FROM OPERATIONS

OTHER INCOME (EXPENSE)
> Commissions
> Interest income
> Rental income
> *Interest expense*
>> Total Other Income (Expense), Net

Net Income Before Taxes
Provision for Income Taxes

NET INCOME

Retained Earnings—beginning of period
Retained Earnings—end of period

PROCEDURES AND CONTROLS

The flow of financial data is illustrated in Figure 15-4. This basic flow is followed by manual or computer processing of financial records. The initial record of each *business transaction* or group of similar transactions is validated by a business document such as an *invoice*, sales ticket, bank deposit, check or receipt verifying *cash payment*, cash receipt, *down payment*, etc. The business document is then recorded in a *journal*. The amounts in the various journals are then transferred by *posting* to the accounts in the *general ledger*. The general ledger accounts are classified (summarized) into totals for the financial statement.

Figure 15-4
FLOW FOLLOWED IN PROCESSING FINANCIAL RECORDS

Business	Prepare	Record in	Post to	Classify into
Transaction →	Document →	Journal →	General Ledger →	Financial Statement

Financial records management must provide for (1) accurate recording and reporting of information, (2) measurement of operational information, (3) assignment of responsibility, and (4) internal control. The manager must assign responsibility for financial record keeping to an individual within the organization. That responsibility includes everything: *preservation* of the assets of the business, insuring a proper *audit trail*, seeing that a *purchase order* is used when ordering supplies, *balancing* the *petty cash* fund, seeing

Figure 15-5. Properly recorded financial transactions are used to generate financial statements, reports, tax returns, etc. (Courtesy, M. Thomas)

a *cash discount* date is not missed when *remitting* to suppliers, preparing financial statements, and any other financial transactions.

Taxation can present further challenges for the manager of a financial record keeping system. Some businesses recognize income and expenses on an *accrual basis* and others on a *cash basis*. Those responsible for financial records must be aware of the reporting method for taxation and insure the necessary information is available for preparation of tax returns.

BALANCE SHEET

The balance sheet is a listing of a business's assets and liabilities. This statement, when properly prepared, reflects a picture, as of a specific date, of what the business owns and owes, as well as the net worth of the business. Figure 15-6 is an example of a balance sheet.

Figure 15-6
BALANCE SHEET FOR FENIX FARM SUPPLY CO.
AS OF DECEMBER 31, 19—

Cash	$263,000	
Net Receivables	349,000	
Inventory	493,000	
Other Current Assets	14,000	
Total Current Assets		1,119,000
Investments	365,000	
Fixed Assets (Net)	1,177,000	
Other Assets	18,000	
Total Long-Term Assets		1,560,000
Total Assets		$2,679,000
Accounts Payable	300,000	
Notes Payable	600,000	
Total Current Liabilities	900,000	
Long-Term Debt	835,000	
Total Liabilities		1,735,000
Capital	489,000	
Retained Earnings	455,000	
Net Worth		944,000
Total Liabilities and Net Worth		$2,679,000

In any given business the breakdown of the items in a financial statement may vary. In this financial statement there are categories that indicate the amount of cash, accounts receivable, notes receivable, inventory, and prepaid expenses. There may be an additional breakdown of these items, but these are the major categories.

In analyzing a financial statement, information is needed that will enable a person to compare changes in the financial statements over a period of time. With many businesses it is more meaningful to compare one year's financial statement with that of a corresponding date for any of several preceding years. Because of the seasonal nature of many businesses, a comparison between consecutive months will quite often be less significant than one for corresponding months between years. Often it is also possible to compare the financial statement of a particular business with the average of a number of businesses in the same industry or with the average of other businesses performing approximately the same services. This provides a measure of how the business compares with other similar businesses. A financial statement without some means of comparison provides relatively little information that can be of major assistance to management.

On the liability side of the financial statement are three major categories. First is current liabilities, which include items such as the current portion of notes payable, accounts payable, and items that are due within the current 12-month period, such as *property tax* and insurance. A second major category is long-term liabilities, which include long-term notes (either secured or unsecured) along with such additional items as long-term bonds and *debentures*. The current liabilities plus the long-term liabilities give the total liabilities figure. The difference between total liabilities and total assets is the net worth, which is made up primarily of two items: One is the par value of stock or other evidence of investment; the other is the retained earnings account, which in effect represents that amount of earnings which has been retained, or reinvested in the business.

The balance sheet provides a measure of the financial organization of the business and a statement of the nature and type of assets available to the business. This is only part of the information that is needed for management analyses and business evaluation. Management is concerned with a number of different types of financial relationships. Each business must determine, on the basis of its operations, which items are most important to the successful management of its particular business. For example, many businesses are concerned with their liquidity position. This is generally defined as the relationship between current assets and current liabilities, and normally indicates the ability of the business to borrow additional short-term money to meet short-term needs.

In addition to the various types of ratios management is concerned with when evaluating the purchase of a *business venture*, owners, shareholders, directors, outside *auditors*, and entrepreneurs need to know to what extent the various asset items are realistically valued. For example, they would need to know the quality and turnover of the accounts receivable, the method for costing inventory, and the extent to which inventory has been verified. They are also interested in how the *valuation* of the fixed assets has been determined—does this represent purchase price less depreciation, or does it represent replacement cost? For example, assume a business has been in operation a number of years and book value is purchase cost less depreciation; with the amount of inflation over the years, this book value would be understated in relation to replacement cost. It is important to insure that everyone understands how these figures are determined and what they really mean when an attempt is made to analyze the financial statement. There are few opportunities for the liabilities on the financial statement to be subject to misinterpretation unless a case arises in which some record keeping inadequacies reveal debts that are improperly listed.

In addition, on financial statements prepared by an outside auditor, it is common to find "notes to the financial statement." These may include such items as method of costing inventory, income tax timing differences, summary of significant accounting policies, a detailed listing of notes payable with maturity dates, classifications of property and equipment, and any *financial restrictions* placed on the business.

Different types of transactions in a financial statement may have different impacts on the relationships involved. For example, collection of accounts receivable through *cash receipts* would reduce accounts receivable and increase cash. A payment (*cash disbursement*) on debt would reduce the cash and the appropriate liability account as well as total assets. Purchase of inventory on credit would increase the inventory account and increase debt and total assets. The reader should practice making various changes in different parts of the financial statement to understand these relationships.

The financial statement data shows trends over the years in the categories of assets, liabilities, and net worth. This data frequently reveals much about management of the business. It indicates the solvency of the business and is an important consideration lenders use in evaluating credit. Generally businesses should have as a goal maintaining sufficient financial cushion to permit taking advantage of unexpected favorable investment opportunities or to permit continued operations when an *economic downturn* occurs.

Frequently businesses, for a number of reasons, find it necessary to make investments in other related business organizations. This is not only true for cooperatives but also for many other corporations. Total current assets are added to the total fixed assets to obtain the total assets.

Therefore, the financial statement is important as (1) a measure of solvency, (2) a means of acquiring access to new capital, (3) an indicator of operations flexibility potential, and (4) a guide as to when a business should take advantage of new investment opportunities.

One approach frequently used in financial analysis is the source and use of funds. Such an approach indicates changes in various items in the balance sheet from one period to another. The following is helpful in classifying sources and uses:

Sources of Cash	Uses of Cash
Net Worth Increases	Net Worth Decreases
Liability Increases	Liability Decreases
Asset Decreases	Asset Increases

Assume a business shows the following changes in their balance sheet from one year to another:

Cash	–10,000
Depreciation	+20,000
Inventory	–10,000
Accounts Receivable	+25,000
Equipment	+15,000
Accounts Payable	+12,000
Notes Payable	– 8,000
Securities	+20,000
Net Worth	+16,000

A source and use of funds would show:

Sources of Cash

Cash	10,000
Depreciation	20,000
Inventory	10,000
Accounts Payable	12,000
Net Worth	16,000
	$68,000

Uses of Cash

Accounts Receivable	25,000
Equipment	15,000
Notes Payable	8,000
Securities	20,000
	$68,000

The sources and uses columns must total the same amount.

Figure 15-7 shows the relationship between various items in the balance sheet and the profit and loss statement. A knowledge of these relationships will assist in understanding this discussion. Management involves much more than the ability to interpret financial records, but such an interpretation is an essential ingredient in successful management.

PROFIT AND LOSS STATEMENT

The profit and loss statement (income and expense summary) is a statement of income and expenses incurred by a business for a specified period of time, such as for a month, a year, or some other accounting period. It usually shows the current month and year-to-date activity for the *fiscal year*. For this statement to really have much meaning, it becomes necessary to compare the results from one year to the next or from one accounting period to the next, as the case may be. It is also necessary to keep in mind any changes that may have occurred that would make the result for one period incomparable with some other period with which it is being compared. While there are many items that might be brought out from a profit and loss statement, an analysis of the expense items provides a basis for determining the areas in which there is a need for further study. For example, in looking at depreciation, a person needs to know the rate of depreciation being used or if there are certain depreciable assets which are practically worn out that will need to be replaced within a short period of time.

Many management decisions that must be made are related to ways changes in operations would affect income. These changes may concern capital needs, nature and type of service provided, pricing policy, or other items of this nature. In attempting to visualize how these changes would affect organization, it is suggested that both a balance sheet and a profit and loss statement be constructed, assuming the proposed changes have been made. Realistic data should be used in making these projections. An analysis of the projected financial records compared with past performance will give some measure of the impact of the proposed change on the organization and operation of the business.

When making these types of projections, it is further suggested that the individual involved use different levels of cost; for example, a labor cost 10 percent higher than existing labor costs, interest cost 1 percentage point higher and 1 percentage point lower, and such other variables as may be important in a particular business. This will give some indication as to how sensitive earnings in the business can be to changes in cost. It is

Figure 15-7
SCHEMATIC RELATIONSHIP BETWEEN VARIOUS FINANCIAL TERMS

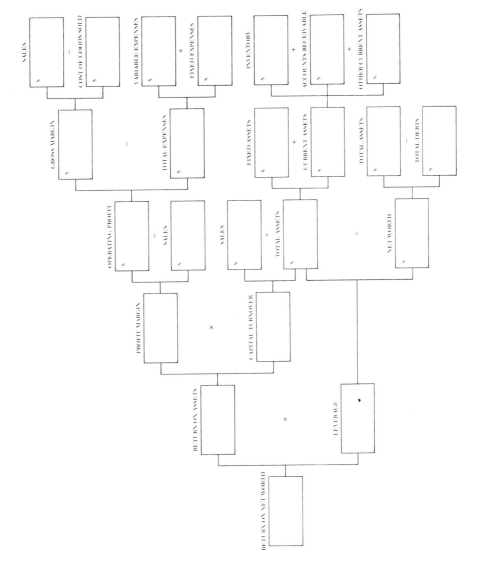

suggested that projections be made, assuming *inelastic demand* of product or services offered; increasing and decreasing the price by 10 percent will provide a measure of *price sensitivity* of the operation. A third type of variable in such projections is various levels of operating capacity; for example, show the effect if the business operates at 50 percent, at 75 percent, and at 100 percent capacity. The use of financial records in making projections of this type provides a major tool for effective management.

In Chapter 5, various ways of using financial records to achieve management controls were discussed. From the profit item, management can calculate returns on total assets or returns on net worth. It is from this *profitability* that dividends are paid.

- Dividends are returns paid to investors for the use of risk capital.

- Interest expense is returns paid for the use of borrowed funds, such as loans from banks or bonds.

- Patronage refunds are earnings distributed to members of cooperatives on the basis of member usage.

These three terms are frequently used interchangeably. However, each

Figure 15-8. Just as the corrosion around the wheel well opening of this truck indicates decreased value, depreciation is the financial method used to reflect the decreased value of capital items as they wear out. (Courtesy, M. Thomas)

represents a specific type of financial activity and has its own tax implications. Interest is a cost of doing business and as such is deducted from income before income tax is computed. Dividends are paid from earnings after income tax is paid. Patronage refunds for eligible cooperatives are deducted from earnings before income tax is computed, but dividends paid on stock investment are paid from earnings after income tax is paid.

A major source of capital for growth of many businesses is internally generated funds. The profit and loss statement shows the amount of such funds that may be available for reinvestment in the business.

Depreciation is a major expense item in many business operations. However, it is not a cash expense but a method of reflecting the decreased value of capital items as they wear out. If such depreciation expense is not used to purchase depreciable capital items or replace *obsolete equipment* in a given year, this represents an addition to funds for reinvestment. Many times businesses may show a loss because of depreciation expense but have an increase in cash or other assets. This has given rise to the statement "When a business has a bad year it lives off depreciation." Because of inflation and technological advances within a particular industry, depreciation may be inadequate to provide replacement funds when existing equipment and facilities are worn out. In the years ahead management should develop a plan for the replacement of such equipment and facilities to insure that they will be *funded*.

CASH FLOW STATEMENT

Another type of financial record needed to better analyze the effect projected changes would have on the organization and operations is a cash flow statement. A cash flow statement indicates the amount of income by sources and the cash uses, including expenses, debt payments, and capital expenditures, by item for each week, month, year or whatever period might be appropriate for that business. Such a statement provides a basis for projecting the need for borrowed funds, when funds will be needed, and what period of time is required for such funds to be repaid. This provides a means for the business and the lender to more accurately plan for and manage debt. Some businesses may find their earnings are satisfactory but their cash requirements for debt service are too great for the business to readily meet. Other businesses may find their seasonal cash requirements are such that lenders are unwilling to finance the operation or the size of the loan is too large for the bank to handle individually, so other or additional arrangements must be made.

Management of a business's capital, debt, and cash—including timing of major purchases, inventory policy, and credit policy—makes an accurate cash flow statement essential. It can be a major financial tool. It may suggest the need for additional net worth or the need to shift more debt to long-term obligations avoiding a *cash flow problem.*

Figure 15-9
A SUMMARY OF THE SOURCES AND USES OF CASH
FOR FENIX FARM SUPPLY'S BALANCE SHEET (FIGURE 15-6)
USING THE CHANGES GIVEN IN THE EXAMPLE

Statement of Cash Flow
for the Fiscal Year Ending December 31, 19—

SOURCES OF CASH (Cash Provided [Used])

Operating Activities	
Net Income from Operations	$16,000
Non-Cash Charge to Operations—Depreciation	20,000
	36,000
Increase of Accounts Receivable	(25,000)
Decrease of Inventory	10,000
Increase of Accounts Payable	12,000
	(3,000)
Total Sources of Cash from Operations, Net	$33,000
Investing Activities	
Purchase of Additional Securities	(20,000)
Purchase of Equipment	(15,000)
Total Uses of Cash from Investment	(35,000)
Financing Activities	
Retirement of Debt	(8,000)
Total Uses of Cash from Financing	(8,000)
NET INCREASE (DECREASE) TO CASH	($10,000)

BUDGET PROJECTIONS

For planning and controlling future operations, most businesses find it advisable to make a projection of revenues and expenses of major financial accounts on an annual basis. Budget projections like this present the plan of financial operations for a specific period and, through accounts and summaries, provide comparisons of actual operations with the predetermined plan. These projections are broken down on a monthly basis for the twelve month period. Such a budget shows the past year's actual activity and the coming year's anticipated target. Then on a monthly basis management can compare the current year's status to what was projected and to the prior year's actual activity. This method permits pinpointing areas of strengths and weaknesses in the operation. If management can identify problem areas early, then corrective action can be taken. However, management must be willing to honestly appraise a situation rather than make excuses for poor performance.

Figure 15-10
COW/CALF OPERATION—BUDGET FOR DIRECT EXPENSES

(Courtesy, M. Woods, Johnson Milling Company, Clinton, Mississippi)

Number of Cows: 34

DIRECT EXPENSES	UNIT	PRICE	QUANTITY	DOLLARS	COST PER COW
Interest	Dollar	$8,700.00	8%	$ 696.00	$20.47
Bull	Head	1,500.00	1	1,500.00	44.12
Pasture	Acre	10.00	200	2,000.00	58.82
Minerals	Bag	10.00	16	160.00	4.71
Protein Meal	Ton	140.00	6.5	910.00	26.76
Veterinary Cow	Head	15.00	34	510.00	15.00
Marketing	Dollar	0.04	$11,623	464.92	13.67
Check-Off	Head	1.00	31	31.00	0.91
Grain	Ton	145.00	7.5	1,087.50	31.99
Veterinary Calf	Head	8.00	31	248.00	7.29
Veterinary Bull	Head	15.00	2	30.00	0.88
Repairs/Equip	Year	1,000.00	1	1,000.00	29.41
TOTAL				$8,637.42	$254.03

PRODUCTION CONTROL RECORDS

Any business that uses raw materials in the process of manufacturing or producing a product must keep accurate records of raw materials used and the costs incurred in the process, both for production labor and materials used. The cost of raw materials and labor vary over time. The purpose of production control records is to accumulate the costs of a product during the manufacturing process and to be able to assign an actual unit cost of production. Knowing the actual cost of production, management can then set the appropriate selling price. During the manufacturing process, expired costs are accumulated in the work in process financial account.

Documents used will vary from one type of business to another. However, they usually include (1) raw material usage, (2) employee labor time sheets, and (3) a job cost summary, including all material and labor costs, as well as number of units produced.

EVALUATING ALTERNATIVE INVESTMENT DECISIONS

As indicated earlier, management must decide how to use scarce resources to achieve the goals of the business. They are concerned with ways to improve existing resource use, to expand or to reduce activities in certain areas, and to add new facilities or new locations. Financial records are important tools in making these decisions.

Three measures will be discussed here: rate of return on investment, pay-back period, and discounted future earnings. In each of these methods it must be assumed the information submitted for evaluation is accurate and realistic. Management is concerned with establishing a list of priorities, with those at the top of the list having a higher priority than those at the bottom.

RATE OF RETURN

This measure shows the percent of return earned by the investment. Assume a business has an option of making the following investments with the specified dollar returns. The rate of return is obtained by dividing return by investment.

Investment	Return	Rate of Return (Percent)	Pay-Back Period (Years)
$10,000	$1,000	10	10
9,000	1,500	$16\frac{2}{3}$	6
12,000	1,800	15	$6\frac{2}{3}$
10,000	1,600	16	$6\frac{1}{4}$
5,000	600	12	$8\frac{1}{3}$

Other factors being equal, the higher the rate of return, the more desirable the investment.

PAY-BACK PERIOD

The pay-back period represents the number of years required for estimated net income to return the investment. This is obtained by dividing the investment by the annual return. Such a procedure may give priority to fast pay back which may not realistically reflect the long-term needs of the business.

DISCOUNTED FUTURE EARNINGS

It is recognized that one dollar today has a greater value than the promise of one dollar one year or five years from now. There are discount tables to replace such values. The higher the discount rate, the less value a dollar has in the future.

The following data suggests the nature of the problem:

| | Alternative 1 | | | Alternative 2 | | |
| | Discounted Value | | | Discounted Value | | |
Year	Earnings	6%	8%	Earnings	6%	8%
1	$ 500	$ 471	$ 463	$ 800	$ 754	$ 741
2	700	623	600	700	623	600
3	800	672	635	600	504	476
4	600	475	441	500	396	367
5	400	298	272	400	299	272
Total	$3,000	$2,539	$2,411	$3,000	$2,576	$2,456

Although in the example both alternatives return $3,000 in the first five years, because of the nature of return, the second alternative would receive the first priority using this criteria. Time value of money can be an important consideration in analyzing the contribution of alternative investment decisions to the business's income.[1]

UNCERTAINTY IN DECISIONS

When making decisions, management can rarely be certain that projected income will materialize. Weather determines acreage and yields, prices for inputs and outputs are volatile, government regulations change frequently, markets are constantly changing, inflation causes disruption of established relationships, advancing technology causes changes, actions of

---

[1] For the reader concerned with more detail on this approach, the tables showing discounted future value (present value of $1 and present value of $1 received annually at the end of each year for *n* years), as well as the use of this approach in making decisions such as when to replace equipment, see *The Financial Management of Agribusiness Firms* by Frank J. Smith and Ken Cooper, pp. 52-69.

competitors alter conditions, and even social changes can cause disruptions. As a result, management must recognize there are elements of uncertainty in making a decision, and there are also implications as to outcome even if no decision is made. Management then must recognize the nature and types of uncertainty involved. In addition, it must make a decision as to the amount of such uncertainty the business either can or is willing to assume. Many times lenders are an important factor in such a decision. What constitutes an unacceptable situation for one business may be perfectly acceptable to another business under similar circumstances.

The approach many businesses use in such an analysis is to develop a best estimate as to the probability that a particular outcome will result and from this to estimate a weighted average expected outcome. The weakness in this approach results from the inability to accurately estimate the probability a specific outcome will occur.

Alternative 1			Alternative 2		
Outcome	Probability		Outcome	Probability	
–300	0.2	–60	100	0.1	10
800	0.4	320	600	0.4	240
1,000	0.2	200	800	0.3	240
2,000	0.2	400	1,000	0.2	200
		$860			$690

The above example suggests that even though the first alternative provides the greater opportunity to make a larger contribution to earnings, it also includes an opportunity for a loss. Some businesses may not be in a position to accept a loss. The decision a business makes may be heavily influenced by whether it is more concerned with maximizing income or minimizing losses.

SUMMARY

Within the constraints placed by the business, financial records can assist management in identifying problem areas, measuring performance, and providing the basis for evaluating alternative investment decisions. Such information is also useful to help owners/stockholders evaluate their investment in the business. Lenders use the information in determining whether or not to make a loan and, once the loan is made, in monitoring the operation to be assured of orderly repayment.

In order to use financial records as tools for better management, it is necessary for the manager to know the relationship between various elements of these records. Becoming familiar with the various elements in Figure 15-7 will provide assistance in reading and analyzing financial records and also facilitate the use of management controls discussed in Chapter 5.

CHAPTER QUESTIONS

1. What are the four major financial records used in making management decisions?

2. What are four methods of measuring the performance of a business?

3. What is a business's chart of accounts?

4. List at least one sub-grouping from each of the three sections of a balance sheet.

5. What is the basic flow followed in processing a business transaction in financial record keeping?

6. What four items must financial records management provide for?

7. What is meant by liquidity of a business?

8. Why is a financial statement important?

9. What is a profit and loss statement?

10. What is the major non-cash expense for most businesses?

11. What are (1) interest expense, (2) patronage refund, and (3) dividends?

12. How is a cash flow statement used by management?

13. What are budget projections?

14. What is the purpose of production control records?

15. What documents are used to chart production costs?

Chapter 16

CREDIT

Extending credit to a customer means that the agribusiness provides goods or services and the customer promises to pay at a later date. Extending credit is a common practice with suppliers of inputs to production and also in other areas of agribusiness, because it is often determined that it is better to extend credit to the customer and maintain the relationship rather than let the customer take his or her business elsewhere.

The nature of agricultural production makes extending credit a common practice. A cotton farmer may only receive income during each year's harvest, so the agribusinesses supplying the cotton farmer take a chance that enough will be made at the end of the season to pay for the goods and services they have already provided.

This chapter discusses the agribusiness's need to extend credit. Several factors to be considered when making credit decisions are presented. The chapter also provides some strategies the business manager can use to reduce the amount of risk taken when extending credit.

OBJECTIVES

1. Understand the need for credit.
2. Understand what is essential in a business credit policy.
3. Identify the factors businesses use to analyze credit.
4. Identify costs associated with extending credit.
5. Learn how to age accounts receivable as a tool of management.

NEED FOR CREDIT

Nearly every agribusiness is forced to make a decision as to whether or not it is going to extend credit to its customers. This decision is forced upon management by the fact that agricultural production is a processing industry in which farmers or ranchers buy a number of inputs, such as feed, fertilizer, herbicides, machinery, and petroleum products, and then combine them in the production processes to develop a number of output items, such as corn, wheat, soybeans, cotton, cattle, hogs, and milk. The time necessary for these production processes ranges from a relatively short period for producing broilers to a relatively long period for raising herds of beef cows and feeding out the calves. There are some processes, of course, that are even longer—such as growing trees for fruit or timber. It is often a wise use of resources for producers with many operations to borrow funds during periods of the production process requiring heavy capital.

Many businesses will regularly deliver various products to farms and over a period of several months will not see any member of the farmer's family. Under such conditions it would be rather difficult to operate on a "cash on the barrel" basis. As a result, a system of convenience credit has been developed by businesses that allows farmers to pay their outstanding accounts once each month.

Many businesses find that they need to extend more long-term credit to their customers. Farmers use in excess of $30 billion worth of supplier credit per year. This represents about 40 percent of the short-term operating and *working capital* used by farmers; therefore, credit is a major item for an agribusiness. Frequently the agribusiness will extend credit to the buyer of its products, particularly commodities such as feed, seed, fertilizer, and petroleum products. In addition, many businesses are called upon to extend credit to customers who will be marketing products through these businesses at some future date. They extend credit to help meet the necessary living and operating expenses of farmers during the production period and are repaid when the products are sold through their business.

The type of credit arrangement may vary quite widely—from a straight open account, where credit requirements may be very informal, to a highly

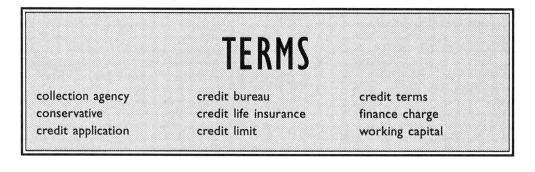

TERMS

collection agency	credit bureau	credit terms
conservative	credit life insurance	finance charge
credit application	credit limit	working capital

structured credit system involving the same type of credit analysis as would be found in a major financial institution. Some of these credit arrangements involve little, if any, control by the business over the borrower. On the other hand, some of the highly integrated operations place the agribusiness in the position of providing a large percentage of the purchased inputs, along with varying degrees of management. In these situations, the agricultural producing firm (the farmer) provides only limited inputs, some of the facilities and the labor, while most of the major management decisions are made by the agribusiness.

One would expect the use of credit by producers to continue to increase, partly because the size of the operations will continue to increase. In addition to this there is strong reason to believe that purchased inputs will continue to make up an increasingly larger portion of the total inputs in the production process (Table 16-1).

In a market where there is less than perfect competition, a manager finds that services provided by the business frequently effect the customer's decisions to buy products or services. The price that a customer pays for a product covers the payment for the goods plus related services; for example, the price for a ton of feed includes the value of the feed ingredients plus transportation, credit, etc. When there are a limited number of businesses, then each business must consider not only how its pricing decision will affect its own operation, but also how its competition will react. The action of the competitors is closely tied to what the original business decides to do. It is not to the business's advantage to engage in competition on the basis of price. The alternative is to compete on the basis of related services. Consequently, for many businesses credit becomes an important sales tool.

REQUIREMENTS FOR EXTENDING CREDIT

The business needs a well-defined credit policy that is understood by both the business's employees and its customers. This policy should indicate the criteria to be used in determining whether or not a customer is eligible for credit (Figure 16-1). There are several important factors that should be evaluated. First is a consideration of the individual's managerial ability, reputation, honesty, integrity, business ability, attitude toward debt, and character. The second factor is the customer's ability to repay the credit extended, and the third is the purposes for which the credit is requested. The fourth factor is financial strength (to support the operation and the

Table
U.S. FARM EXPENDITURES, IN

Year	Feed	Livestock	Seed	Fertilizer and Lime
1954	3,906	1,563	525	1,209
1959	4,744	2,693	491	1,291
1964	5,715	2,420	566	1,701
1969	6,634	4,174	697	2,013
1974	12,902	4,925	2,233	6,847
1979	19,314	13,012	2,904	10,805
1984	19,383	9,478	3,386	13,048
1989	21,002	13,138	3,558	12,686
1991	19,800	14,358	3,975	13,732

[1]Source: *Agricultural Statistics*, 1992, U.S. Government Printing Office, Washington, DC
[2]After 1974, does not include repairs used on the farm.

loan), and fifth is collateral that might be pledged to support the credit or secure the debt. Answers to these questions are usually obtained by using a *credit application* form developed by the business which also sets forth the *credit terms* and the *finance charge*. Another source of historical credit information for a new customer is available through the *credit bureau* in the customer's area.

Figure 16-1
FIVE FACTORS FOR BUSINESSES TO USE
TO ANALYZE CREDIT CUSTOMERS

THE INDIVIDUAL	*Managerial ability in business, honesty, integrity*
REPAYMENT	*Ability to meet expenses and repay debt*
PURPOSE	*How funds are to be used*
FINANCIAL POSITION	*Financial strength to support operation and debt*
COLLATERAL	*Assets pledged as security to protect lender*

Credit should be extended with repayment expected when the products used to repay the credit are marketed. Extending credit to a farmer to buy fertilizer at planting time for a wheat crop with repayment expected a year

16–1
MILLIONS OF DOLLARS, SELECTED YEARS[1]

Fuels/ Repairs[2]	Labor	Taxes	Interest	Miscellaneous
3,506	2,596	1,084	371	2,077
4,069	2,882	1,401	572	2,724
3,940	2,913	1,833	952	3,515
4,828	3,192	2,753	1,602	4,576
6,988	6,516	3,197	3,637	10,966
5,635	8,981	3,871	6,190	27,066
7,296	9,427	4,337	10,733	35,779
4,798	11,110	5,127	7,781	36,077
5,472	12,595	5,980	7,319	36,841

later would violate this principle. Such a repayment plan encourages many producers to use their income in a way that would not necessarily work to the advantage of the business providing the credit. By the same token, a line of credit to purchase feed for hogs should be repaid at the time the hogs are sold.

Once credit terms have been agreed upon by both the producer and the business, any change in terms must be agreed upon by both parties. If the repayment terms are not followed, then the business should immediately determine from the customer why these terms were not followed and discuss with that customer what alternatives are available to them. Many businesses follow the policy of charging 1 or 1½ percent interest per month on the outstanding balance for all accounts over two months old. Other businesses have found that it is advantageous to them to take a promissory note on all accounts over two months and then rediscount and sell these notes to a financial institution. In addition, some financial institutions may offer or require a *credit life insurance* for customers applying for credit to cover payment of a loan or other obligation in case of death of the creditor.

Some businesses have developed working relationships with existing financial institutions whereby the financial institution has established an operating line of credit for the customer; then, on a monthly basis, the business sends a list of existing outstanding account balances for all of the customers so approved. The financial institution then disburses to the business an amount sufficient to cover all of the outstanding balances. This system works very well for a number of businesses.

Some businesses follow the policy of rating their customers in such a manner that some customers can have as much credit as they want, some have a *credit limit*, and still others may be rated not to receive credit at all. The credit limit must be established by the type of business, the amount of credit usually required, and the repayment period. Not all customers are necessarily equally good credit risks for all amounts of money. As the need for credit continues to grow, it will become more important that businesses follow sound methods of evaluating customer credit requests.

Businesses need to carefully analyze credit policy according to how it will affect their capital needs. If a business is extending credit, then the amount of equity capital must be sufficient to either extend the credit without borrowing additional funds, or to provide the necessary financial strength to borrow the money, which will in turn be used to provide credit. There are few businesses that can extend additional credit without placing added burdens on the capital needs of the business.

ORGANIZATION FOR CREDIT

The credit department in a business should be separate from the marketing and sales departments if possible. Essentially, employees concerned with sales are optimists. A sales representative must be sold on the business's product and well informed on how it will fill a customer's need or help increase the customers' earnings. The sales staff has a tendency to look at the expected outcome on an exceedingly favorable basis; he or she is being paid for selling products or services. On the other hand, people working in the credit department are more *conservative* in their approach; they recognize that normal conditions are something other than the most favorable. Their primary responsibility is to minimize losses from the credit operations. A person will seldom find in one individual those characteristics that make that person an ideally motivated sales representative and credit manager. For this reason there is the need to separate these two operations, so far as the organizational structure is concerned. Many managers feel that sales representatives are not necessarily good collectors because the sales staff is reluctant to take any action against a customer that might affect future sales. However, there is also the argument that if a sales representative knows he or she is required to collect all open accounts, that individual might be much more reluctant to make some of the sales on an open account basis, where even a minimal investigation would indicate the sale should be made only if the buyer has the necessary cash to make the payment at the time of sale.

COST OF EXTENDING CREDIT

Any business that is extending credit should be well aware of what it costs to provide this service. The cost of extending credit varies by years, areas, and type of business organization. Many studies indicate that it costs between 2 and 3 percent of sales to extend credit, approximately half of which is interest cost. The other half is made up of extra bookkeeping costs, collection expenses, and the investigations associated with a sound credit policy. When this information is readily available and generally recognized, it provides the basis for more realistically appraising the cost of extending credit and from this making adjustments in pricing policy to recognize these different costs.

One of the factors that many businesses must consider is the relationship between prices to cash customers and prices to credit customers. If it costs more money to service credit customers than cash customers, then the question may be raised as to why both groups should be required to pay the same prices. One of the arguments for both groups' paying the same price is that the business has excess capacity when operating only on a cash basis, and if it adopts a credit policy, there will be sufficient volume that per unit operating costs will decline enough to permit the business to have greater earnings, even though it costs more per unit at a given volume to operate on a credit basis than on a cash basis. Many businesses, however, are not in a position to realistically appraise the relative values of different pricing programs because they do not have sufficient information to answer the question as to what it costs to extend credit.

AGING OF ACCOUNTS

A sound credit policy dictates that every business age its accounts on a regular basis, usually monthly. This involves listing the number and amount of accounts that are less than 30 days old, those 30 to 60 days old, and those 60 to 90 days old, and listing by name and amount those accounts that are 90 to 120 days old, those 120 to 180 days old, those 6 months to 1 year old, and those over 2 years old. This may not be the proper breakdown for all businesses; some may find an alternative break-down to be more realistic. If a business follows a policy of listing its accounts by age, or at least by amounts, over a period of years this would provide some very useful management data in evaluating current operations. If it is found that the percentage of the accounts in the older age groups is increasing at a rather rapid rate, this points up some danger signals that need careful consideration. Most studies indicate that as the age of the accounts receivable increases, their value tends to decrease; for example, it may be that in a particular business any accounts receivable under 90 days old, on a historical basis, are 100 percent collectible; whereas, those between 3 to 6 months old are 90 percent collectible, those that are over 2 years old are 50 percent collectible, and those that are over 5 years old are virtually uncollectible. Before this happens, a business—after exhausting its internal procedures—should contact a *collection agency* and turn these ac-counts over to them for collection.

Once a creditor's history has been established, it provides the company with a basis for establishing a pricing policy for credit sales, and setting up necessary reserves. Any business needs to determine, on a historical basis, the relationship that is realistic for its particular business. This pro-vides a basis for a better analysis of the validity of the financial statement.

In any analysis of credit policy there is need to determine who the major users of credit are and if accounts receivable present a particularly serious problem. There is a need to determine how these major users differ from other customers. Accounts receivable have been a particularly serious problem for many businesses in the last several years, since there has been such a very rapid increase in the demand for sufficient financial strength to provide adequate capitalization, not only to take care of the credit needs of customers but also to provide for growth to more adequately provide the goods and other services that the customers require.

CREDIT LIMITS

In determining credit policy, management must establish some criteria for determining who will be eligible for credit. The five factors that provide a basis for these criteria have been previously discussed. In addition, it is suggested that the credit manager may wish to classify customers into a number of categories; for example, those with unlimited credit, those with up to $10,000 credit, those with a $5,000 credit limit and those ineligible for credit. Certainly all sales reps should be acquainted with the credit limits for their particular customers and have an understanding with each of them as to what those credit limits are.

Earlier in the discussion there were some comments as to the cost of extending credit. Some of these costs are directly related to the amount of money involved, for example, the cost of money—as the volume of credit increases, the cost increases. Other costs, such as bookkeeping costs and to a certain extent collection costs, do not vary with the amount of money involved. This suggests that the business might wish to have a policy that provides no credit for those customers whose business is primarily handled as an accommodation and where the costs of handling the credit are greater than the income received from the transaction. The business should determine fixed costs for handling a credit transaction; if the overhead cost of handling a credit transaction was 50 cents and the gross margin was 5 percent, then the company could very easily take the position that it would not handle a credit transaction for any item of less than $10. An exception might be made for those customers who conduct a relatively large annual business with the organization but who occasionally request a small credit transaction. It would hardly be good business to refuse credit to a customer for a small transaction if that customer's total business with the organization during the year was $2,000. So the policy might be modified to provide that small credit transactions would be acceptable if the customer's annual business with the organization was equal to a certain specified minimum.

CHAPTER QUESTIONS

1. What are the five factors a business should use to analyze whether a credit sale should be made?

2. What are two sources which may be used to evaluate customer credit?

3. Why should the marketing and sales department not be in charge of extending credit?

4. What are some of the costs of extending credit?

5. What is the purpose of aging accounts receivable?

Chapter 17

PRINCIPLES OF COMPUTER OPERATION

Computers are everywhere! Most people cannot spend a day without coming in contact with some type of computer. A trip to the grocery store includes having the items scanned by a computer component. Modern cash registers have a computer inside. A catalog order will be punched into a computer. Bills that come in the mail almost surely have been generated by a computer. If a credit card is used for a gasoline purchase, the cashier sends the information via telephone to a computer. On some dairy farms, a computer reads the tag on an individual cow, determines how much feed she has eaten that day and how much more she is allowed to eat.

Many individuals use computers for word processing, keeping records, or generating financial statements to help them accomplish their work on a given day. Since 1981, computers have become affordable for almost every business and many individuals. These people are taking advantage of the benefits of using a computer to make them more efficient.

In the previous chapters of this book, many agribusiness management functions and strategies have been discussed. The computer can help the agribusiness manager with almost all of these functions. This chapter provides an introduction to computers and how they work for individuals who have little background in using computers.

OBJECTIVES

1. Define computers.

2. Discuss the history of computing.

3. Describe how computers work.

4. Describe the parts of a computer (hardware).

5. Identify the various classifications of software.

6. Discuss the factors to consider when buying a computer.

COMPUTERS AS A BUSINESS TOOL

A computer, simply defined, is an electronic device that executes programs. A *program* is a detailed set of instructions written by a computer *programmer* which may be simple or complex.

The computer is useful as a tool in business and other areas because the programs it executes can perform a wide variety of tasks. If the pro-

TERMS

artificial intelligence
application
backup
binary logic
bit
bitmapping
byte
commercial software
cathode ray tube (CRT)
cursor
cursor control keys
daisy wheel printer
data
data files
disk drive
documentation
dot matrix printer
dot pitch
floppy disk
FORTRAN
freeware
function keys

gigabyte (GB)
graphical user interface
   (GUI)
graphics
hard disk
hardware
icons
inkjet printer
input device
integrated software
kilobyte (K)
laser printer
liquid crystal display
   (LCD)
machine language
math coprocessor
megabyte (MB or Meg)
memory
microchip
microprocessor
millions of instructions
   per second (MIPS)
mouse

near letter quality
numeric keypad
operating system
output device
peripherals
pixel
program
programmer
random access memory
   (RAM)
resolution
read-only memory
   (ROM)
semi-conductor
software
software piracy
terminal
terminate-and-stay-
   resident (TSR)
transistor
user-supported software
virus

Figure 17-1. In the 1990s, most executives have computers available for ready access.

grammer can imagine it and write the program, the computer can perform the task (with a few limitations).

A person can do anything a computer can do, but there are several ways in which a person or business can use computers to become more efficient. First, a computer, when programmed correctly, never gives a wrong answer. Second, unlike humans, the computer doesn't get fatigued, even when doing mundane tasks. A computer will perform a simple arithmetic problem thousands of times without complaining or getting tired. Third, the computer does these things at incredible speeds. A computer can add two numbers in $\frac{1}{2,000,000}$ of a second—the time it takes light to travel 12 feet.

Computers are not smart, but they do follow directions. A computer is only as smart as the people who programmed it and the people who operate it. Anyone who has had problems with service from a business has probably heard something like, "I'm sorry, our computer is down," or "Our computer won't do that for us." These people are allowing computers to dictate their work *to them* instead of doing work *for them*. Used properly, the computer is a tool that makes work easier, not harder.

HISTORY OF COMPUTING

The earliest computing involved counting and developing a place system, probably to keep track of time. Before long, humans felt a need for assistance in their computations. Many devices were created to aid in computing long before the computer, as we know it today, came along. These early machines and computing devices, however, did lead us to the modern day computer.

EARLY COMPUTING DEVICES

The abacus, developed around 1000 B.C., was probably the first computing device, and almost certainly was the first portable computing device. It used beads strung to a frame and worked on the principle of place value, with different beads having different values. The beads were called calculi. Calculi is the plural of calculus, which is the area of math that deals with small differences. Calculus is the root word for calculate and calculator.

Figure 17-2.   An abacus—probably the earliest portable computing device.

Although the abacus had been used in the Orient for many years, it wasn't until the early 17th century that Europeans invented any type of calculating machine. They caught up quickly, however. In 1617, Napier, a Scottish nobleman, developed an instrument for performing multiplication and division. The instrument matched up numbers on rods that were side by side, then the results were read from the other side. This device, called Napier's Bones, was the prototype of the slide rule.

Around 1642, Blaise Pascal, a French scientist and philosopher, invented the first gear-driven or mechanical calculator. He was 19 at the time and built the machine to help his father, who was a mathematician. The machine was called a Pascaline. Each gear had ten teeth representing a number between 1 and 10. When one gear completed a rotation, the next gear would move one notch, much like a car odometer. This machine did addition and subtraction. This was the first machine to raise a stir because it caused fear of automation and thus unemployment.

Leibniz, a philosopher and mathematician who invented differential and integral calculus (independent of Sir Isaac Newton), invented a device called Leibniz's Wheel in 1673. It was a gear-driven machine that was superior to Pascal's because it could also multiply and divide. This was basically the forerunner of the hand-operated adding machines and calculators used into the 1970s.

Another device important to computing was Jacquard's Loom, developed around 1801. It had a device to control the weaving pattern of a loom. Jacquard used a perforated card to control the selection of threads used to create a pattern of thread. Changing cards changed the pattern. This invention caused widespread riots because of fear of automation. Workers threw boots (*sabots*) into looms. This is where the word sabotage originated. Card-driven equipment is still used in the textile industry today.

For over 40 years, from around 1790 until into the 1830s, Charles Babbage and Ada Byron worked on the Analytical and Difference Engines. Babbage is considered the Father of Computers because of his invention of these machines, while Byron is considered the first computer programmer because of her analyses and explanations of his work. The difference engine, a model of which was built, solved polynomial equations by the method of differences. The analytical engine, never built, was designed to be a general purpose computing device.

The analytical engine design was the prototype of the modern computer. It contained five parts common in today's computers: (1) an *input device* using punched cards, an idea taken from Jaquard's Loom; (2) a processor, which was a mill containing hundreds of vertical axles and thousands of gears, that stood over ten feet tall; (3) a control unit, in this case a barrel-like device with slats and studs, operating like a complex player piano; (4) a storage device with more axles and gears, designed to hold 100 40-digit numbers; and (5) an *output device* that made a set of plates designed to fit a printing press. Babbage was so far ahead of his time that the machining and tooling available was not good enough to build his machine.

Necessity was the mother of invention in the case of the Hollerith Card, invented around 1890. Herman Hollerith, an employee of the U.S. Census Bureau, won a competition to develop a method that would be faster than hand-tabulation for use in the 1890 Census. He expanded upon Jacquard's idea and developed the punched card, a code, and a machine to read the code. With the punched card, the 1890 Census results were announced within six weeks (whereas the 1880 Census took over seven years). Hollerith left the Census Bureau and formed his own company, the Tabulating Machine Company, known today as International Business Machines or IBM. Cards

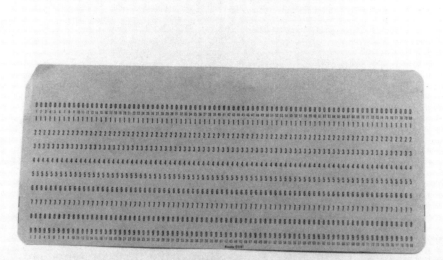

Figure 17-3. A punched card, designed on the same principles Hollerith used to tabulate the 1890 U.S. Census. These cards were the primary method of data entry for computers until the floppy disk replaced them. Some were still in use into the mid-1980s.

were still a primary method of entering information into computers in the 1980s.

Early Computers

The first electronic digital computer was the Atanasoff-Berry Computer (ABC), developed in 1942. The ABC was developed at Iowa State University by Dr. John Atanasoff and his assistant, Clifford Berry. Atanasoff built the computer so his students wouldn't have to take so long in solving long mathematical problems.

By 1944, Howard Aiken, a professor at Harvard University, had developed the Mark I for IBM. The Mark I was really electro-mechanical in that it used thousands of mechanical switches, called relays. When operating, the Mark I supposedly sounded "like a roomful of ladies knitting." One day the Mark I stopped running because a moth was caught in one of the switches. The student who was working in the laboratory wrote "got d'bug out" in his log. The term debug, meaning to correct a problem, was born.

Dr. John Mauchly from the University of Pennsylvania, with the help of a graduate student, J. Presper Eckert, Jr., developed the ENIAC - Electronic Numerical Integrator And Computer in 1946. The ENIAC was built as a wartime secret to figure trajectory tables for the Army. The first large-scale electronic digital computer, it could do 5,000 additions/minute and 500 multiplications/minute. The ENIAC weighed 30 tons and occupied 1,500 square feet of floor space. It contained over 18,000 vacuum tubes requiring a huge amount of electricity and generating a large amount of heat. It operated, on average, seven minutes before a vacuum tube would burn out. The ENIAC was easily the most famous of the early computers and is known as the first general-purpose computer.

The Computer Generations

The UNIVAC, Universal Automatic Computer, was developed in 1951. It was the first commercially available computer. The development of the UNIVAC began what is now called the first generation of computers. First generation computers used vacuum tubes for processing and memory and magnetic tapes for storage.

The first generation also saw the development of the first computer programming language to use English commands—*FORTRAN*, an acronym for Formula Translation. Before FORTRAN was developed in 1957, computer programmers used machine language (zeroes and ones, open or closed). The number of computer programs developed increased dramatically.

In 1959, the *transistor* was invented. This very important invention marked the beginning of the second generation of computers. The transistor replaced vacuum tubes as the primary electronic component in computers. This change allowed computers to be smaller, faster, and to produce less heat. All vacuum tubes in computers were replaced within a few years. The IBM 1401 and Honeywell 400 were both second generation computers.

The second generation lasted until around 1965, when the *microchip* was developed. The microchip contained minute integrated circuits on a silicon chip often smaller than a dime. This made third generation computers smaller and faster. Silicon was used because it is a *semi-conductor*. Today, these chips contain the computer's memory and microprocessor. The IBM 360 was the dominant machine of the generation. The "360" was used to represent the degrees in a full circle, because it was supposed to meet everyone's needs.

The development of very large scale integration (VLSI), led to the fourth generation of computers. VLSI made it possible to put a much larger number of circuits in a smaller space. The IBM 370 was the first computer to make use of this technology.

Computers of the fourth generation are commonly called microcom-

Figure 17-4. A 5.25-inch floppy disk.

Figure 17-5. A compact disk (CD). These optical disks are used to store large quantities of information but are still portable. This disk contains over 30,000 files.

puters, personal computers, or desktop computers because of their small size. The fourth generation continues today, with most experts waiting for computers to exhibit true *artificial intelligence* before signalling the start of a fifth generation. The fourth generation has improved since its inception in the early 1970s. The *floppy disk*, developed in 1973, made it possible to transfer data to and from computers without bulky tapes.

The development of Compact Disk—Read Only Memory (CD-ROM) technology around 1983 made it possible for computer users to have portable storage of large amounts of information. One CD can hold 680 *megabytes* of information, or about 275,000 typed pages of text. This amount is the equivalent of about 1,800 floppy disks. As an example, the entire U.S. telephone directory can be stored on two CDs.

The CD has become popular for storage of large *graphics* files, allowing for interactive video/hypermedia computing. They are also used to hold large databases, allowing for one-time searches of huge quantities of information. Other developments, such as graphical user interfaces and hard disks will be discussed later in this chapter.

Early Microcomputers

The Altair 8800, introduced in 1975, was a do-it-yourself kit designed for electronic buffs. It is generally recognized as the first microcomputer.

In 1976, Steven Jobs and Stephen Wozniak built the Apple computer in their garage. It was mounted on a piece of plywood and built out of spare parts. According to legend, Jobs and Wozniak offered their computer to Hewlett-Packard, the company they worked for at the time, but management there didn't foresee a market for microcomputers. They went on to develop Apple Computer Corporation, one of the largest computer companies in the world.

Radio Shack introduced its TRS 80 series in 1977. Through the mid-1980s, Radio Shack used their system of retail centers to sell many of their TRS-80 microcomputers. It was one of the top early microcomputers.

In 1981, IBM introduced the IBMpc (personal computer). IBM took advantage of its credibility with larger computers to sell many of these poorly-developed models, but did improve upon it with the IBMpc XT and IBMpc AT. IBM and its clones (IBM-compatibles) captured much of the

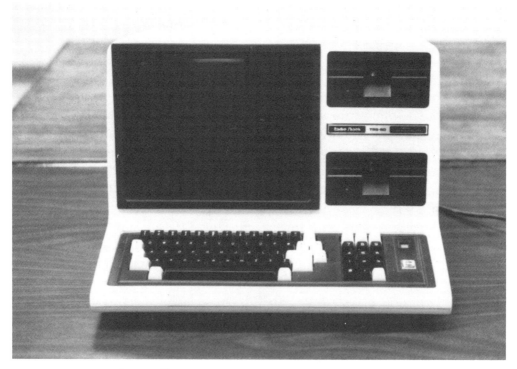

Figure 17-6. A Radio Shack TRS-80 Microcomputer.

Figure 17-7. The original IBMpc. IBM used this machine to
vault to the top in microcomputer sales in the
1980s.

market during the latter half of the 1980s due to agreements with Microsoft
Corporation. Microsoft writes programs to run on these computers and has
a policy of letting anyone write and market programs using its operating
system (MS-DOS).

IBM contracted with Bill Gates, a college dropout, to develop the
operating system for the IBMpc. Gates is now chairman of the board of
Microsoft Corporation. With a net worth of over seven billion dollars,
Gates is the richest man in America.

In 1984, the Apple company developed the Macintosh. With this computer, they introduced the *graphical user interface* (GUI, pronounced gooey),
touted for its "user-friendliness" or ease of operation and learning. This
interface is characterized by the use of a *mouse* to access its pull-down
menus and *icons* (symbols representing commands) as opposed to DOS's
command line and character-based user interface. Microsoft soon copied
the idea and developed its own GUI program—Microsoft Windows.

Figure 17-8. An Apple Macintosh. Note the "mouse" to the right of the keyboard. It is used to input commands using on-screen icons.

HOW COMPUTERS WORK

Computers use a series of microchips to translate electrical impulses into information that is meaningful to the user. The process involves microchips that serve as the computer's *memory* and as the *microprocessor* (the "brains" of the computer).

BINARY LOGIC

The basic process used by computers is *binary logic*. Binary, meaning two, is the number of distinctions the computer can make on the signals it receives. When the computer's microprocessor receives a signal, it can only determine whether it is on or off, open or closed. The concept is similar to the electrical circuit behind a light switch—the light is off when the circuit is open and on when it is closed. With computers, 0 represents open and 1 closed.

One signal, open or closed, is called a *bit*, short for binary digit. This amount of information is not very useful in itself, so early computer engineers developed a system whereby a series of bits could be used to represent certain information. They determined that a combination of eight bits could be used to represent all of the characters, such as letters, numbers, and other symbols, needed to program a computer. Collectively, these eight bits are called a *byte.*

A standard code was developed for each particular character. Every computer comes with a built-in ability to translate these characters into information the computer can use. For example, when a computer user types an "A" the computer translates this into *machine language,* which for A is 01000001, then it translates it back to the "A" that shows up on the monitor. The standard codes are called ASCII (pronounced ask-key), which stands for American Standard Code for Information Interchange.

MEMORY

The usefulness of a computer is determined to a large extent by the amount of memory it contains. Memory is the place where information is held so it can be accessed quickly by the computer for the purpose of manipulating the information or executing the program. The two types of memory are Read Only Memory (ROM) and Random Access Memory (RAM).

Read Only Memory (ROM)

ROM is permanent memory which is built into the computer. It is called non-volatile because it remains in the computer when the power (electricity) is turned off. ROM is expensive, so it only contains information that is fundamental to the operation of the computer. These operations include the BIOS (basic input/output system) which allows the computer to relate to peripherals, ASCII codes, and the basic mathematical functions. The ROM resides in microchips in the system unit. These chips can only be read, not written to or altered, once they leave the factory.

Random Access Memory (RAM)

RAM is temporary memory that is used to receive information and execute programs. A program is usually placed in RAM from a disk and resides in RAM until it is replaced by a new program. RAM is volatile—when you turn off the computer, it is erased. Any information in RAM that needs to be saved so it can be used again must be stored on a disk or some other

Figure 17-9. A microchip which is used
for RAM memory.

device so it can be loaded into the RAM again at a later time. The random access label comes from the fact that the computer can call up information from any location in memory in the same access time, regardless of which memory location was accessed previously.

Memory Capacity

The memory capacity of a computer is determined by the number of bytes that will fit into the RAM at any one time. Capacity is usually listed in K, or *kilobytes*. One kilobyte is equal to approximately 1,000 bytes (actually, it is 1,024 bytes, or 2 to the 10th power). New computers often list RAM capacity in MB, or *megabytes*. One megabyte is equal to 1,024 K or 2^{20}. As an example, a computer with 1MB of RAM can hold 1,048,576 bytes at one time. A *gigabyte* is equal to 1,024MB or 2^{30}. Some large computers will list their storage space in gigabytes.

Both the program being executed and the *data* it uses must be stored in RAM at the same time. Also, the *operating system* takes part of the RAM, so a computer with 640K will not be able to use all 640K for a program and data. The minimum requirement for most programs today is 640K of RAM, with some programs recommending or requiring 2MB to 4MB. New computers regularly have 2MB to 4MB, and most can be expanded to 16MB. The ability to expand is very important as new programs are developed that require increasing amounts of memory.

PARTS OF A COMPUTER

At first glance, the computer may resemble a television sitting on a box, attached to a typewriter. In fact, these earlier machines did influence the modern look of a computer. The four primary *hardware* components of a computer system are the system unit, the monitor, the keyboard, and a printer.

SYSTEM UNIT

The system unit contains the actual computer, with other parts considered *peripherals*. Normally, a system unit includes the power supply unit, the motherboard, the disk drives, and the input/output ports.

Figure 17-10. A system unit built in a mini-tower format.

Power Supply

The power supply unit simply transmits electricity from the power source to the motherboard to allow the computer to operate. In some countries, the power supply must also have an adapter to convert from direct current (DC) to alternating current (AC) electricity.

The power supply is usually sealed at the factory. Amateurs should not attempt to repair this part or even to try to open it. If a problem occurs, the user should call a technician for any necessary repairs.

A constant source of power is important for the operation of a computer. If the power goes off, all information in RAM is lost. The computer user

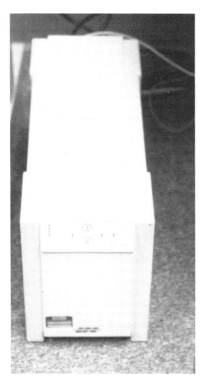

Figure 17-11. An Uninterrupted Power Source (UPS),
with a battery backup to circumvent a
power loss.

should save his or her data often to reduce the catastrophic effects of power loss. Some computer systems, especially networked systems, use an uninterrupted power source (UPS) to avoid data loss. The power source runs through the UPS before entering the computer system. The UPS contains batteries to keep the system running for a period of time with no power coming in from the power source.

A surge protector is another good investment for the computer user. It will not protect against power loss, but will keep surges in electricity from harming the system or turning the system off momentarily.

Motherboard

The motherboard contains the primary microchips that operate the computer; the microprocessor, the memory chips (ROM and RAM) and expansion slots. It contains connections to every part attached to the computer.

Microprocessor. The microprocessor is the chip which processes all of the information given to the computer and transmits all of the output. It is sometimes called a central processing unit (CPU). The microprocessor's operating speed and rate of handling information determines the speed at which the computer operates. Most IBM and compatible computers use microprocessors developed by the Intel corporation.

The original IBMpc microprocessor, the Intel 8086, was very slow by today's standards. It handled 16 bits of information at a time and operated at a clock speed of 4.77 megahertz (mHz). The 8086 had 29,000 transistors on one chip and could perform at .33 million instructions per second (*MIPS*).

The 8086 was followed by the 8088, the 80286, the 80386, and the 486; there were several varieties of each. The latest Intel microprocessor, the Pentium, has a 64-bit data handling capability and operates at 60 to 100 mHz. Introduced in 1993, the early versions have 3.1 million transistors on one chip and operate at 112 MIPS. Later versions will be even more powerful.

Other companies developing microprocessors for IBM-compatible computers include Advanced Micro Devices (AMD), NEC, and Cyrix. Apple Macintosh microprocessors are made by Motorola.

Figure 17-12. A surge protector protects against loss of data due to surges in electrical power.

Figure 17-13.   A microprocessor and math coprocessor plugged into a motherboard.

Early microprocessors may be enhanced in their ability to handle math-intensive operations by adding a *math coprocessor*. The microprocessor will divide calculations between itself and the math coprocessor, almost doubling the processing speed of drafting programs and other math-intensive software.

Memory. The computer's RAM and ROM chips are also located on the motherboard. They determine the amount of information a computer can hold for immediate access at any one time. The amount of ROM varies from computer to computer, but all hold basic input/output information, arithmetic functions, and logical operators such as equal to and greater than/less than functions. Because ROM is read-only, the user cannot use it for programs or data. The operating system, various *terminate-and-stay-resident (TSR)* programs, *application* programs, and data all reside in RAM. The amount of RAM in computers varies, but as a general rule, the more the better. Most new computers come with 4MB or 8MB of RAM, but can be expanded to 16MB or more.

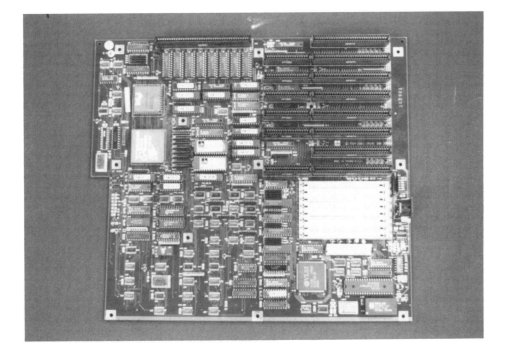

Figure 17-14. Above is a motherboard that has not been installed into a system. Below is a small footprint computer with the cover removed. Note how many expansion slots are filled with cards.

Expansion Slots. Expansion slots allow the motherboard to be expanded to connect to other devices or for additional memory. A card is inserted into a slot that connects it to the motherboard. The card may have a port to connect it to another device out of the back of the computer. Most computers come with eight or more expansion slots, but several of these will already be filled. A computer buyer should determine how many expansion slots are available before buying a new computer. (Most computer descriptions will give total and available expansion slots.)

A small footprint IBM compatible computer (which takes up less desk space) with a bus modem, a mouse, and an internal modem that is connected to a network may have only one expansion slot available, even though it started with eight.

- One expansion slot is usually taken for output—the parallel port. This is usually used to connect the computer with a printer, but may be used for other output devices such as a plotter.

- Computers with a small footprint will often use a slot for some of the memory because of the small size of the motherboard.

Figure 17-15. A mouse and mousepad.

Figure 17-16. An internal modem. The modem plugs into an expansion slot on the motherboard.

- One expansion slot is usually taken for the graphics card, which has an output port connecting it to the monitor.

- One expansion slot is used for a connection to the various disk drives a computer may have.

- If the computer has a bus mouse, it will take up an expansion slot. The card will have an input port to connect the mouse.

- An internal modem or FAX/modem card will also use a slot. It will have ports for incoming and outgoing telephone lines.

- If the computer is connected to a network or a printer-sharing device, these may need to use an expansion slot.

Disk Drives

The primary location for storing information for the computer to use is on disks. The data is stored as electronic impulses on magnetic disk material. The device used to read and write information using disks is called a *disk drive.*

Most computers have a least one, usually two, floppy disk drives and one hard disk drive. Some computers may also have a CD-ROM drive or a tape drive (used almost exclusively to *backup* a hard disk in case of failure). These are located in drive bays in the system unit. A personal computer will usually have three full-height drive bays and one or two half-height drive bays. The full height bays are used for 5.25-inch drives or hard disk drives. The half-height bays are usually used for 3.5-inch drives.

Floppy disks must be formatted in order to store information. Formatting maps the disk into sectors and tracks that the drive uses to locate information on the disk. The number of sectors and tracks depends on the size and type of the disk and determines the amount of information which can be stored on the disk.

Disk drives contain a read/write head which simultaneously reads or writes to both sides of a disk. This makes the disk system much faster than the tape systems which were used in the earlier generations of computers, because the tapes must access information sequentially. The tape drive may have to rewind almost the entire length of the tape to get to a certain piece of information.

While the disk spins on the drive, the read/write heads move from outside to inside to get the information quickly. Because the disk spins faster than the read/write heads move, information is stored from outside to inside on both sides at the same time. This allows for the fastest access to information.

Floppy Disk Drives. Floppy disk drives generally come in two sizes, 5.25-inch and 3.5-inch (sometimes called microdiskettes). Older computers may have double-density disk drives, which will only read and write on double-density disks. Most newer computers come with high-density disk drives, which can read and write on high- or double-density disks. When purchasing a new computer, most buyers opt for one disk drive in each size. This allows them to use either 5.25-inch disks or 3.5-inch disks.

Floppy disks may contain space for 360K of information (5.25-inch, double-density) or up to 2.88MB of information (3.5-inch, super high-density). Table 17-1 contains an explanation of how the various floppy disks store information.

Special care must be taken to avoid damage to floppy disks. With improper handling, data may be lost or destroyed and impossible to recover. The smaller 3.5-inch disks are sturdier and have a sliding cover for the

Table 17-1
FLOPPY DISK SIZES AND STORAGE CAPABILITIES

Size	Density	Tracks/ Side	Sectors[1]/ Track	Storage Capacity
5.25"	Double	40	9	360K
5.25"	High	80	15	1.2MB
3.5"	Double	80	9	720K
3.5"	High	80	18	1.44MB
3.5"	Super-High	80	36	2.88MB

[1]Each sector contains 512 bytes.

write/protect notch, but still can be damaged. Some special concerns when handling floppy disks:

- Keep disks away from magnets or magnetized objects (such as a ringing telephone or magnetized screwdriver). Magnetized objects can erase all of the electronic impulses.

- Don't smoke around the disk. Smoke particles are larger in size than the distance between the read/write head and the disk surface. The same is true for food and drink particles.

- Never touch the actual disk surface. Body oils can damage the surface.

- Use a soft-pointed pen, such as a felt tip, to label disks.

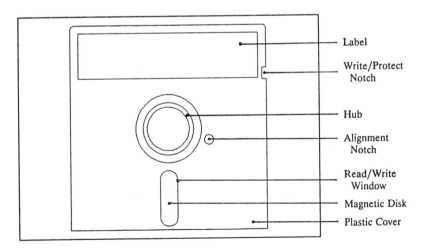

Figure 17-17. Parts of a floppy disk.

Figure 17-18.   A 3.5-inch floppy disk.

Hard Disk Drives. Most computers have a hard disk drive with a fixed *hard disk*. This means that the disk and drive are not portable; they stay in the computer at all times. Computers running new programs must have a hard disk drive, because the operating system and programs will not fit on a floppy disk. Many users also store most of their *data files* on the hard disk.

Hard disk drives work the same way as floppy disk drives, but the hard disk usually has several platters. The platters are made of aluminum or ceramic and coated with a magnetic surface material. The disk drive has two read/write heads for each platter on the hard disk. The read/write heads work like a phonograph needle, except they don't actually touch the hard disk, although they do come very close. A smoke particle is larger in diameter than this distance, which is why a computer user shouldn't smoke around the computer. (Of course, smoking is also bad for the health of the user and others who work around that person.)

The first hard disks contained space for 10MB to 30MB of information.

Today's personal computers may have up to several gigabytes of storage space. The most common hard disks, however, have from 120MB to 500MB of storage space.

Hard disks usually are located in one of the available disk drive bays. Some hard disks, however, are located on a card which fills an expansion slot. These are referred to as hard cards. Some computers make use of portable hard disks, called Bernoulli disks. These disks may be used for primary storage or to backup the fixed hard disk.

A disk cache is used on newer computers to speed up operations that are slowed down by accessing the hard disk drive. The disk cache keeps copies of recently accessed sectors on the hard disk in a reserved area of memory called cache RAM. When the program tells the computer to access the hard drive, the cache program first goes to cache RAM to see if the information needed is located there. If the information is in cache RAM, the operation occurs faster because accessing RAM is much faster than accessing a hard disk.

Figure 17-19. A hard disk drive with the cover removed. Note the three platters and read/write heads for each exposed side.

Other Storage Devices. The other two primary storage devices used on computers are the tape drive and the CD-ROM drive.

The tape drive is used primarily to backup a hard drive as insurance against loss of data if disk failure occurs. It may use cassettes or tape cartridges. Newer tape drives may use 8mm tapes similar to the ones used in video cameras. These tapes may hold several gigabytes of information. An internal tape drive will be located in one of the disk drive bays. An external tape drive will be attached to the computer through the serial port.

The CD-ROM drive reads the optical compact disks (CD) mentioned earlier in this chapter. The CD can store digitized text, graphics images, and sound. Like the tape drive, it may be internal or external.

Input/Output Ports

The system unit may have several input/output ports to connect pe-

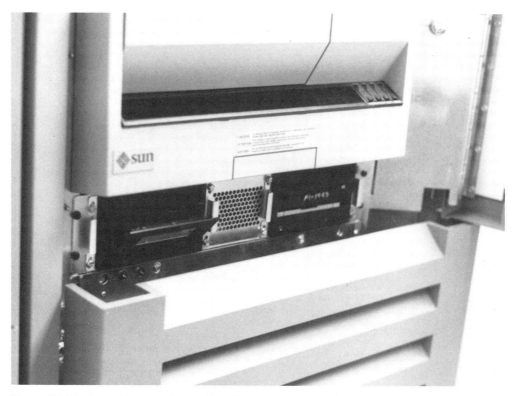

Figure 17-20. Tape drives used to backup files on a network file server. The one on the left uses an 8mm cartridge and the one on the right a 1/4-inch cassette.

Figure 17-21.   An external CD-ROM drive, connected to the computer's serial port.

ripherals to the computer. The two standard ports are the serial port and the parallel port.

Serial ports. The serial port is an asynchronous communications port. A mouse, an external modem, or a character printer can be connected to the computer through this port. The term serial is used because data is transferred one bit at a time over a single line.

Serial ports use an RS-232 interface, which is a standard that was developed to allow devices to be used interchangeably on different computers. The computer addresses the serial ports as COM1, COM2, etc. Although most use fewer, one computer can address up to four COM ports.

Parallel ports. Parallel ports are normally connected to a printer of some type. The term parallel means that bits of data are transferred over more than one line at a time. This process makes parallel ports faster than serial ports. The parallel port is often connected to the motherboard with a controller card, thereby using one of the expansion slots.

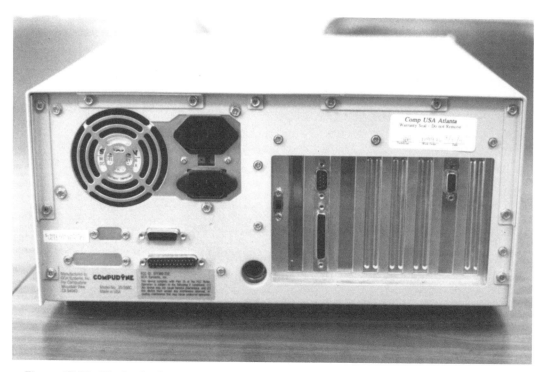

Figure 17-22. The back of a computer. Note the input/output ports available for various connections.

MONITOR

A computer monitor, or screen, is an output device which allows the computer user to see the results of processing. For example, when the user types in a command, the command shows up on the screen so the user can see what was typed. When the command is processed, the results of the process show up to let the user know what occurred or why the command did not work.

The four primary types of monitors or screens found on personal computers are the *cathode ray tube (CRT)*, the electroluminescent (EL) display, the *liquid crystal display (LCD)*, and the gas-plasma display.

Cathode Ray Tube (CRT)

The most common type of monitor for personal computers is the CRT. The CRT is based on the same technology found in a television set—some can even be used to receive television signals. They usually display 25 lines of text with each line 80 characters long. A 12- to 15-inch size, measured diagonally, is the most common, although some are larger.

The surface of a CRT screen is coated with a phosphorescent coating. When the monitor receives a signal from the computer, an electron gun generates an electronic beam on the phosphors, which causes them to glow. Each phosphor glows for a short period of time and then must be refreshed. The refresh rate is one of the factors that determines how easy the monitor is to look at for extended periods of time. A standard refresh rate to keep the image from flickering is 60 times per second, but superior monitors may be much faster.

Color CRT monitors contain red, green, and blue electron guns. Each color produced on the monitor is some combination of these colors at various strengths. For example, white is the result when all three guns are turned on high. Various shades of gray occur when all three are reduced by the same amount.

Monitors with graphic capabilities have bitmapped displays. The graphics standard information is located on a graphics card in an expansion slot. The screen has a number of dots that are illuminated to create a graphic or text. Each dot that can be illuminated is called a *pixel*. The number and size of the pixels determines the sharpness of the image produced, also called the *resolution*. The size of the pixel is called the *dot pitch*. A smaller dot pitch and higher resolution produce a sharper picture. Table 17-2 contains a summary of the various monitor standards and resolutions.

Table 17-2
VIDEO DISPLAY STANDARDS

Standard	Description	Year	Resolution	Pixels
MDA	Monochrome Display Adapter	1981	720 × 350	252,000
CGA	Color Graphics Adapter	1981	640 × 200	128,000
EGA	Enhanced Graphics Adapter	1984	640 × 350	224,000
VGA	Video Graphics Array	1987	640 × 480	307,200
SuperVGA	Extended VGA/VGA Plus	1988	800 × 600	480,000
			1024 × 768	786,432

Source: *PC Glossary*, Disston Ridge, Inc.

Electroluminescent (EL) Display

The EL is often called a monochrome monitor, meaning one color. It is the most reliable type of display and is found on many computers in operation. Most EL monitors do not have graphics capabilities, but are excellent for text, providing a sharp image.

EL monitors have a phosphor film between a reflective back film and a transparent front film. A grid of electrodes contains the pixels which can be lighted individually. These monitors usually emit an amber or green color on a black background, which is easy on the eyes of the user.

Liquid Crystal Display (LCD)

LCDs use a liquid crystal material sandwiched between two pieces of glass to form the screen. The image is activated by polarizers and an external light source. LCD's are commonly found on portable, especially notebook, computers because they have a flat screen that is not bulky when compared to a CRT. The same technology is found in wristwatches, clocks, microwaves, and many other devices.

Figure 17-23. A notebook computer with an LCD screen.

On the first LCDs, the image could only be viewed from directly in front of the screen. Newer versions have backlighting and advanced electronic signals to produce a much better image than the early models. LCD's are now available in color and monochrome versions.

Gas-Plasma Display

Gas-plasma displays use a trapped gas, usually neon or argon/neon, which lights up when electricity is applied to it. The electricity causes the individual pixels to glow an orange-red color.

As a monochrome screen, the gas-plasma has a sharper image than the LCD. Like the LCD, it is a flat screen and is used almost exclusively on portable notebook computers.

KEYBOARD

The keyboard is the computer user's most common input device. Along with a mouse, it is the means by which the user can tell the computer what to do. The keyboard is the detachable device that looks similar to the keypad of a typewriter. The primary difference is that the computer keyboard contains some specialized keys for use with computer *software.*

Like a typewriter, the computer contains the letter and number keys, special character keys, a shift key, a caps lock key, a backspace key, a tab key, and the spacebar. On a computer keyboard, however, the return key is replaced with an enter key, which signals to the computer that a command is complete. The computer keyboard also contains 10 or 12 *function keys,* a control key, an alternate key, and *cursor control keys.*

The cursor control keys include arrows and other keys used to move the *cursor* around. The other cursor control keys are the home key, the end key, insert and delete keys, and the page up and page down keys. The cursor control keys may be located on a *numeric keypad,* found on most keyboards, with a switch to toggle the keys between their different functions. The keyboard may have dedicated cursor control keys in addition to those on the numeric keypad. On some notebook computers, the computer will not have a number pad, and the cursor control keys will be located on the letter keys, usually under the right hand.

Most keyboards use the standard typewriter configuration for the letter keys, called a QWERTY keyboard. (The first five letters in the top row are q, w, e, r, t, and y.) The QWERTY keyboard was first developed to slow down fast typists, because they were jamming the keys on mechanical

Figure 17-24. A 101-key, QWERTY computer keyboard. Note the numeric keypad
on the far right and the dedicated cursor control keys between the
letter keys and the numeric keypad.

typewriters. Some other configurations include the Dvorak, Maltron, and
AZERTY keyboards.

PRINTER

The printer is a common output device that provides the computer
user with a hard copy of information. This protects the user by providing
another copy of data, in case the original is lost or erased from the
computer's storage. It also provides a portable copy that can be shared with
those who do not have a computer or appropriate software to read the
electronic copy.

The four major types of printers are daisy wheel, dot matrix, laser, and
inkjet.

Daisy Wheel Printer

The *daisy wheel printer* is an impact printer based on technology available
in many typewriters. A circular disk (the wheel) has two characters on each
individual spoke. To print a letter, the printer strikes the individual spoke
against an ink ribbon. This action results in a complete letter printed on
the paper.

The daisy wheel is a letter-quality printer. This means that the output
is comparable to a typewriter's output—the letters are fully-formed and
easy to read.

Daisy wheel printers commonly use either a tractor-feed mechanism to
move continuous form paper through the printer or a single sheet feeder.
Some use a friction feed system, much like that of a typewriter.

Daisy wheel printers may come in standard carriage, which handles a page 8.5 inches wide, or wide carriage, which can handle a 14-inch wide page. Standard paper can hold about 80 characters on one line, while wide paper can hold about 132 characters.

Dot Matrix Printer

The *dot matrix printer*, the most common printer for individuals, prints characters composed of dots. It prints characters one at a time by pressing wires, also called pins, against an ink ribbon and onto the paper. The wires are arranged in a rectangle.

Dot matrix printers come in two major varieties, 9-pin and 24-pin. The 24-pin printers are more expensive and produce a higher quality output. Most dot matrix printers are bidirectional, meaning that they can print

Figure 17-25. Nine and one-half by 11-inch continuous form paper for use with a computer's printer. Note the perforated edges which allow the printer to use a tractor feed mechanism. When the perforated edges are removed, the paper is a standard 8.5 by 11 inches.

Figure 17-26. A 24-pin, dot matrix printer.

lines of text from left to right or right to left, which increases printing speed.

Dot matrix printers usually have two modes, draft and *near letter quality*. In draft mode, dot matrix printers are fast, but the output is of lower quality. In near letter quality mode, the print is improved because each line is printed two times. With a new ribbon, a 24-pin printer is very close to letter quality, and is usually considered acceptable for correspondence.

Dot matrix printers can print medium-to-high quality graphics. The printer uses *bitmapping*, where the computer tells the printer whether or not to print each dot on the page.

Like daisy wheel printers, dot matrix printers commonly use either a tractor-feed mechanism or a single sheet feeder, although some use a friction feed system. Many dot matrix printers can change from one method of feeding paper to another. Also, like daisy wheel printers, dot matrix printers may be standard carriage or wide carriage.

Laser Printer

The *laser printer* prints output one page at a time, rather than one character at a time. It works somewhat like a photocopier, with the image coming from the computer, rather than another piece of paper. When the computer sends a signal to the printer, it focuses a laser beam on its drum. Each position on the drum touched by the laser becomes negatively charged and attracts toner. Then heat and pressure transfer the toner to the paper and fuse it to the paper's surface. This is why some people refer to the laser as "burning" an image on the paper.

Laser printers are popular because they are very flexible, easily combining letter quality text in various sizes and high quality graphics on one page. Like a dot matrix printer, the laser prints graphics by letting the computer tell it whether or not to print each dot. With a laser, however, many more dots must be bitmapped. Standard resolutions of laser printers

Figure 17-27. A laser printer. Note the sheet feeder loading paper into the front of the machine.

range from 300 dots-per-inch (dpi) to 1200 dpi. Because the entire page is printed at once, the printer must have enough memory to bitmap an entire page. For high-quality graphics, the laser should have at least 2MB of memory and may need more.

Lasers typically use a sheet feeder that handles paper 8.5 inches wide and may hold from 100 to 500 sheets of paper at one time.

Inkjet Printer

Inkjet printers use a spray nozzle to spray ink on the paper to produce a character or graphic. An ink cartridge slides across the page as the paper moves up one line at a time. The ink may be one color or several different colors.

Color inkjet printers are popular with users who do graphics work requiring different colors. Like dot matrix printers, they bitmap the graphic and print it one line at a time. They also can do overhead transparencies in colors.

Inkjet printers can be made very small. This feature makes them popular for use with laptop computers.

Inkjets vary in the quality of their print, but have improved greatly in the 1990s. The output of high-quality inkjet printers is considered letter quality.

COMPUTER SOFTWARE

Software refers to computer programs that allow the computer user to accomplish specific tasks. In general, software can be classified by how the user purchases or obtains the software and by its function.

METHODS OF OBTAINING SOFTWARE

Software may be *freeware, user-supported software,* or *commercial software.* Each has features that make it different from the others.

Freeware

Freeware refers to a freely-distributed software that has been placed in the public domain. This means that the author has not attached a copyright notice to the software and does not retain any legal rights to the program(s). The software may be used, freely copied, and distributed by anyone. While the user is not required to pay a fee to use the program, the author may attach a request for comments about the usefulness of the program to the software.

User-supported Software

With user-supported software, the author retains the copyright. The program can be freely copied and distributed, but the user is expected to register with the author and pay a fee for using the software.

Payment of the user fee gives permission to use the software and typically includes a full set of *documentation* upon registration. The user may also receive the newest version of the program and future updates. With some programs, registered users are offered telephone support for the software and a commission for registering other users.

User-supported software is sometimes referred to as shareware, which is actually a marketing system for software authors. Shareware distribution allows the author to market a program with minimal expense. Many of these software authors belong to ASP, the Association of Shareware Professionals.

Figure 17-28. PC Glossary is a user-supported package containing user terms and definitions. It is available through Disston Ridge, Inc.

Commercial Software

Most successful application programs are commercial software which is copyrighted by the company or person who distributes it. It is illegal to copy these programs, other than to make backup copies for personal use. The software cannot be given to others without the permission of the copyright holder. Unauthorized duplication is known as *software piracy*.

Commercial software companies have enormous amounts of money invested in the development of software. Like book publishers, the copyright is their primary means of protecting that investment. One way they have tried to avoid software piracy is by using copy-protect codes in their

Figure 17-29. Norton Antivirus, a program designed to detect and prevent viruses from infecting a computer system.

software, but computer users found ways around these codes soon after they were developed.

FUNCTIONS OF SOFTWARE

Many types of software are available in today's market, each with its own special capabilities and functions. In general, however, the software types can be classified into six categories: operating systems, word processing, electronic spreadsheets/recordkeeping, database management, graphics, and communications/networking. A brief description of each of these is provided below. The remaining chapters in this text go into more detail about these special functions.

Operating Systems

The *operating system* is the basic software which allows the computer to operate. Other applications run under the operating system platform; it provides a system from which the computer interacts with the software and the user.

The most common types of operating systems are: Microsoft Disk Operating System (MS-DOS), used with older IBM and IBM-compatible computers; System, used with Apple Macintosh computers; OS/2, used with newer IBM computers; and UNIX, used with networked computer systems.

Also included in this category are utilities programs designed to enhance the functions of the operating systems and hardware. These utilities may be user interfaces, menu programs, *virus* protection programs, and file management programs.

Word Processing

Word processing is the most commonly used function of desktop computers. Over 80 percent of the desktop computers in operation are used at least part of the time for word processing.

Word processing is simply using the computer as a "turbocharged" typewriter. The computer allows the user to select different sizes of print, make revisions easily, and saves the user time because documents that need only a few revisions do not have to be entirely retyped. WordPerfect and Microsoft Word are the two most popular word processing programs in use today.

Desktop publishing software is specialized word processing software for people who produce more complex documents combining text and graphics. It combines some of the features of a word processor with a graphical user interface and what-you-see-is-what-you-get (WYSIWYG, pronounced whizzy-wig) placement and formatting. PageMaker and Ventura Publisher are two popular desktop publishing programs.

Spreadsheets/Recordkeeping

The computer's speed and accuracy when performing mathematical functions allows it to be an excellent tool for keeping numerical records. The two primary types of software for this function are electronic spreadsheets and accounting packages.

Electronic spreadsheets are enhanced versions of the paper spreadsheet that has been used in recordkeeping for many years. The spreadsheet, a very flexible program, allows the user to develop his or her own categories, headings, and formulas within the form. Lotus 1-2-3, Quattro Pro, and Microsoft Excel are three very popular electronic spreadsheet programs.

Accounting packages come with ready-to-use recording systems based on general accounting practices. Their primary feature is that the program sets up accounts and ledgers for the user, saving time. Various levels of flexibility are built into the programs, and some have advanced features such as electronic payments, check writing, and tax computation. Quicken is probably the most popular accounting package used today.

Database Management

Database management programs are designed as flexible programs that enable the user to create a database of information about a set of subjects, then have ready access to the information. These programs allow the user to sort, search, choose, update, and report information in a variety of ways.

Database management software is useful for text and numerical information, with tools to manipulate both types. The user decides on what information is needed about each subject, divides the information into logical areas, and inputs the information. DBase, Paradox, and Oracle are popular database management programs.

Graphics

Graphics programs allow the user to generate a variety of charts, graphs,

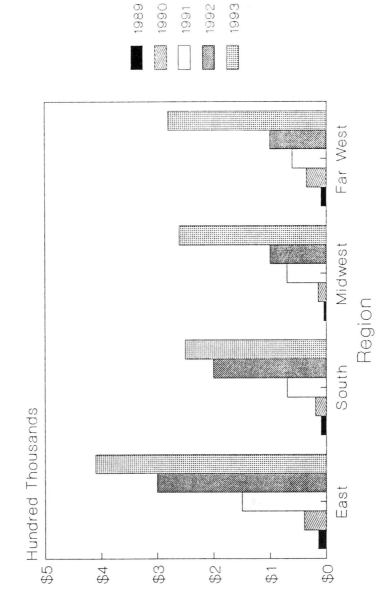

Figure 17-30. Output from a computer graphics program.

and line art. Some of the programs have a set of graphics available; others allow the user to create original drawings; and some do both. Certain graphics programs allow the user to input numbers which are then converted into data graphs, such as bar, pie, or line graphs.

Different graphics programs allow the user to choose from a variety of output forms. The output may be designed to be shown on the computer monitor, projected on a wall screen, printed, plotted, or converted to 35mm slides. Harvard Graphics, Corel Draw, MacPaint, and AutoCAD are popular graphics/drafting programs.

Communications/Networking

The practice of using computers as long-distance communications tools is growing rapidly. In such systems, the personal computer, or a terminal, is connected with a file server, usually through telephone lines. This file server may serve a small area in a local area network (LAN), or a larger area in a wide area network (WAN). Novell, with its NetWare system, controls about 80 percent of the LAN market.

Networking has three primary functions: file transfer, where files are shared between two or more computers; program sharing, where more than one person can use an application; and electronic mail, where messages can be sent electronically in just a few seconds.

BUYING A COMPUTER SYSTEM

One of the many decisions an agribusiness manager has to make is whether or not to buy a computer and, if buying, which computer to purchase. Many factors must be considered, including the type of business, the computer abilities of personnel, future needs, and costs. A good rule is to buy enough computer to accomplish the needed work, while considering future upgrades and prices. When a new microprocessor comes on the market, like the Pentium did in 1993, a smart manager can often get the next lowest technology (in that case a 486DX) at a very good price and still get plenty of computer to do the job.

Below is a brief discussion of the questions a manager should answer before purchasing a new computer system.

1. **What do we need from a computer?** Examples include the ability

to produce letters, billing statements, inventory printouts, financial records, communications, and service manuals.

2. **What applications are necessary to provide what we need?** A word processing program will produce letters and service manuals, but if the company produces several newsletters or brochures, a desktop publishing package may also be needed. For recordkeeping, an electronic spreadsheet may be the choice if someone in the office has experience using one; if not, one of the accounting packages might be more appropriate.

3. **What software do we want to provide our applications?** This choice is often based on the personal preference of the manager and office staff. Two things the manager should keep in mind are the amount of training required and the stability of the software company. The manager wants to avoid lengthy and costly training if possible. Having someone in the office who can use a software package may influence the manager to buy that package. Buying from a stable company means that future service needs and upgrades will be available. One thing the manager might consider is using an *integrated software* package that combines several applications at one price.

4. **What hardware do we need to run the software?** Although it is nice to have state-of-the-art equipment, managers can often save money and get adequate or better service by buying equipment with slightly older technology. Software developments usually run a few years behind the hardware; therefore the programs available may not be able to take advantage of the latest equipment. Of course, if the hardware is needed and will be needed for several years, it pays to buy good equipment.

    The software chosen and amount of data required will determine the specification of the hardware. This includes the type of peripherals, amount of memory, and the size of the hard disk. For example, if Windows-based graphics programs are chosen, a large hard disk and a fast processor are important. If the output needed is 35mm slides, a film recorder must be one of the pieces of hardware.

    Hardware decisions can be a matter of personal preference, sometimes determined by physical characteristics of the user.

5. **What support service is available for the hardware and software?** Service is very important. The software should have toll-free telephone support and good documentation. The hardware should have

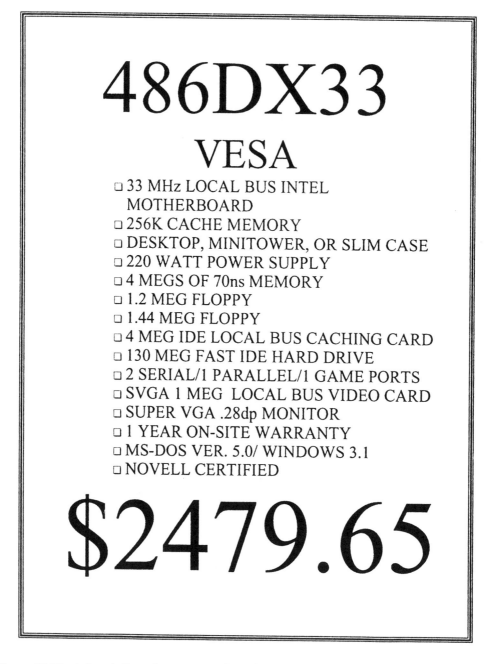

486DX33
VESA

- 33 MHz LOCAL BUS INTEL MOTHERBOARD
- 256K CACHE MEMORY
- DESKTOP, MINITOWER, OR SLIM CASE
- 220 WATT POWER SUPPLY
- 4 MEGS OF 70ns MEMORY
- 1.2 MEG FLOPPY
- 1.44 MEG FLOPPY
- 4 MEG IDE LOCAL BUS CACHING CARD
- 130 MEG FAST IDE HARD DRIVE
- 2 SERIAL/1 PARALLEL/1 GAME PORTS
- SVGA 1 MEG LOCAL BUS VIDEO CARD
- SUPER VGA .28dp MONITOR
- 1 YEAR ON-SITE WARRANTY
- MS-DOS VER. 5.0/ WINDOWS 3.1
- NOVELL CERTIFIED

$2479.65

Figure 17-31. A description of a computer for sale in May 1993. Note how the various parts of the system are specified. This allows the buyer to compare prices and features among dealers.

Figure 17-32. Local dealers are often a good choice when buying a computer because of the service they can provide.

a warranty, preferably specifying on-site service, and a good record of reliability. A good policy is to buy locally, when possible. This practice usually ensures good service, but at a slightly higher price.

6. **What money is available to spend on the system?** The manager should avoid making decisions based on price alone, even though it is an important factor. After the other considerations are made, the manager must make a decision that is cost-efficient and still meets the goals of the business. Sometimes the decision is easy. For example, a computer used exclusively for word processing does not need a fast microprocessor and may not need a color monitor. The printer for this system, however, should be of good quality.

The manager's job is to provide office staff—including the manager—with the tools they need to do their work efficiently. This usually means buying computers. The tough decisions are determining what software and hardware to buy and from whom it should be purchased.

CHAPTER QUESTIONS

1. What is a computer program?

2. Describe three early computing devices.

3. What was the importance of the punched card?

4. Describe each of the four generations of computers.

5. What two inventions led to the development of the microcomputer?

6. When was the first microcomputer developed?

7. When was the IBMpc first introduced?

8. What is binary logic?

9. Explain the terms ROM and RAM.

10. Briefly describe the parts of a computer.

11. How much faster is a Pentium microprocessor than an 8086?

12. How is information stored on a floppy disk?

13. What are the input/output ports on a computer used for?

14. Which type of monitor is most prevalent on today's computers?

15. Describe the four types of printers in terms of print quality.

16. Which type of printer can print in multiple colors?

17. Briefly explain the three methods of obtaining software.

18. What are the six major functions of software?

19. Describe the steps in the process of buying a computer.

20. Suppose you were running a local farm supply business. What type of computer would you buy? Justify your decision.

Chapter 18

OPERATING SYSTEMS

Most computer users find a certain system they like and use it exclusively. They have determined what they want the computer to do and which applications they need to accomplish this work.

The operating system is the software that connects applications with the computer hardware. It is sometimes called the platform. Some computer users are not even aware of the operating system, while others make extensive use of the system to customize their computer for maximum productivity.

In the past, the operating system determined which software a computer user was able to use. Now, most computer software companies develop versions of their software that are compatible with most of the existing platforms. As an example, the WordPerfect corporation has different versions of its popular word processing program, WordPerfect, for computers using MS-DOS, Macintosh System, and Unix operating systems.

This chapter takes a look at the most common operating systems used on today's computers. A description of each operating system is given, and a more extensive description is provided for MS-DOS, the most popular operating system currently in use. Several utilities available that enhance the operating system and hardware are also discussed.

OBJECTIVES

1. Describe the functions of an operating system.

2. Discuss the various means of classifying operating systems.

3. Identify the most popular operating systems and user interfaces.

4. Describe the process a computer undergoes when it is started up.

5. Utilize MS-DOS files.

6. Associate MS-DOS commands with their functions.

7. Associate MS-DOS error messages with their causes and possible solutions.

8. Identify popular utilities programs and their functions.

FUNCTIONS OF OPERATING SYSTEMS

The operating system is a set of files that serves as the connection between the user, application software, and the computer hardware. It coordinates the functions of the microprocessor, memory, input/output devices, and the software running on the computer. It does this by providing a standard, or platform, for software developers to use when writing programs.

The central core of information, called a *kernel*, of the operating system must reside in RAM at all times. This is the information that manages the computer for the applications running under the operating system.

The operating system also contains various commands that the user can use to manage files and disks, optimize memory, or configure hardware. Knowledge of these commands and their functions makes a user proficient in using an operating system.

The three primary functions of the operating system are allocation of

TERMS

address	filename	prompt
AUTOEXEC.BAT	IBM compatible	pull-down menu
booted	computer	root directory
buffer	internal commands	spooling
command files	kernel	subdirectory
CONFIG.SYS	login	switch
conventional memory	logout	system security
device drivers	Microsoft Windows	time slices
extension	multitasking	user-friendly
external commands	on-line time	virtual memory
file allocation table (FAT)	parameter	management
file	point-and-click	virus protection
file management	program file	wildcard

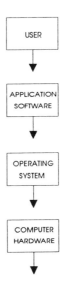

Figure 18-1. The operating system keeps the user and application
connected to the computer hardware.

computer resources, monitoring of system activities, and management of files.

ALLOCATION OF COMPUTER RESOURCES

The operating system manages the computer's microprocessor, memory, input/output, and storage access to keep the programs and instructions from getting mixed up during processing.

Microprocessor

The microprocessor can only carry out one instruction at a time, although it does so very quickly. When the microprocessor receives more than one instruction, the operating system coordinates the activity. This happens frequently when more than one user or application is trying to access the same processor, although it can happen to a lesser extent with one user and one application.

The operating system allocates *time slices* to each user and application using the microprocessor. These time slices are measured in milliseconds. Each user typically receives a time slice in rotating order. In newer machines with fast microprocessors, the users don't realize that they are sharing with someone else because in real time the microprocessor stills performs very fast.

Memory

A computer's RAM must hold several things at one time. The operating system, the instructions from application programs in use by one or more users, data being processed, data being sent to output devices, data being received from input devices, space for procedures such as calculations and sorting, and TSR programs all must be available in RAM. The operating system keeps this information sorted. The system's primary function is to make sure that information from one application or user does not replace other information in memory that is needed by another application or user.

The operating system may do this in one of two ways. One is to maintain an *address* of all information located in RAM at any one time so that the operating system can determine RAM space that is available. The other way is to use *virtual memory management*. In virtual memory management, the operating system increases available memory by allocating some of it to a hard disk. This method is commonly used in systems with multiple users.

Input/Output

While input devices such as the keyboard, mouse, modem, and disk drives may be sending information to the computer, output devices such as the monitor, printer, mouse, and disk drives may be receiving information from the computer. The operating system coordinates these processes.

The operating system handles this information by creating *buffers* and by *spooling*. The buffers are parts of RAM used for temporary storage of information. They are usually used for information going to disk drives and monitors, while spooling is used for information going to slower devices, such as printers and modems. When spooling, the operating system sends some of the information to temporary storage on the hard disk (or a floppy disk).

Storage Access

The operating system also gives a user or users access to storage devices such as disk drives and tape drives. Disk drive access is usually given on a first come, first served basis, with each user getting his or her turn as the instructions are processed. Tape drive storage needs more management because it is a sequential access device. The tape drive is usually reserved for specific users or applications.

MONITORING OF SYSTEM ACTIVITIES

With systems that have more than one user, the operating system may be required to monitor the time of use and provide system security. Some network systems are set up so the users pay for *on-line time* or for microprocessor time. In these systems, the user must *login* to the system to begin using it and *logout* when finished in order for the system to keep an accurate record of time used.

Having to login and logout leads to some possible security problems. The operating system manages *system security* by requiring passwords for login. The password should be known only to the user. (Of course, the system operator should have the ability to delete passwords when someone quits using the system.) The user should be careful not to let others know his or her password and thereby have access to confidential information or send messages using his or her login name. Some systems are set up with default times so that a user can be timed out when not using the system for a certain period of time. This prevents someone else from coming in and using a person's access because they forgot to logout when finished.

MANAGEMENT OF FILES

The operating system provides the user and application with a set of *file management* techniques that help them keep their data organized. These techniques include copying, saving, renaming, deleting, and sorting files, formatting disks, and moving files from one storage device to another. The applications also have access to these file management functions. For example, when using a word processing program, the user can usually save, delete, rename, move or copy files; in most cases, the application uses the operating system commands to carry out these functions.

Most operating systems also include a file editor for editing certain command files and system files. These file editors can also be used to create files. Specific file management techniques are described later in this chapter.

CLASSIFICATION OF OPERATING SYSTEMS

The different operating systems are designed for various purposes. Computer operators must select a system based on its purpose and the availability of needed applications for the system. Usually, the operating systems are classified in one of three ways. These classifications include the number of tasks or programs the system can run at one time, the number of users the system can handle at one time, and the type of interface provided to the user.

NUMBER OF TASKS

The two categories in this classification are *multitasking* and single tasking systems. Multitasking refers to the operating system's ability to concurrently execute more than one application. For example, on a multitasking system, the user can have a word processing program open and an electronic spreadsheet open at the same time. The user can be printing something with the word processing program and entering data in the spreadsheet at the same time. The microprocessor must switch back and forth between application instructions.

Of the more popular operating systems, Unix, OS/2, and System (Macintosh) are all multitasking systems. MS-DOS is a single tasking system.

NUMBER OF USERS

Computer systems are usually divided into single user systems and multi-user systems. By nature, multi-user systems must also be multitasking systems, where more than one application can be used at the same time. Multi-user systems usually will also allow more than one individual to use the same application. This function is very important to a catalog sales operation, for example, where several operators are taking orders using the same ordering program.

Unix and OS/2 are both multi-user systems. MS-DOS and System are single user systems.

INTERFACES

The operating system's interface refers to what the user sees on the monitor and how the user interacts with the system. A graphical user interface (GUI) refers to an interface characterized by use of a mouse to *"point-and-click"* on icons or to access *pull-down menus* to give commands to the system. A character-based user interface (CUI) refers to a system where the user gives commands by typing them at a *prompt*.

System and OS/2 have GUIs. Unix and MS-DOS are considered to have CUIs, although newer versions of both have incorporated pull-down menus and other GUI features. Microsoft Windows, an operating environment used with MS-DOS computers, is a graphical user interface with multitasking capabilities.

POPULAR OPERATING SYSTEMS AND ENVIRONMENTS

MS-DOS

Microsoft Disk Operating System (MS-DOS) is usually referred to as DOS for short. DOS was developed as PC-DOS by Microsoft for IBM for use on the original IBMpc in 1981. DOS was later marketed as MS-DOS by Microsoft for companies developing *IBM compatible computers* or IBM clones.

DOS quickly became an industry standard in the early 1980s. The leaders at IBM and Microsoft decided to allow anyone to have access to the code, and thereby, any computer programmer could write programs for DOS machines. This led to much more software being written for it than any other operating system, which in turn made DOS-based machines big sellers. The rest of the computer world has yet to catch up. DOS is by far the most popular operating system, running on over 80 percent of all desktop computers in operation. It also has the widest variety of software programs written for it of any operating system.

DOS is actually a 16-bit revision of an 8-bit operating system called CP/M (short for control program/microcomputer). CP/M was developed by Gary Kildall, the founder of Digital Research. Today, Digital Research makes an operating system called DRDOS, which competes with MS-DOS and will run the same software.

The original version of DOS was MS-DOS 1.0. In 1993, Microsoft introduced version 6.0. In between, several versions have been developed. Versions 2.1, 3.3, and 5.0 were very popular. The most commonly used DOS commands are described later in this chapter.

Figure 18-2. Microsoft's version 6.0 of MS-DOS, the
world's most popular operating system
software.

MICROSOFT WINDOWS

Microsoft Windows, or Windows for short, was the DOS community's answer to the popular GUI introduced by Apple for their Macintosh computer. The GUI is considered more *user-friendly* than the CUI used by DOS for many years. Windows works as an operating environment, providing a multitasking graphical user interface that still uses DOS operating system commands.

Windows became very popular in the early 1990s. Users like it because they can still exit it to run their DOS software, and also take advantage of its graphical capabilities with newer, Windows-versions of programs with which they are already familiar. Windows 3.0 was one of the best-selling programs of 1992 and 1993, and software companies have invested major resources into developing programs for use with Windows. Most popular DOS programs, for example WordPerfect, Lotus 1-2-3, and DBase IV, have Windows versions available.

As an operating environment, Windows acts as integrated software, with common commands for different applications that requires the user to learn fewer commands to run applications. This gives the user the ability to use powerful applications without as much training.

OS/2

In 1988, IBM introduced the IBM PS/2 which included OS/2, a multitasking, multi-user, operating system. Many computer experts tout OS/2 as the best operating system because it will run DOS programs and Windows programs as they were intended. Even so, OS/2 has not sold as well as expected, probably because of the established base of DOS and Windows users who upgrade primarily with newer versions of those programs.

OS/2 is a very powerful operating system. It is the only popular operating system that combines a GUI (its Presentation Manager), multitasking, and multi-user capabilities. (Windows NT, expected to be released in late 1993 or early 1994, is supposed to do all three as well.) Although it is provided with new IBM computers, IBM's share of the PC market is not as extensive as it was in the 1980s. Within the next few years, however, all PC's will probably be sold with an operating system like OS/2, although it may be simply an upgrade of DOS.

SYSTEM (Macintosh)

In 1983, Apple introduced the Lisa computer, an innovate product that never sold well because of its $10,000 price. Lisa was discontinued in 1984. That same year Apple took the best parts of the Lisa and packaged them into a lower-priced computer system called the Macintosh (Mac for short). The Mac was also overpriced and scoffed at by IBM and compatible users as a toy, fun to play with but weak in computing power.

One thing the Mac had going for it, however, was the first GUI, which was easier to understand and use than DOS's command line. For the first time, novice computer-users did not have to know what command to type and how to type it. They could simply select from a menu of commands or choose an icon by clicking on it with the mouse.

At first, Mac users were almost like a cult, refusing to learn DOS commands in order to use a computer, but without many software options available to them. At first, Apple wrote its own programs for the Mac, and other software companies were not invited. Then, even after Apple paved the way for other companies to write software, the companies did not invest much time and effort in Mac applications. DOS had a much greater base of users, and good DOS-based applications were sure to sell more than those developed for Macs.

The Macintosh overcame these early hurdles because of agreements with some software companies and a small but growing base of users who were loyal to the Mac way of computing. By the 1990s, Macs had made inroads into business operations that were formerly all-IBM.

Figure 18-3. The Macintosh from Apple Computers was the first computer to use the graphical user interface (GUI), touted for its ease of use.

UNIX

Unix was developed in the early 1970s by scientists at Bell Laboratories, a part of AT&T. AT&T, under federal regulations, couldn't commercially market Unix until its divestiture as part of the deregulation of the telephone industry in the early 1980s. Prior to this time, Unix was a popular system in use on many university campuses as a multi-user, multitasking system suitable for large networked computers. Many of its features were forerunners of features in the popular operating systems for personal computers.

Unix has grown in popularity since coming on the commercial market in the 1980s. Versions of Unix are run on almost every size of computer, although it is still primarily used in large networks. For this reason, Unix is discussed further in Chapter 23, Communications and Networking.

STARTUP OF
THE COMPUTER

A knowledge of what the computer does when started up, or *booted*, will help the user to understand how the operating system works and the importance of various operating system commands and files. A description of the startup of a computer using the MS-DOS operating system is given below. Other systems will be different, but will execute most of the same functions.

LOADING THE SYSTEM

When the power to the computer is switched on, it first accesses ROM memory to give the initial instructions to be followed. These initial instructions are called the boot record. The boot record tells the computer to go to the default disk drive and load the operating system into the computer. On most computers the default drive is the A: drive, usually a floppy disk drive. If the A: drive contains a system disk, the system is copied from the disk to the computer's RAM. If not, the computer will usually go to the hard disk, drive C:, and get the system. This procedure is important in that the user will normally have the system wanted on the hard disk, but if he or she wants to change for some reason, they can use the A: drive to boot with the different system.

The boot procedure loads three DOS files into RAM. The three files are COMMAND.COM, IO.SYS, and MSDOS.SYS. Having these three files on a disk makes it a system or startup disk. A directory listing of the files on the disk will only show the COMMAND.COM file because IO.SYS and MSDOS.SYS are hidden files. These files contain the kernel of the operating system that resides in RAM at all times.

CUSTOMIZING THE STARTUP PROCESS

After loading the system, the startup procedure can stop after loading the system at an A: or C: prompt. At this point the user enters a command or executes a program to continue use of the computer. Most users, however, have utilized advanced features of DOS to customize their startup procedures. Two files give users this flexibility: CONFIG.SYS and AUTOEXEC.BAT. When the computer has the system loaded, the boot procedure tells it to look for these files and execute them as part of the startup process.

The *CONFIG.SYS* file is created when DOS is installed to the computer, but the user can edit this file to customize his or her system. CONFIG.SYS can be customized to do many different things. Some of the more common ones include: (1) indicate a country code, with symbols and conventions pertaining to a particular country; (2) specify different *device drivers* to handle memory or hardware; (3) specify the number of files that may be open at one time; (4) load DOS and various TSRs in high memory; (5) specify the number of buffers in RAM; and (6) indicate the location of files and other information.

Figure 18-4. To interact with peripherals such as these tape drives, the operating system must have device drivers, special programs written for each type of peripheral.

The *AUTOEXEC.BAT* program is created by the user of a system to save time during the startup process. AUTOEXEC.BAT contains a list of commands which are executed at startup, rather than the user having to execute each command individually every time the system is booted. These commonly include commands to establish a current path and/or default directory, set screen attributes, start TSR programs such as screen savers, run disk utilities, customize the prompt, and access a menu or operating environment.

MS-DOS FILES

A *file* is a collection of logically related information stored together on a disk. The information is stored magnetically, much like a tape recording. The location of a file (which sectors and tracks contain the file) on a disk is called the address. When a file is written to a disk, the address is recorded in the *file allocation table (FAT)*.

Files may be either data files, program files, or command files. Data files contain information entered by the user of the computer system. *Program files* are files used to operate an application program. *Command files* are files used by the operating system and utilities.

DOS FILENAMES

DOS files may have a *filename* and *extension*. The filename can be up to eight characters in length, the extension up to three. The filename and extension are separated by a period. Extensions are optional; they are recommended for naming files and not recommended for naming directories. Filenames may be typed in upper or lower case letters. MS-DOS converts the characters to upper case.

Valid characters for filenames include all letters and numbers and these symbols:

$ % ' - @ { } ~ ' ! # ( ) &

Spaces cannot be used in filenames. Also, several symbols cannot be used. The following symbols *cannot* be used in naming files:

. " / \ [ ] : | < > + = ; ,

These symbols are used for other purposes in DOS and might confuse the system if used in filenames.

When using DOS commands, a *wildcard* may be used. Wildcards include the asterisk (*) and the question mark. The asterisk is used to represent multiple letters in filenames and extensions. The question mark is used to represent a single letter in a filename or extension. For example, *.* is used to include all files, while *.txt will include only filenames with the extension .txt. On the other hand, ?.* will include only one-letter filenames, while *.t?? will include all files with an extension beginning with a "t."

DOS FILES EXECUTION

Some DOS files can be executed by typing the name of the file and pressing <ENTER>. These files, called executable files, can be identified by their extension. Executable files will have one of three extensions: .COM, .EXE, or .BAT. When naming data files, the user should avoid using any of these extensions.

.COM Files

The .COM extension is usually reserved for external DOS commands and utilities command programs. For example, the DOS command to format a floppy disk is actually an executable file named FORMAT.COM. Typing FORMAT at the prompt will execute the file and begin the process of formatting a disk.

.EXE Files

The .EXE extension is used primarily by applications programs to indicate files that will start up (boot) some portion or all of the program. For example, the file that starts WordPerfect is WP.EXE. Typing WP at the prompt will execute this file and begin WordPerfect.

.BAT Files

Files with the .BAT extension are usually created by the user and are called batch files. Batch files are a collection of DOS commands and procedures stored in a file. They help the user take short cuts and save time. Instead of typing in each command, batch files allow the user to type a single command which tells DOS to run the entire batch of commands. The AUTOEXEC.BAT file mentioned earlier is an example of a special batch file that is executed automatically by DOS whenever the system is booted.

The computer user can create batch files to perform many tasks. Batch files are used to provide the menus and options for different situations. If a user has to enter multiple commands in sequence on a regular basis, he or she has a use for a batch file. This is often true when loading a special program or looking for a menu of possible executable files on a disk.

Although almost any DOS command can be included in a batch file, some special commands make batch files more efficient for the user. A brief description of each follows.

CALL—executes another batch file, then continues with the current batch file.

ECHO—displays messages on the screen. ECHO OFF hides subsequent commands and messages.

FOR—executes a series of commands.

GOTO—jumps to the designate label.

IF—a conditional statement, based on input from the user.

PAUSE—temporarily stops the execution of the batch file.

REM—used to imbed a remark or comment into the batch file. The user cannot see the comment during normal execution of the batch file.

SHIFT—moves the command line arguments one position to the left.

```
ECHO OFF
CLS
PATH=C:\;C:\DOS;C:\WP51;C:\UTIL;C:\NAV;C:\DBMENU;
MOUSE
PROMPT $P$G
MENU.BAT
```

Figure 18-5. An example of an AUTOEXEC.BAT file, read as part of the startup procedure.

MS-DOS DIRECTORY STRUCTURE

In DOS, all disks have a directory, much like a table of contents, where the information is listed in the FAT. In many cases, however, having one directory is not a good way to keep files organized. In addition to having the *root directory* (created when the disk is formatted), the user may also create a *subdirectory* for each group of files that contain related information.

For example, the WordPerfect word processing base program contains over 100 files. Rather than putting all of those files in the root directory, most users will create a subdirectory just for WordPerfect files. Under that directory, the user will probably create more subdirectories for graphics files and document files. The document subdirectory may be further divided into more subdirectories for individual projects and the files that relate to them.

Another way to designate the relationship is to refer to directories as parent and child directories, which relates to a family tree. If a directory is created within another, the created directory is referred to as a child directory of the original directory, while the original directory is a parent directory. Just like a family tree, a child directory must have a parent directory. In the example given above, the WordPerfect directory would be a child directory of the root directory, but a parent of the WordPerfect documents directory.

Each directory has a path, a way to determine the tree leading to that particular directory. Some common paths are given below.

C:\—The root directory

C:\WP51—WordPerfect subdirectory (child of the root directory)

C:\WP51\DOCUMENT—Document subdirectory (child of the WordPerfect sub-directory)

C:\WP51\DOCUMENT\LETTERS—Letters subdirectory (child of the Document subdirectory)

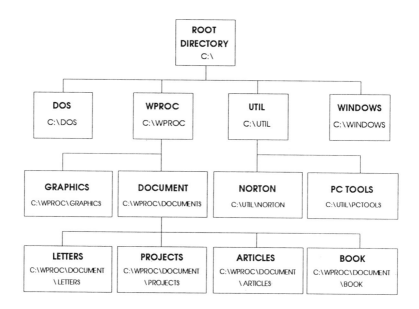

Figure 18-6. A possible directory structure (tree) for a hard disk designated as drive C:. The path for each directory is given under the directory name.

MS-DOS COMMANDS

Common DOS commands allow the user and applications software to participate in file, environment, and hardware management. These commands may be typed in at the prompt or accessed through the DOS shell (or Windows).

DOS commands take a general form: the command, a space, the *parameter*(s) (if any), a space, the *switch*(es), (also called options, if any), and press <ENTER> to activate the command. As an example, the DOS command for listing the files is DIR. To list files in the current directory, the user would enter:

DIR

The user often is working in one directory and wants to see a list of files in another drive or directory. The other drive is listed as a parameter of the DIR command. If the user is working in A: drive but wants to list files in the DOS directory of drive C:, he or she would enter:

DIR C:\DOS

When a directory contains more files than can be listed on the screen at one time, the above commands will allow the first files listed to scroll off of the screen without giving the user time to read the filenames. This problem can be remedied by adding a switch or option to the command. To have the listing of files stop when the screen is full and wait for the user to go to the next screen, the user would enter:

DIR C:\DOS /P

Note that the switches are separated by a slash (/). The space is optional.

Unlike some other operating systems, DOS does not distinguish between upper and lower case letters when processing commands. DOS actually changes lower case commands to upper case before processing them.

DOS has two types of commands: internal and external. Some of the most commonly used commands are described below. The user should consult a DOS manual for more details about these and other commands.

INTERNAL COMMANDS

The commands most commonly used by users and application programs are called *internal commands*. These commands are loaded in RAM when the system is booted and are part of the DOS kernel that must be available in RAM at all times. These commands and their functions are described below.

COPY

This command duplicates a file from one disk or directory to another or from the keyboard to a disk. It requires parameters of the source directory/filename and target directory/filename. (The current directory is the default.) No switches are used with COPY. To copy a file named CHAPTER.TXT from the drive A: root directory to the DATA directory in drive B:, the user would enter:

    COPY A:\CHAPTER.TXT B:\DATA\CHAPTER.TXT

The target filename can be changed if desired. If left off entirely, the target filename will be the same as the source filename.

With the COPY command, the wildcards * and ? can be used.

CHDIR (CD)

The CD command changes the current directory to the directory specified. For example, the command

    CD C:\DOS

will change the current directory to the DOS subdirectory in drive C:. The CD command requires a parameter of the desired directory but the full path is optional if going up or back one level in the current directory structure. Some other parameters include .. and \. As examples,

    CD ..

changes the current directory back one level to the parent directory, and

    CD\

changes the current directory to the root directory in that drive.

CLS

The CLS command clears the screen. Although it can be used at the prompt, it is used almost exclusively in batch files to clear the screen after a command has been processed. The user generally inserts the batch file command PAUSE before using CLS, because CLS will clear the screen before the results of the previous command can be seen.

DATE

The DATE command allows the user to change the date in the computer. In computers with battery backups, this command is seldom needed, except when the battery runs down. In computers without a battery backup, the DATE command is often part of the AUTOEXEC.BAT file, allowing the user to input the date each time the system is booted.

DEL (ERASE)

The DEL and ERASE commands are interchangeable. Both remove a file or files from a directory. The parameter required is the directory and filename. The current directory is the default directory, there is no default filename.

The wildcards * and ? can be used to remove multiple files, but should be used carefully. For example,

```
DEL *.*
```

will remove all of the files from a directory.

DIR

The DIR command is a very useful command in file management. It provides a list of the files in a directory so the user can determine which files to move, copy, delete, etc. The parameter required is the directory; the default is the current directory. Switches include /P to keep the list from scrolling off the screen, /W to give filenames in more than one column, /A to select by attributes, or /O to select in some specified order. For example,

```
DIR C:\DOS /W
```

will provide a list of the files in the DOS directory in drive C: in a wide column format.

MKDIR (MD)

The MD command creates a child directory (also called subdirectory) of the current directory. This allows the user to keep files that are related in a specific place for easy access. The command parameter is the name of the directory. Directories can be named just like files, but most experienced DOS users have adopted a practice of naming directories without extensions and files with extensions. This practice makes it easier to tell at a glance whether a name is referring to a file or a directory.

PATH

The PATH command tells the computer what directories, other than the current directory, should be searched when looking for a filename. This command is commonly used in AUTOEXEC.BAT files to give a list of probable directories. A common PATH given in an AUTOEXEC.BAT file might look like the following:

    PATH C:\;C:\DOS;C:\UTIL;D:\WPROC

Loading this path in when the computer starts tells it to look in each of these directories when searching for a command or file not found in the current directory.

PROMPT

The PROMPT command changes the prompt seen by the user. It is commonly used in AUTOEXEC.BAT files. The default prompt is A or C. If the user wants the prompt to display the current drive and directory and then keep the greater-than sign at the end, this line should be part of the AUTOEXEC.BAT file:

    PROMPT PG

RENAME

The RENAME command changes the name of a file. The parameters are the old filename's drive and directory and the new filename's drive and directory. The default is the current drive, with no default filename. This command can be used to move files as well. For example, to move a file called CHAPTER.TXT from the root directory in drive A: to the root directory in drive B:, the user would enter

RENAME A:\CHAPTER.TXT B:\CHAPTER.TXT

RMDIR (RD)

The RD command removes the specified directory, if it is empty (containing no files or subdirectories). The current directory must be the parent directory of the one that is being removed, or the entire path for the directory to be removed may be entered.

TIME

The TIME command is similar to the DATE command in that is it seldom needed in a computer system with a battery backup and used as part of the AUTOEXEC.BAT file in systems without a battery. The TIME command is used more in systems with a battery than DATE, however, because the internal clock in computers loses a little time each day. The user will find it necessary to adjust the clock periodically using the TIME command.

TYPE

The TYPE command prints the specified file on the screen. The parameter is the location and name of the file. The type command can also be used to print the file to a printer or other output device or to a disk using the > (redirect) sign. For example, the command

TYPE A:\CHAPTER.TXT

will print the contents of the file CHAPTER.TXT on the screen. To send the file's contents to the printer, the user would enter

TYPE A:\CHAPTER.TXTPRN

(The redirect command [>] can also be used to send output from other commands to the printer or to a disk file.)

If the file is a long file that scrolls off the screen, the MORE command can be used in conjunction with the type command to stop the scrolling at the end of each full screen. To use this to view the file CHAPTER.TXT on the screen, the user would enter

TYPE A:\CHAPTER.TXT|MORE

Note that the symbol used is the pipe (|) symbol, not a colon (:).

Table 18-1
QUICK SUMMARY OF INTERNAL MS-DOS COMMANDS

Command	Function
COPY	Makes a duplicate copy of a file
CHDIR (CD)	Changes the current (working) directory
CLS	Clears the screen
DATE	Allows user to set the date
DEL (ERASE)	Removes a file from a disk
DIR	Lists the files in a directory
MKDIR (MD)	Makes a new directory
PATH	Changes the current path
PROMPT	Allows user to customize prompt
RENAME	Changes a filename
RMDIR (RD)	Removes a directory from a disk
TIME	Allows user to set current time
TYPE	Sends contents of a file to screen

EXTERNAL COMMANDS

External commands are not used quite as commonly as internal commands and are not part of the operating system kernel. Each external command has its own separate filename as part of the DOS files. To use these commands, the files for the commands must be in the current directory or the directory containing the commands must be in the system's current path (as described in the section on the PATH command) so the system will know where to look for the commands.

Some of the more commonly used commands are described below. The user should consult a DOS manual for more information about specific commands.

BACKUP

The BACKUP command makes a copy of specified files or directories, compressing them so fewer disks are used than with the COPY command. This procedure is essential to hard disk users, who should *always* have a backup of the information on their hard disk. Hard disks (floppies, too) sometimes crash and lose all of their data.

Older versions of DOS had a poorly-developed BACKUP function and experienced users usually had a utility for this process. Version 6.0 has a very usable backup system designed like the ones used by the utilities. It has pull-down menus and allows the user to specify files or directories to be backed up.

CHKDSK

The CHKDSK command performs routine checks of the status of a disk. It provides the user with a summary of the total space on the disk, the space available, what the space is being used for, total memory of the system, and available memory. It will also give the serial number of the disk.

DBLSPACE

DBLSPACE is a disk compression utility that is new with DOS 6.0. It allows DOS to compress files before writing them to a disk and uncompress them after reading them from a disk. With a compression ratio of approximately 1.8:1, this utility allows the user to store almost twice as much information on a given disk.

DEFRAG

As files are written to and deleted from a hard disk, it becomes fragmented. This means that files may be located in more than one sector on different parts of a disk. After a file is deleted, the space it was using is open to the next file saved to the disk. The new file may be longer (or shorter) than the deleted file. DOS will write some of the file in the space where the deleted file was located, and then write the rest of it to a new location. As more and more files are written this way, the disk operates slower than if each file was written to one location. The DEFRAG utility rewrites the entire disk with files all moved to one location. This speeds up access time when using the hard disk.

DISKCOPY

The DISKCOPY command copies the entire contents of a disk to another identical size and type disk. The command erases all of the information on the disk being copied to, if it has any. DISKCOPY will also format the disk being copied to, if it is not already formatted. If a computer has two of the same type disk drives, the command can be entered as

DISKCOPY A: B:

If the computer has only one disk drive of each type (as is most common on newer computers) then the user can enter

DISKCOPY A: A:

DOSSHELL

The shell program in DOS is its answer to the popular GUI environments many users prefer. A mouse and pull-down menus are used to execute commands and programs. The shell contains a directory tree of the current directory, a list of files in the current directory, a menu bar with pull-down menus, icons for changing to the various disk drives in the system, and a selection of utilities for the user. DOSSHELL is actually the name of the .EXE file that executes when the command is entered by the user.

Most users who use the shell include the DOSSHELL command as the last line of their AUTOEXEC.BAT file. This tells the computer to enter the shell after completing the startup procedure.

EDIT

In versions 5.0 and 6.0, DOS includes a text editor with pull-down menus for editing ASCII files, such as batch files, from the DOS prompt. The EDIT command activates this editor.

FDISK

The FDISK command is used to establish partitions in a hard disk. It is used when setting up a new hard disk or when changing the partitions in an existing hard disk. Either way, any information saved on the hard disk will be erased when running FDISK.

FORMAT

The FORMAT command prepares a disk for use by dividing it into sectors and tracks. It will erase any information that might be on the disk. The parameter is the drive. Switches include /S to make the formatted disk a system disk (with the DOS kernel on it), /V to prompt the user for a volume label on the disk, /Q to quickly format an already-formatted disk by erasing the file allocation table, and /B to save room for the system without making it a system disk. For example, to format a disk in drive A: and make it a system disk with a volume label, the user would enter:

    FORMAT A: /S /V

HELP

The HELP command is used when the computer user needs quick information about other DOS commands. The parameter is the command about which the user wants information. For example, when information about the TYPE command is needed, the user would enter

    HELP TYPE

and DOS would give the user a brief description of the command. The HELP command is not designed to replace the DOS manual, however.

MEMMAKER

Older versions of DOS recognized 640K as the maximum memory available in RAM. The first 640K is referred to as *conventional memory*. As programs started requiring more memory, a way to address more memory using DOS was needed. After conventional memory, DOS recognizes the next 384K as expanded memory. Any memory beyond that is referred to as extended memory.

The MEMMAKER program analyzes the memory available in a system and allocates DOS and other programs to maximize the memory available to the user. This procedure is important because many applications are designed to run in conventional memory only.

MORE

The MORE command is a filter command often used with the TYPE command to keep long files from scrolling off the screen. In newer versions of DOS, however, the MORE command can be used by itself to view large files. To view a file called CHAPTER.TXT, 24 lines at a time, the user would enter

    MORE<CHAPTER.TXT

and the file would show up on the screen with "—More—" shown on the last line. To view the next screen of information, the user would strike any key.

MSAV

The MSAV command activates the *virus protection* utility available in DOS 6.0, allowing the user to scan disks for viruses. The parameter for the command is the disk drive. DOS 6.0 also has a TSR program—VSAFE.COM— that a user can load using the AUTOEXEC.BAT file which will provide ongoing protection from the introduction of viruses through floppy disks.

PRINT

The PRINT command allows the user to make a printed copy of an ASCII text file. To print a copy of the AUTOEXEC.BAT file, for example, the user would enter

    PRINT C:\AUTOEXEC.BAT

and the PRINT command will send the specified file to the printer. Of course, the same result can be obtained by using the TYPE command and redirecting it to the printer. (TYPE C:\AUTOEXEC.BATPRN)

RESTORE

In versions of DOS prior to 6.0, the RESTORE command is used to replace files copied using the BACKUP command. The parameters are the drive containing the disks the information was backed up to and the destination of the files to be restored. To restore files backed up to drive B: from C:\WPROC, the user would enter

    RESTORE B: C:\WPROC

and the system would copy the backed up files from drive B: to the C:\WPROC directory. DOS will replace any files with the same name on C:\WPROC with the backed up files, so users must be careful.

In DOS 6.0, the restore function has become more integrated with the BACKUP function, complete with pull-down menus for selecting drives and directories.

SYS

The SYS command copies the hidden system files (IO.SYS & MSDOS.SYS) to the specified disk. The parameter is the disk drive specification. For example, to copy the system files to a disk in drive A:, the user would enter

    SYS A:

The SYS command does not copy COMMAND.COM, the other file necessary to make a disk a true system disk.

TREE

The TREE command lists all of the directories and subdirectories on a disk. The parameter is the disk drive specification. TREE can also be used to list the files within the subdirectories by using the /F switch. To list all the files in all of the directories and subdirectories on drive A:, for example, the user would enter

    TREE A: /F

UNDELETE

The UNDELETE command allows users to rectify a common error: erasing an important file by mistake. The parameter is the directory from which the file was erased. Undeleting a file is possible because the DEL or ERASE command does not actually erase the file from a disk, just its address from the file allocation table (FAT). As long as no other file has been written over it, a deleted file remains on the disk. When the user enters an UNDELETE command, such as

UNDELETE A:\

DOS will list the deleted files that can be recovered. It will prompt the user about whether or not to restore each deleted file.

Table 18-2
QUICK SUMMARY OF EXTERNAL MS-DOS COMMANDS

Command	Function
BACKUP	Makes backup copies of files/directories
CHKDSK	Checks disk space and system memory
DBLSPACE	Compresses information on a disk
DEFRAG	Rewrites disk files to defragment
DISKCOPY	Makes a duplicate of a disk
DOSSHELL	Allows user to use the shell interface
EDIT	Allows user to edit an ASCII file
FDISK	Partitions a hard disk
FORMAT	Sets up a disk to receive information
HELP	Provides information about DOS commands
MEMMAKER	Optimizes available memory of a system
MORE	Stops output at 24 lines (one screenful)
MSAV	Scans a disk to detect viruses
PRINT	Prints the contents of a file
RESTORE	Restores files backed up with DOS 5.0 or earlier
SYS	Loads the system files on a disk
TREE	Provides a list of directories and subdirectories
UNDELETE	Restores a file that has been removed from a disk

ERROR MESSAGES

DOS has two versions of error messages. When the shell is being used, a command error will result in the error window being shown with the type of error and options for the user, usually including: try again, don't try again, OK, Cancel, and Help. When an error is made in a command line entry, the type of error is shown on the screen and options may or may not be given, depending on the message.

Some of the common error messages and prompts are given below, with the reason for the message and possible solutions to the problem.

Abort, Retry, Fail?

Abort, Ignore, Retry, Fail?

These prompts follow a number of error messages, including disk drive not ready, and printer not found. A prompt selection can be chosen by typing the first letter. The ignore and fail options are used mainly by computer programmers.

Problem: DOS can't read a disk or communicate with a peripheral, such as a printer.

Solution: First, try to fix the problem, such as closing the door on the disk drive. Then type R several times. Then try A. Most users should avoid I or F as this can result in data loss.

Bad command or filename

Problem: DOS can't recognize the command or filename typed. This is the most common error message. Misspellings, forgetting to use the DOS command before the filename, or being in the wrong directory are common reasons.

Solution: Check spelling of command or file, do a DIR to check which directory is current and the location of the desired file.

Attempted write protect violation

Problem: Disk is locked by the write/protect tab or switch.

Solution: Remove write-protect tab from 5.25-inch disk, move write-protect switch on 3.5-inch disk.

File not found

Problem: The DOS command worked, but the file name specified is not in the directory specified.

Solution: Check filename spelling, do a DIR to see if file is where expected.

Invalid directory

Problem: DOS can't find directory named in the command.

Solution: Check spelling of directory name, do a DIR or TREE to see
if directory exists or if the right path is selected.

Non-system disk or disk error
(Replace and strike any key when ready)

Problem: The disk being accessed does not have the system on it.
Usually occurs because a data disk was left in the A:
drive when booting the computer.

Solution: Reboot with a good system disk or remove data disk from
drive A: so the computer will go to C: where the system
is located.

UTILITIES FOR
MS-DOS COMPUTERS

Over the years, experts have found areas in which they needed a little
more than DOS was providing. Several software vendors have met these
needs with programs called utilities. Utilities are designed to allow users
to optimize their existing hardware and software by making it more powerful
and easier to use. In turn, DOS has included some of these capabilities in
its newer versions and will continue to do so. In many cases, however, the
DOS version does not have all of the features available in some of the
specialized programs from other vendors.

Utilities programs may be very simple or very complex. Their functions
may be very specific or general. Some utilities programs fall into the
expensive category of commercial software. Others may be user-supported
software or freeware.

Common functions of utilities software include file management, hardware diagnostics/optimization, virus protection, memory management, and
menu building. These functions are described below. Each description includes the appropriate DOS utility name (if any) and the name of popular
programs by other vendors.

FILE MANAGEMENT

File management refers to the ability to copy, view, delete, move, and rename files. Also included is the ability to undelete files. Many utilities offer file management. Most don't do anything special that can't be done using DOS, they just offer the user another way to do these things that the user may find a little easier. DOS has developed its shell in later versions to perform basically the same function.

Two of the most popular utilities programs are Symantec's Norton Utilities, designed by computer guru Peter Norton, and Central Point Software's PC Tools. Both are general programs with a variety of functions and excellent file management capabilities.

HARDWARE DIAGNOSTICS/ OPTIMIZATION

Hardware diagnostics/optimization software includes programs that analyze disk drives to check for defects, such as Norton Utilities, with its Disk Doctor program. Disk Doctor has more features and is much easier to use than the DOS programs used for disk diagnostics and repair. Some users run Disk Doctor as part of the startup procedure each time the system is booted.

This category also includes utilities software that is used for disk data

Figure 18-7. Addstor's Superstor is a popular disk compression utility.

compression, such as Stac Electronic's Stacker and Addstor's Superstor PRO. These programs led to DOS 6.0's DBLSPACE utility. Also included in this category would be disk defragmentation utilities such as Norton's SpeedDisk and PC Tools' Compress, another feature DOS 6.0 has included with its DEFRAG utility.

VIRUS PROTECTION

Computer viruses are prevalent in systems around the world. Virus protection is important to avoid loss of programs and data. With version 6.0, DOS incorporated this function with its MSAV and VSAFE utilities. Other excellent virus protection can be obtained from the commercial software Norton Antivirus, Central Point Anti-Virus for DOS, and VIREX, and the user-supported F-PROT.

MEMORY MANAGEMENT

Getting the most out of available memory has been important to users

Figure 18-8. WordPerfect Corporation's Library program provides users with the ability to easily set up and edit menus.

for many years, especially as programs became larger and DOS still would only recognize 640K as conventional memory. DOS 6.0 includes the MEMMAKER function to optimize available memory. Other programs that do this well include Qualita's 386MAX, Quarterdeck Office System's QEMM-386, and, for networked systems, Helix Software's NetRoom.

MENU BUILDING

Menu building programs allow the user to customize his or her working environment by developing menus from which to select applications. Most of the large applications software developers have menu programs available, including WordPerfect, Lotus Development, Microsoft, and many others. Also, many functional programs can be found from shareware distributors and from computer bulletin boards as freeware. Experienced DOS users often develop their own menus using ASCII text files and batch files.

CHAPTER QUESTIONS

1. What are the five most popular operating systems/operating environments in use today? Which one is used by the most people on their personal computers?

2. Briefly describe the three functions of an operating system?

3. What are the three ways operating systems can be classified? Briefly describe each.

4. What are the three system files in MS-DOS?

5. What is the purpose of the CONFIG.SYS file?

6. How does the AUTOEXEC.BAT file save time for the computer user?

7. What is a file?

8. How many letters long may an MS-DOS filename be?

9. What symbols can *not* be used in filenames?

10. What tells the user if a file is an executable file?

11. Write a short batch file that will: (a) list the files in drive A:, (b) clear the screen (after letting the user see the file list), (c) show the contents of a file in drive A: called MENU.TXT, and (d) put in a comment with the filename and purpose that the user cannot see when executing the file.

12. Describe four basic utilities functions. Include the DOS command (if any) for activating these utilities and other programs that have these capabilities.

13. Using the descriptions in the chapter, give the result of each of the following commands:

   a. DIR A:\DATA /W

   b. TYPE C:\WPROC\DATA\CHAPTER.TXTA:\C1.TXT

   c. TREE A: /F

   d. MORE > C:\WPROC\DATA\CHAPTER.TXT

   e. CD..

   f. PROMPT

   g. MD BULLDOG

   h. DISKCOPY B: B:

   i. FORMAT A: /S

Chapter 19

WORD PROCESSING

Word processing is far and away the most common use of personal computers. Over 80 percent of personal computers are used at least partly for word processing. Most offices have one or more computers dedicated exclusively to word processing. Even people who use other applications often spend most of their time word processing.

For several reasons, using a word processing application is more efficient than using a typewriter. With a computer, written documents can be saved and reloaded later for revisions. Similar letters sent to several different clients do not have to be retyped entirely. The user can take advantage of the computer's speed in checking spelling and grammar, and also performing other functions. The computer's flexibility, combined with that of the printer, allows the user to customize letters with graphics and different text sizes and functions.

This chapter describes some of the common functions and features of word processing application software. The interaction between the word processing application and computer hardware, especially printers, is also discussed.

OBJECTIVES

1. Define word processing.

2. Describe the major functions of word processors.

3. Describe the common features of word processors.

4. Describe selected advanced features of word processors.

5. Describe a common page of paper for use in a word processing program.

6. Discuss terms associated with printer typefaces, typestyles and fonts.

WORD PROCESSING AS A COMPUTER APPLICATION

Word processing is the automated processing or manipulation of words using a specialized application program designed to compose, revise, print, and file written documents. It is a specialized form of data processing where the data are characters and words.

In word processing, characters are typed on a keyboard or input into the computer through other hardware. The characters can be grouped into words, sentences, paragraphs, and pages. The largest grouping is called a *document*. Each document generally is stored as a file, although very large documents may be split into several files.

WORD PROCESSING SOFTWARE

Word processing is accomplished by using a word processing application program. Each software package has particular features and interfaces that make it unique, but most have the standard set of features discussed later in this chapter.

The most commonly used word processing package today is WordPerfect, developed by the WordPerfect Corporation. It is a very powerful program with many capabilities. Other highly-rated and popular programs are

TERMS

ASCII files	fixed-pitch font	page description
bitmapped font	font	languages
blocking	font renderer	proportionally-spaced
characters per inch (cpi)	footers	font
code	grammar checker	scalable font
concordance file	headers	scrolling
document	macro	search and replace
document layout	margins	text features
editing	merging documents	thesaurus
		undelete

Figure 19-1. WordPerfect (left) is the most popular word processing program. Microsoft
Word (right) is the second most popular word processing program.

Microsoft Word, Ami Professional, WordStar and MacWrite. Many other
programs are available as well.

When choosing a word processing program, the user should look for
the number of features in relation to the cost, the stability of the vendor,
and the support offered by the vendor. One reason WordPerfect is such a
popular program is the 24-hour help line offered by the company to assist
users who are having difficulties.

COMPUTER HARDWARE REQUIREMENTS

To run the latest versions of word processing applications, the computer
must have a hard disk to store the program files. A minimum of 30MB in
storage space is recommended, although more will probably be necessary
if the computer is used for other applications.

Most word processors make use of spooling to reduce the amount of
RAM necessary to operate the program. A minimum of 640K of RAM will
handle the program and most files. However, for those users with large files,
1MB of RAM is recommended. Newer versions will probably have more
features and require probably 2MB to 4MB of RAM.

Table 19-1.
POPULAR WORD PROCESSING APPLICATIONS SOFTWARE PACKAGES

Package	MS-DOS	Windows	Macintosh
WordPerfect	Yes	Yes	Yes
Microsoft Word	Yes	Yes	Yes
WordStar	Yes	No	No
MacWrite	No	No	Yes
Ami Professional	No	Yes	No
MultiMate	Yes	No	No
PC Write	Yes	No	No
Leading Edge	Yes	No	No
DisplayWrite	Yes	No	No
Q and A Write	Yes	No	No

Word processing can be done on monochrome monitors, which is a good choice because they are considered easy on the eyes. The computer buyer should be careful, however, to make sure other applications can also use the monitor; many other types of programs require a color monitor.

A printer is a must when using a word processing package. The capabilities of the printer are actually one of the most limiting factors in using the software. For letters and documents to be sent outside of the agribusiness, a minimum quality printer would be a 24-pin dot matrix. A true letter quality printer such as a laser or daisy wheel is recommended. Laser printers offer the most flexibility and best quality, but are more expensive. For word processing of text only, a daisy wheel is sufficient, however, graphics and some text features will not be available. Also, in a business where several people are in the same office, laser or inkjet printers are good choices because they operate much more quietly than impact printers like daisy wheel and dot matrix.

MAJOR FUNCTIONS OF WORD PROCESSORS

Word processing applications can be used for almost anything put down in writing. The five major functions of a word processing application are creating, editing, formatting and printing a document, and also document/file handling.

Figure 19-2. A daisy wheel printer gives high-quality text, but will not handle all of the features of a powerful word processor.

CREATING

Creating a document involves opening, naming, and typing or keystroking it. Most word processors start with a blank screen that allows the user to begin typing the new document immediately.

EDITING

Editing a document means making changes to an existing document. This function includes deleting, overwriting, moving, and inserting additional text.

FORMATTING

Formatting a document refers to the word processor's ability to change the look of a document. This includes alignment or positioning of the text.

```
Format

    1 - Line
            Hyphenation                    Line Spacing
            Justification                  Margins Left/Right
            Line Height                    Tab Set
            Line Numbering                 Widow/Orphan Protection

    2 - Page
            Center Page (top to bottom)    Page Numbering
            Force Odd/Even Page            Paper Size/Type/Labels
            Headers and Footers            Suppress
            Margins Top/Bottom

    3 - Document
            Display Pitch                  Redline Method
            Initial Codes/Font             Summary

    4 - Other
            Advance                        Printer Functions
            Conditional End of Page        Underline Spaces/Tabs
            Decimal Characters             Border Options
            Language                       End Centering/Alignment
            Overstrike
Selection: 0
```

Figure 19-3. The format menu from WordPerfect.

```
05-26-93  02:24p            Directory C:\WP51\*.*
Document size:    40,680    Free:  1,458,176 Used:   6,268,682      Files:      108

   .    Current   <Dir>                     °    ..    Parent    <Dir>
 LEARN    .        <Dir>   03-19-92 10:57a ° 8514A    .VRS     5,226   03-09-92 12:00p
 ALTB   .WPM          73   05-11-93 10:22a ° ALTC     .WPM        75   05-16-93 09:21a
 ALTD   .WPM          67   03-19-92 07:03p ° ALTH     .WPM       128   06-30-92 07:26a
 ALTI   .WPM          99   03-11-92 07:54p ° ALTM     .WPM       285   03-18-93 09:57a
 ALTP   .WPM         105   08-28-92 01:25p ° ALTQ     .WPM       107   01-25-93 08:44a
 ALTS   .WPM         257   06-24-92 08:59a ° ATI      .VRS    37,635   03-09-92 12:00p
 CALC   .WPM       7,972   03-09-92 12:00p ° CHARACTR.DOC    47,008   03-09-92 12:00p
 CHARMAP .TST     39,271   03-09-92 12:00p ° CODES    .WPM    28,149   03-09-92 12:00p
 CONVERT .EXE    109,591   03-09-92 12:00p ° CURSOR   .COM     1,452   03-09-92 12:00p
 EDIT   .WPM      10,826   03-09-92 12:00p ° EGA512   .FRS     3,584   03-09-92 12:00p
 EGAITAL .FRS      3,584   03-09-92 12:00p ° EGASMC   .FRS     3,584   03-09-92 12:00p
 EGAUND  .FRS      3,584   03-09-92 12:00p ° ENDFOOT  .WPM     4,169   03-09-92 12:00p
 ENHANCED.WPK      3,837   03-09-92 12:00p ° EPFX286E.PRS    11,746   03-19-92 11:05a
 EQUATION.WPK      2,974   03-09-92 12:00p ° FASTKEYS.WPK     2,999   03-09-92 12:00p
 FIXBIOS .COM         50   03-09-92 12:00p ° FOOTEND  .WPM     3,829   03-09-92 12:00p
 GENIUS  .VRS     12,885   03-09-92 12:00p ° GRAB     .COM    16,450   03-09-92 12:00p
 GRAPHCNV.EXE    122,368   03-09-92 12:00p ° HPLASEII.PRS    59,587   01-14-93 10:02a
 HPLASIII.PRS    145,300   07-04-91 12:09a   HRF12    .FRS    49,152   03-09-92 12:00p

1 Retrieve; 2 Delete; 3 Move/Rename; 4 Print; 5 Short/Long Display;
6 Look; 7 Other Directory; 8 Copy; 9 Find; N Name Search: 6
```

Figure 19-4. By pressing F5 (function key 5) in WordPerfect, the program gives a list of
            subdirectories and files in the current directory, with a menu at the bottom for
            selecting file handling commands.

Examples include setting margins, line spacing, page breaks, tab stops and many other features.

PRINTING

Printing means producing hard copy on paper from a document loaded and active in the word processor or a document stored on a disk.

HANDLING

Handling refers to the file management capabilities of the word processing application. By interacting with the computer's operating system, the word processor can copy, delete, move or rename files. Some word processors also have a view capability, allowing the user to look at a document without having to load the document into the word processor.

COMMON FEATURES OF WORD PROCESSORS

Although all word processors operate a little differently and with a few different functions, there are some features which are common to most.

CURSOR MOVEMENT

As mentioned earlier, the cursor indicates where the user is typing on the computer's screen. Word processors make use of the arrow cursor movement keys to allow the user to move the cursor up, down, right, and left. The page down and page up keys allow the user to move through a document one page (or screen) at a time. The home key usually moves the cursor to the beginning of a line. The end key moves the cursor to the end of a line.

Many programs also allow for more advanced movement. In Word-Perfect, using the control key with the left and right arrow keys can move the cursor one word at a time. Using the home key with the up or down arrow keys will move the cursor one screen at a time. The control key plus the home key allows the user to specify which page in the document to go to. Pressing the home key twice plus an up arrow key moves the cursor to the first line of the document. Doing the same with the down arrow key moves the cursor to the last line of the document.

HELP

Most word processors have a help command or function key to provide the user with a summary of commands and their functions. Although it does not replace a user's manual, the help screen can sometimes remind the user of the capabilities that go with commands.

```
Up/Down Arrow

        Moves the cursor up/down one line.

If you press:                       The cursor will move to . . .
Home, Up/Down Arrow                 The top/bottom of the screen.
Home, Home, Up/Down Arrow           The beginning/end of the document.
Home, Home, Home, Up Arrow          The beginning of the document before any codes.

Esc, n, Up Arrow ()                 n lines up.
Esc, n, Down Arrow ()               n lines down.

GoTo, Up Arrow ()                   The top of the current page or column.
GoTo, Down Arrow ()                 The bottom of the page or column.




Selection: 0                                    (Press ENTER to exit Help)
```

Figure 19-5. A summary of the cursor movement capabilities of the up/down arrows in WordPerfect. (Taken from a WordPerfect Help screen.)

SCROLLING

As the document is typed, it appears on the screen. When the screen gets full, the computer stores information in memory and gives the user a clean, fresh area on which to type. *Scrolling* allows the user to view the information ahead and back, as well as sideways. Most video screens display 24 lines, with 80 characters or less on one line, depending on the size of text used. Most documents are over 24 lines long and some type sizes allow more than 80 characters per line. In either case, scrolling allows the user to see all of the document on the screen, although usually not all at one time.

DELETING/INSERTING

Text can be deleted in a word processor in several ways. Pressing the backspace key deletes text to the left of the cursor one character at a time. Pressing the delete key deletes the character under the cursor and moves the next character to the right to the position under the cursor. Most word processors have a *blocking* or marking function, that allows a section of text to be blocked so the entire block can be deleted.

Most word processors allow for two methods of typing. The typeover method allows the user to type over existing text, deleting the old text while typing the new text. The insert method allows the user to type in new text while pushing any existing text to the right. This feature is usually controlled by the insert key. Text may also be inserted into a document from another document file stored on a disk.

COPYING AND MOVING

The blocking feature mentioned above can also be used to move or copy a section of text to another location in the existing document or another document. Text may be blocked and moved using the mouse or a function key command and arrow keys.

SEARCHING/REPLACING

Searching is the ability of the word processor to search through a document looking for a word or *code*. This feature is especially useful for documents which will include a glossary. The user can insert a code, such as italics, for each word in the text to be included in the glossary. Then a search for the italics code will take the user to each word to be included in the glossary.

Another time-saving part of this feature is the *search and replace* capability. The user may decide to use one word instead of another, or may want to replace a capitalized word with lower case. The computer will search for the word and replace it. The user can usually choose to confirm each replacement or allow the computer to replace the word throughout the entire document without confirmation. For example, the word "operator" could be replaced with the word "user" throughout the text, or just in particular instances.

TEXT FEATURES

Commands that change the text from normal to text with special characteristics are grouped together and called *text features*. These features allow the user to emphasize certain parts of the text. Text features include changing size, underlining, capitalizing, boldfacing, superscripts, subscripts, and italics.

Although the word processor has the ability to create all or almost all of the features mentioned above, the printer may not. This is a common way in which the printer may limit the capabilities of the word processor.

DOCUMENT LAYOUT

Document layout refers to the commands used to position text and/or graphics in certain ways. These commands include centering, determining and changing margins, justifying margins, tab settings, paragraph indentions, setting spacing between lines and paragraphs and many others. In some programs, these settings are displayed in a "status line/bar" or "ruler."

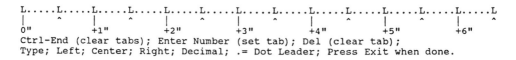

```
L.....L.....L.....L.....L.....L.....L.....L.....L.....L.....L.....L
|       ^     |       ^     |       ^     |       ^     |       ^     |       ^
0"          +1"         +2"         +3"         +4"         +5"         +6"
Ctrl-End (clear tabs); Enter Number (set tab); Del (clear tab);
Type; Left; Center; Right; Decimal; .= Dot Leader; Press Exit when done.
```

Figure 19-6. The tab ruler in WordPerfect. Each "L" represents a tab stop, with an editing commands menu below the ruler.

CHECKING SPELLING

Most word processors come with a built-in spell checker. When the command is given, the word processor checks each word in the document to see if the word is included in its dictionary. This feature is very useful for poor spellers and/or poor typists. What the spell checker will not do, however, is check to see if the correct version of the word or the correct word is used. For example, when the user means to use the word "from" but instead types "form," the spell checker does not indicate that the word is incorrect. Likewise, when "too" is supposed to be used, but "to" is used instead, the spell checker will not catch it.

Some users get frustrated by the number of words the spell checker does not have in its dictionary, but this problem can be solved. When a word that is spelled correctly is not recognized by the spell checker, the operator generally has the opportunity to add it to the dictionary. (This feature should be used carefully.) Also, supplemental dictionaries with specialized words are available to increase the words in a particular user's dictionary. For example, an agricultural scientist may buy a special dictionary that includes correctly spelled words used in scientific classification of plants and animals.

PRINT OPTIONS

Most word processors offer the user a variety of print options. These include printing all or selected pages of a document, printing a document from a disk, selecting the quality of print, switching between types of printers, and printing or omitting graphics. These features allow the user to save time and computer paper.

ASCII FILES

Some word processors use *ASCII files* exclusively, but most save files

```
Print

        1 - Full Document
        2 - Page
        3 - Document on Disk
        4 - Control Printer
        5 - Multiple Pages
        6 - View Document
        7 - Initialize Printer


Options

        S - Select Printer            HP LaserJet III
        B - Binding Offset            0"
        N - Number of Copies          1
        U - Multiple Copies Generated by  WordPerfect
        G - Graphics Quality          Medium
        T - Text Quality              High




Selection: 0
```

Figure 19-7. The print options menu available in WordPerfect.

created by the word processor as word-processor-text files, to maintain the various codes included in the formatting of the document. These word processors should also have the capability of importing or exporting files in what is known as ASCII or DOS format, with the specific codes of the word processor not included.

This feature is important because ASCII files can be viewed using the DOS TYPE command and, in the case of batch files, executed by the operating system. In addition, ASCII files can be transferred from one type of operating system to another without problems. Users who wish to type a document and then transport it over a network should use this feature.

THESAURUS

The *thesaurus* allows the user to mark a word and then obtain a list of synonyms (and sometimes antonyms) for a word. Most word processors with a thesaurus will allow the user to replace the marked word with one from the thesaurus by typing a corresponding number or letter.

The thesaurus for a particular program will be limited by the number of words/uses stored in the thesaurus file, but many programs have extensive capabilities. In addition, some programs offer specialized thesaurus files for different types of users.

UNDELETE

When a user deletes text, using either the delete key, the backspace key, or the blocking command, some word processors do not automatically delete it from memory. The information is stored in a buffer in RAM, and the user may recall the text using the *undelete* feature. Deleted text typically remains in the buffer until replaced with newly deleted information. Some word processors will keep three to five deletions separate in the buffer, with newly-deleted text replacing the oldest deletion.

ADVANCED FEATURES OF WORD PROCESSORS

While almost every commercial word processing program has some version of the common features mentioned above, some of the more popular (and more expensive) word processors have features that are advanced beyond standard features. Some of these are described below.

ADVANCED LAYOUT FEATURES

Advanced layout features include the ability to imbed *headers* and *footers*, *widow/orphan protection*, re-numbering pages in the middle of a document, WYSIWYG viewing of pages without having to print them, incorporation of graphics, changing paper sizes and types, and options about printing page numbers, to name a few.

```
Format: Page

       1 - Center Page (top to bottom)      No

       2 - Force Odd/Even Page

       3 - Headers

       4 - Footers

       5 - Margins - Top                     1"
                     Bottom                  1"

       6 - Page Numbering

       7 - Paper Size                        8.5" x 11"
                     Type                    Standard
                     Labels

       8 - Suppress (this page only)



   Selection: 0
```

Figure 19-8. The page format menu from WordPerfect. Note the ability to select different paper sizes, headers, footers, and page number positions.

GRAPHICS

The ability to import graphics into a document separates the most powerful word processors from the rest. This feature typically uses a graphics file that is separate from the document file and merges the two files when printing. Some programs have extensive graphics files that come with the program or that can be bought separately. Some have the ability to import a graphic generated by another program. WordPerfect features a grab utility that allows the user to copy a graphic from the computer screen and save it as a WordPerfect graphics file.

COLUMNS

The columns feature allows the user to type in two or more columns on the same page. The columns may be newspaper format, where the text in column one carries over to the next column, or parallel format, where the text in one column continues over to the next page in the same column.

Number of Cows:	34				
DIRECT EXPENSES	UNIT	PRICE	QUANTITY	DOLLARS	COST PER COW
INTEREST	DOLLAR	$8,700.00	8%	$696.00	$20.47
BULL	HEAD	$1,500.00	1	$1,500.00	$44.12
PASTURE	ACRE	$10.00	200	$2,000.00	$58.82
MINERALS	BAG	$10.00	16	$160.00	$4.71
PROTEIN MEAL	TON	$140.00	6.5	$910.00	$26.76
VETERINARY COW	HEAD	$15.00	34	$510.00	$15.00
MARKETING	DOLLAR	$0.04	11623	$464.92	$13.67
CHECK-OFF	HEAD	$1.00	31	$31.00	$0.91
GRAIN	TON	$145.00	7.5	$1,087.50	$31.99
VETERINARY CALF	HEAD	$8.00	31	$248.00	$7.29
VETERINARY BULL	HEAD	$15.00	2	$30.00	$0.88
REPAIRS/EQUIP.	YEAR	$1,000.00	1	$1,000.00	$29.41
TOTAL				$8,637.42	$254.03
Courtesy, M. Woods, Johnson Milling Company, Clinton, Mississippi.					

Figure 19-9. A table with a file imported from a spreadsheet.

TABLES

The tables feature automatically sets up tables with a specified number of rows and columns. A good word processor will allow the user to import a spreadsheet or database file into the word processor in column format. Some of the more popular word processors can import selected spreadsheets without losing any of the spreadsheet features. For example, in WordPerfect, a Lotus 1-2-3 file can be imported maintaining the same characteristics found in the spreadsheet. WordPerfect even keeps the formulas and relationships between parts of the spreadsheet intact.

GRAMMAR CHECKER

A *grammar checker* picks up the editing/proofreading function where spell checkers leave off. In addition to checking spelling, the grammar checker will check the meaning of words to see if they are used correctly in a sentence, check for passive writing, and grammatical and punctuation errors. Very few word processors have this feature built into the program. A couple of very good supplemental programs are available, however. Two of the most popular are Grammatik and RightWriter. RightWriter includes a copy of Strunk and White's *Elements of Style.*

MERGING DOCUMENTS

Merging documents requires the word processor to work like a database. A file containing fields of information can be merged with a file containing field variables to create multiple documents or pages without having to retype each one with just a couple of changes. The most common use is the merging of address and letter files. One file has each person's name and address while the other file may have a letter with field variables which are filled when the file is merged with the address file. (See Figure 19-10.) Some programs can be used in conjunction with a data base manager to accomplish the same result.

SPLIT SCREEN/WINDOWS

Use of a split screen or windows allows the user to work with more than one document at a time. In some programs, two documents can be loaded but only one shown on the screen at one time. A key is designated to switch back and forth between documents. Other programs allow the user to split the screen to see two (or more) documents at once. Word processors running under Microsoft Windows can open several documents at once.

MACROS

A *macro* is a file created with a set of commands or keystrokes that is combined into one keystroke to save the user time. Macros work on the same principle as batch files. In word processors, macros are generally used for commonly repeated keystrokes. For example, a user may create a macro

```
Database File (Secondary File)

Alicia Harvester(END FIELD)
133 Combine Road(END FIELD)
Farming Village, MS 39999(END FIELD)
(END RECORD)
_____
Johnny Appleseed(END FIELD)
Route 3(END FIELD)
Tractortown, OH 43210(END FIELD)
(END RECORD)
_____
```

```
Text File (Primary File)

                                   November 21, 1993

(FIELD)1~
(FIELD)2~
(FIELD)3~


Dear (FIELD)1~:

      You have been selected to participate in the National Agriscience
Project Contest sponsored by American Farm Bureau................
```

```
Merged File (Page 1)

                                   November 21, 1993

Alicia Harvester
133 Combine Road
Farming Village, MS 39999

Dear Alicia Harvester:

      You have been selected to participate in the National Agriscience
Project Contest sponsored by American Farm Bureau................
```

Figure 19-10. Parts of two files ready for merging are shown. The fields in the database file (secondary file) above are incorporated into the field variables in the text file (primary file).

with his or her signature line for letters to avoid typing in the signature line every time. Instead of typing "sincerely, name, and title" the user would type one or two keys to get the same result. In WordPerfect, a signature line might be stored in the macro file ALTS.WPM, and the user would type S while holding the Alt key to run the macro (which would print the signature line).

In addition to user-defined macros, some programs come with built-in macros containing commonly used sequences. These may include an on-screen calculator, print routines, and help screens. Users may use these "as-is" or edit them using a macro editor.

AUTOMATIC SAVE

In the setup menu of some word processors, the user can designate a set time when the word processor saves the current file to a disk. For example, if the user has designated 10 in the automatic save selection, then the word processor will save the current file after 10 minutes. This feature is very useful for those who forget to save regularly!

If a power loss occurs and the computer reboots, the word processor has the automatically saved file available for the user. This prevents losing work that wasn't saved. If the user exits from a document, the word processor erases the automatically saved file and restarts the clock when a new document is loaded.

```
Setup: Backup

        Timed backup files are deleted when you exit WP normally.  If you
        have a power or machine failure, you will find the backup file in the
        backup directory indicated in Setup: Location of Files.

        Backup Directory

    1 - Timed Document Backup              Yes
        Minutes Between Backups            15

        Original backup will save the original document with a .BK! extension
        whenever you replace it during a Save or Exit.

    2 - Original Document Backup           No




    Selection: 0
```

Figure 19-11. The backup screen from WordPerfect's setup menu. Note that this user wishes to have the current file saved automatically every 15 minutes.

INDEX CREATION

Some word processors give the user the opportunity to create an index of important words used in a document. The program may do this in one of two ways. One way is to have the user mark the words in the document with an index code. At the end of the document, the user can give the index command and the word processor will generate an index that is alphabetized with page numbers after the words.

Another way is for the user to create a *concordance file* for the document. The concordance file contains a list of the important words. When using the index command, the user types the name of the concordance file and the program uses the words in the concordance file to generate the index. The first method is usually preferred because the concordance file method will list the page numbers of every occurrence of the words in the document, whereas the user may only want to index certain occurrences of the word.

THE WORD PROCESSED PAGE

A standard page of typing paper is 8.5 inches wide and 11 inches long. Using defaults of 10 *characters per inch (cpi)* and 6 lines per inch, the page will hold 66 lines of 85 characters each with no *margins*.

With standard default margins of 1-inch on the top, bottom, and each side, the page will hold 54 lines of 65 characters each. If 12 cpi characters are used, lines with a 1-inch margin on each side will hold 78 characters. (This is probably the justification for making a computer screen 80 characters wide.)

Other common margins are 1.5 inches for the left margin, especially when the printed pages are to be bound. Some style manuals require a bottom margin of 8 lines, or 1.33 inches.

PRINTER TYPEFACES, TYPESTYLES AND FONTS

Every computer printer comes with one or more built-in fonts. The word processor has drivers for different printers that allow it to work with the printer. When a different printer is selected, the word processor may have to change the document layout to fit the fonts available to the new printer. The following should help the reader understand what is meant by the term font.

- The typeface is a specific design for a set of letters. Common typefaces include Courier, Prestige, Times-Roman, and Helvetica. There are hundreds of different typefaces.

- A typestyle is a particular variation of a typeface. For example, a printer may have Prestige normal, Prestige bold, and Prestige italic.

- A *font* is a complete alphabet of a typestyle in one size. The size is usually designated in characters per inch (cpi) or point sizes. A point is equal to 1/72 of an inch, so a 12 cpi font is roughly equivalent to a 10 point font.

FONT DESCRIPTIONS

Various terms are used to describe fonts. One of these is serif, which refers to the extensions (or finishing strokes) on each letter in some typefaces. For example, Times-Roman has serifs. Sans-serif refers to a font without serifs. Helvetica is a sans-serif font.

```
Printer Fonts
```

Courier 10 cpi (normal)
Courier 10 cpi (bold)
Courier 10 cpi (italic)
Prestige Elite 10 point (normal)
Prestige Elite 10 point (bold)
Prestige Elite 10 point (italic)
Times Roman 12 point (normal)
Times Roman 12 point (italic)
Times Roman 14 point (bold)
Helvetica 12 point (normal)
Helvetica 12 point (italic)
Helvetica 14 point (bold)
Universal Scalable 18 point (bold, italic)
Universal Scalable 22 point (normal)

Figure 19-12. An example of selected fonts. Note that Helvetica and Universal Scalable are sans-serif fonts, while Courier, Prestige Elite, and Times-Roman have serifs.

Fonts may also be described based on letter spacing. A *fixed-pitch font* uses the same space on a page for each character, regardless of the actual space the character occupies. A *proportionally-spaced font* varies the space given to each letter based on the width of the letter.

Another way to describe fonts is by how they are developed and interpreted by the printer. In a *bitmapped font*, each character is described as a pattern of dots in a specific point size. The font must be available in a certain point size before it can be used. A *scalable font* has each character described as a mathematical formula. The user can designate any size type by changing the point size. Scalable fonts require the printer to have a *font renderer*, a scheme to interpret the mathematical formula into a printable character. For this reason, scalable fonts usually take longer to print than bitmapped fonts.

PAGE DESCRIPTION LANGUAGES

Printers are often described by the *page description languages* they can use to interact with software. Page description languages are programming languages that describe the placement and appearance of text and graphics on a page. For laser printers, the most common are Adobe PostScript, Hewlett-Packard Printer Control Language (HP PCL), and Hewlett-Packard Graphics Language (HP-GL).

Adobe PostScript was developed as a common language for describing pages to almost any output device, including printers, typesetters, and slidemakers. It has been the language of choice in the publishing industry for several years. Adobe PostScript delivers high-quality text and graphics and supports thousands of fonts and many software applications.

HP PCL was developed for HP LaserJet printers. The HP LaserJet III and IV use PCL 5, which is similar to PostScript. HP GL is a new language designed to improve the graphics capabilities of Hewlett-Packard printers. The combination of HP PCL 5 and HP GL give these printers a very flexible language.

CHAPTER QUESTIONS

1. How do word processing programs work?

2. What is the most popular word processing program in use today?

3. What type of computer would you buy to use primarily for word processing? Give specifications and justify your choices.

4. Briefly describe the five major functions of word processors.

5. Describe six common features of word processors.

6. Describe six advanced features of word processors.

7. Describe a typical page of a word processed document.

8. What is the difference between a typeface, a typestyle, and a font?

9. What is the difference between a bitmapped font and a scalable font?

Chapter 20

ELECTRONIC SPREADSHEETS/ RECORDKEEPING

The paper spreadsheet has been used in accounting for many years. It consists of a series of columns and rows, with space for column and row headings to keep track of accounts.

In 1979, Dan Bricklin and Bob Frankston introduced VisiCalc, the first electronic spreadsheet, designed to run on an Apple II computer. The idea was simple, to create an electronic version of the paper spreadsheet that had been a standard for decades. The introduction of VisiCalc is probably the most important reason that computers have become popular for businesses.

The flexibility and powerful features of the modern electronic spreadsheet continue to make it a popular choice for business. This chapter provides an overview of how electronic spreadsheets work and describes some of the most useful features of spreadsheets.

OBJECTIVES

1. Define electronic spreadsheets.

2. Describe the basic components of electronic spreadsheets.

3. Describe the major functions of spreadsheets.

4. Identify essential features of spreadsheets.

5. Associate standard spreadsheet commands with their functions.

6. Associate selected advanced spreadsheet commands with their functions.

7. Identify features of popular accounting software.

ELECTRONIC SPREADSHEETS: A FLEXIBLE RECORDKEEPING TOOL

An electronic spreadsheet—spreadsheet for short—is an all-purpose computer application that can be used for almost any task involving the organization of numbers. It is based on a paper spreadsheet with columns and rows. The user keys in the titles and numbers and any calculations that might be needed.

One advantage of the spreadsheet is that once it is set up properly, the user can save time by never having to set up the spreadsheet again. For example, suppose the user has an employee's schedule of time worked set up in a spreadsheet. When one month is over, the user can simply copy the spreadsheet to another file or another location on the same spreadsheet and enter the numbers for the next month. The spreadsheet will automatically recalculate where it is supposed to so the user will know how much to pay the employee, the amount of taxes to pay, etc. In a company with many employees, a blank schedule of time worked can be developed with all the titles and formulas and no data. This blank schedule is an example of a *template*. The template can be copied to each employee's spreadsheet file and then the data may be entered.

Another advantage of the spreadsheet is its capability of exploring "what-if" scenarios. Once the formulas have been entered into the spreadsheet, the user can change input information to see the results of possible changes without having to implement the changes. This feature is useful in budgeting, determining prices of products, and submitting bids for services.

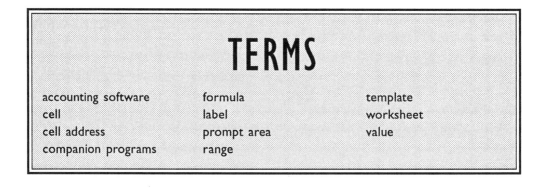

TERMS

accounting software	formula	template
cell	label	worksheet
cell address	prompt area	value
companion programs	range	

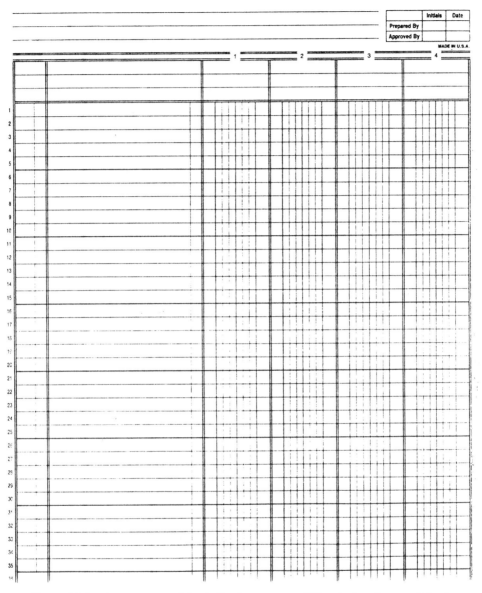

Figure 20-1.   A paper spreadsheet, the forerunner of the electronic spreadsheet.

SPREADSHEET SOFTWARE

The most popular spreadsheet available today is Lotus 1-2-3, marketed by Lotus Development Corporation. Other popular spreadsheets with powerful features include Quattro Pro from Borland, Microsoft's Excel, and SuperCalc from Computer Associates.

Figure 20-2. Lotus 1-2-3 is the most popular spreadsheet on the market today.

Because the basic spreadsheet is a fairly simple application, packages such as InstaCalc from FormalSoft, Lucid 3-D from DacEasy and the shareware program PC-Calc provide users with a functional spreadsheet for a low price. These packages don't have all the features of the big packages, but provide a lot of program for the money. Table 20-1 contains some of the more popular spreadsheet application software packages.

HARDWARE REQUIREMENTS

Full-featured spreadsheet applications such as Lotus 1-2-3 and Quattro Pro will recommend 4MB of RAM and up to 10MB of hard disk space to run the latest versions. These programs will not function as intended on

Table 20-1
POPULAR SPREADSHEET APPLICATION SOFTWARE PACKAGES

Package	MS-DOS	Windows	Macintosh
Lotus 1-2-3	Yes	Yes	Yes
Quattro Pro	Yes	Yes	No
Microsoft Excel	Yes	Yes	Yes
SuperCalc	Yes	No	No
Lucid 3-D	Yes	No	No
InstaCalc	Yes	No	No
PlanPerfect	Yes	No	No

machines with no hard disk drive. Some of the less expensive programs will work on a computer without a hard disk and only 640K of memory. The smaller memory may, however, limit the amount of data that can be entered at one time.

Spreadsheet calculation times can be improved with the addition of a math coprocessor for machines using a microprocessor without a built-in math coprocessor (486sx or lower for DOS machines). The math coprocessor is not recommended, however, for users who have small worksheets or who plan to use the programs less than two hours per day. These users are unlikely to notice the time that is gained with a math coprocessor.

Spreadsheet programs designed to run under Microsoft Windows or on the Macintosh will benefit more from a laser printer than DOS-based programs. The Windows programs provide excellent font/graphic support in conjunction with the Windows software. Newer DOS versions of Excel, Quattro Pro, and Lotus 1-2-3 also provide fairly good printer and graphics support. For DOS-based programs, however, a good 24-pin dot matrix printer is probably the best choice for the money.

BASIC COMPONENTS OF ELECTRONIC SPREADSHEETS

When a user loads a spreadsheet application, the screen will be divided into two parts. The *prompt area* will take the top 3 or 4 lines of the screen. It contains the command line or ruler (accessed by pressing the slash [/] key), that shows the user which commands are available. It also contains

Figure 20-3. Microsoft Excel, a popular spreadsheet package.

the entry/status line (two lines in some programs), that tells the user what is in a cell or shows what is being typed into a cell.

The *worksheet* area is divided into columns and rows. Columns are vertical areas extending from the top of the spreadsheet to the bottom. Columns are labeled with letters (column A, column B, etc.). Rows are horizontal areas extending from the left side of the spread sheet to the right side. Rows are labeled with numbers (row 1, row 2, etc.) A border around the worksheet area keeps the row and column labels visible at all times.

A *cell* is the place where a column and a row intersect. Cells are labeled by their column and row. For example, cell B22 is at the intersection of column B and row 22. The label B22 is an example of a *cell address*. This cell address is important, as it can be used to identify the contents of the cell.

Cells may have one of three types of information. Descriptive text used primarily to provide headings for the various rows and columns is referred to as a *label*. A number that is entered into a cell is referred to as a *value*. A *formula* is a mathematical expression or calculation entered into a cell. The number displayed as a result of the formula is called a variable.

MAJOR FUNCTIONS OF ELECTRONIC SPREADSHEETS

As noted earlier, spreadsheets are flexible programs that can perform almost any function requiring the organization and manipulation of numerical data. The data is organized in table format in a document called a worksheet. Like word processing programs, spreadsheet software has five major functions, which are described below.

CREATING

Creating involves starting with a blank worksheet and entering all of the labels, values, and formulas necessary to make a functional worksheet. For common operations, spreadsheet templates can be used to avoid some of the problems associated with developing worksheets from scratch.

The spreadsheet software allows the user to change formats such as

```
Number of Cows:       34
-----------------------------------------------------------------------------
DIRECT EXPENSES   UNIT        PRICE   QUANTITY        DOLLARS    COST PER COW
#############################################################################
INTEREST          DOLLAR   $8,700.00        8%        $696.00         $20.47
BULL              HEAD     $1,500.00        1       $1,500.00         $44.12
PASTURE           ACRE        $10.00      200       $2,000.00         $58.82
MINERALS          BAG         $10.00       16         $160.00          $4.71
PROTEIN MEAL      TON        $140.00      6.5         $910.00         $26.76
VETERINARY COW    HEAD        $15.00       34         $510.00         $15.00
MARKETING         DOLLAR       $0.04    11623         $464.92         $13.67
CHECK-OFF         HEAD         $1.00       31          $31.00          $0.91
GRAIN             TON        $145.00      7.5       $1,087.50         $31.99
VETERINARY CALF   HEAD         $8.00       31         $248.00          $7.29
VETERINARY BULL   HEAD        $15.00        2          $30.00          $0.88
REPAIRS/EQUIP.    YEAR     $1,000.00        1       $1,000.00         $29.41
-----------------------------------------------------------------------------
TOTAL                                                $8,637.42       $254.03
#############################################################################
```

Courtesy, M. Woods, Johnson Milling Company, Clinton, Mississippi.

Figure 20-4. A printout of a Lotus 1-2-3 worksheet containing an expense budget for a cow/calf operation. (Courtesy, Matt Woods, Johnson Milling Company,

column widths and types of numerical displays. Users can also insert columns and rows as needed to make a worksheet more functional.

REVISING

Revising refers to making changes in an existing worksheet. These changes may be in the format of the worksheet, in the values and labels entered, or in the formulas.

```
  Number of Cows:        38
-----------------------------------------------------------------------------
DIRECT EXPENSES    UNIT        PRICE   QUANTITY        DOLLARS    COST PER COW
#############################################################################
INTEREST           DOLLAR   $8,700.00      10%         $870.00         $22.89
BULL               HEAD     $2,000.00        1       $2,000.00         $52.63
PASTURE            ACRE        $10.00      200       $2,000.00         $52.63
MINERALS           BAG         $10.00       16         $160.00          $4.21
PROTEIN MEAL       TON        $140.00      6.5         $910.00         $23.95
VETERINARY COW     HEAD        $15.00       34         $510.00         $13.42
MARKETING          DOLLAR       $0.04    11623         $464.92         $12.23
CHECK-OFF          HEAD         $1.00       31          $31.00          $0.82
GRAIN              TON        $145.00      7.5       $1,087.50         $28.62
VETERINARY CALF    HEAD         $8.00       31         $248.00          $6.53
VETERINARY BULL    HEAD        $15.00        2          $30.00          $0.79
REPAIRS/EQUIP.     YEAR     $1,000.00        1       $1,000.00         $26.32
-----------------------------------------------------------------------------
TOTAL                                                $9,311.42        $245.04
#############################################################################
```

Courtesy, M. Woods, Johnson Milling Company, Clinton, Mississippi.

Figure 20-5. A revised version of the spreadsheet in Figure 20-3. Note the results of changes in the number of cows, the interest rate and price of the bull.

FORMATTING

As already mentioned, spreadsheet software makes it easy for the user to change the format of the spreadsheet. Commands are available to change column width, fonts, label placement, and numerical displays (decimal places, percentages, dollar signs, etc.).

PRINTING

Worksheets and graphics from worksheets may be printed to a printer, plotter, or disk. The printer is the most common output device. A plotter is sometimes used to produce color charts, but not commonly used to print the actual data in the worksheet. A spreadsheet may be printed to a disk as an ASCII file, where it can be used by a word processor or transferred to another computer over a network. The resulting ASCII file, however, does not include the formulas and other codes contained in the spreadsheet.

HANDLING

Spreadsheet software has file management functions for copying, deleting, moving, and renaming files. These functions are performed in conjunction with the operating system or environment (such as Windows).

ESSENTIAL FEATURES OF SPREADSHEETS

Although the basic operating principles of spreadsheets haven't changed much since VisiCalc, the popular spreadsheet packages continue to add features to make the programs more powerful and easier to use. Some features that are essential to all spreadsheets are discussed below. Some of the advanced features are discussed later in this chapter.

CURSOR MOVEMENT

In a spreadsheet, the cursor can be moved to different cells using the cursor control keys: the arrow keys, page up/page down keys, the home key, and the end key. Users often find it much easier to use a keyboard with dedicated cursor control keys—those not shared with a number pad. Because spreadsheets use a lot of numbers, most users wish to keep the number pad reserved for number entry only.

The other way to move around a spreadsheet is by using the "goto" command. Because each cell has its own address (its column and row), the user can give the goto command followed by the cell address to send the cursor directly to that cell. For example, in Lotus 1-2-3, the goto command is F5, followed by the cell address. To move to the cell at the intersection of column K, row 28, the user would press F5 and type K28.

SCROLLING

It is possible to create a worksheet that is much larger than the computer monitor's screen. For example, the Quattro Pro spreadsheet has a possible worksheet size of 230 columns (A through IV) and 8192 rows, a total of 1,844,160 cells! All of these cells couldn't possibly be shown on the screen at one time. Scrolling allows the user to see columns and rows not visible when the spreadsheet is in the home position.

So the user will know what the data in columns means, he or she can set titles of columns and/or rows that remain on the screen at all times. Some spreadsheets also allow the user to use multiple windows—to see two or more worksheets or two parts of the same worksheet at the same time.

DATA ENTRY

Text entered into a worksheet is referred to as titles or labels. Some spreadsheets require the user to put an apostrophe (') or quote (") symbol before the text to indicate that it is a label and not a value. (The apostrophe or quote does not show up on the worksheet, only on the entry line.)

Numbers entered into a worksheet are considered values. These values can be part of formulas entered in other cells of the worksheet. Formulas are mathematical expressions used to create variables. The user indicates to the spreadsheet that a formula is being entered by typing a left parenthesis symbol [(], an at sign [@], or a math symbol such as a plus sign [+]. After this symbol, basic mathematical rules apply, such as having to close parentheses after opening them. As with any mathematical formula, calculations within parentheses are performed before those outside, and division and multiplication are performed before addition and subtraction. Spreadsheets also have built-in commands, called @ commands. These make formula writing easier by reducing the number of keystrokes required to obtain the same answer. For example, if the user wants to add the values in cells E1 through E10, he or she could enter

+E1+E2+E3+E4+E5+E6+E7+E8+E9+E10

Table 20-2
COMMONLY-USED @ SPREADSHEET COMMANDS AND FUNCTIONS

Command	Function
@COUNT	Gives a count of the number of cells in a specified range
@DATE	Enters the current date in a cell
@EXP	Raises a number to a specified exponent
@MAX	Finds the maximum value in a range of cells
@MIN	Finds the minimum value in a range of cells
@SQRT	Finds the square root of a value or variable
@SUM	Adds the value of cells in a specified range
@TIME	Puts a clock in a cell

An easier way to do this would be to use an @ command called @SUM. To use this command, the user would enter

@SUM(E1..E10)

Both would give the same result. Table 20-2 contains a summary of commonly used @ commands.

Another data function is the built-in error warning given when a user enters a label (text) in a cell where the spreadsheet is expecting a value. The cell containing the formula will display "ERR" instead of the expected variable.

```
Number of Cows:        34
--------------------------------------------------------------------------
DIRECT EXPENSES    UNIT        PRICE    QUANTITY        DOLLARS    COST PER COW
##########################################################################
INTEREST           DOLLAR    $8,700.00         8%        +C5*D5         +E5/B1
BULL               HEAD      $1,500.00          1        +C6*D6         +E6/B1
PASTURE            ACRE         $10.00        200        +C7*D7         +E7/B1
MINERALS           BAG          $10.00         16        +C8*D8         +E8/B1
PROTEIN MEAL       TON         $140.00        6.5        +C9*D9         +E9/B1
VETERINARY COW     HEAD         $15.00         34       +C10*D10       +E10/B1
MARKETING          DOLLAR        $0.04      11623       +C11*D11       +E11/B1
CHECK-OFF          HEAD          $1.00         31       +C12*D12       +E12/B1
GRAIN              TON         $145.00        7.5       +C13*D13       +E13/B1
VETERINARY CALF    HEAD          $8.00         31       +C14*D14       +E14/B1
VETERINARY BULL    HEAD         $15.00          2       +C15*D15       +E15/B1
REPAIRS/EQUIP.     YEAR      $1,000.00          1       +C16*D16       +E16/B1
--------------------------------------------------------------------------
TOTAL                                                  @SUM(E5..E16)  @SUM(F5..F16)
##########################################################################
```

Courtesy, M. Woods, Johnson Milling Company, Clinton, Mississippi.

Figure 20-6. The same spreadsheet shown in Figure 20-4, with the formulas shown in cells rather than the variables resulting from the formulas.

STANDARD SPREADSHEET COMMANDS

Commands on almost every type of spreadsheet program can be accessed using the slash (/). Pressing the slash key will list the command menus in the prompt area. In many programs, the command ruler is shown on the screen at all times and can be accessed with either the slash key or a mouse. Most programs contain the following menus: worksheet, range, copy, move, file, and print. Others contain more menus which are discussed in a later section of this chapter.

WORKSHEET

The worksheet menu allows the user to make several changes to the entire worksheet. The following submenus are included in the worksheet menu.

Global

The global subcommand allows the user to make format changes to the entire worksheet. These include column width, column justification, and value characteristics such as number of decimal places, percentages, and dollar signs.

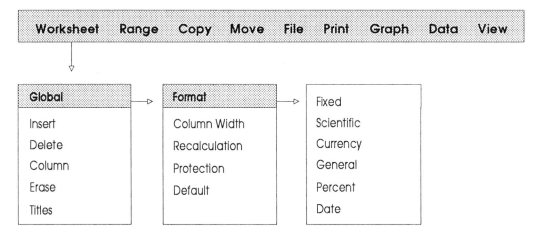

Figure 20-7. An abbreviated tree for the worksheet command and global subcommand in Quattro Pro for DOS.

Insert/Delete

The insert subcommand inserts a column or row at the cursor location or at another place specified by the user. The delete subcommand will erase a column or row.

Titles

The titles subcommand allows the user to specify a number of columns or rows that remain on the screen at all times. These serve as the titles for the scrolling columns and rows.

Erase

The erase subcommand is used to erase a worksheet from RAM. It does not erase the worksheet from the disk. Users should be careful to save any changes in the worksheet to a disk before using this command or the changes will be lost.

RANGE

The *range* command is similar to the global command. It allows the user to make format changes to a cell or group (range) of cells instead of the entire worksheet. The user can also name or erase a range of cells.

COPY

The copy command allows the user to copy a cell or range of cells to another location. One important feature is the ability of this command to adjust formulas to the different location. Some spreadsheets do this automatically, while others ask the user each time the command is used.

MOVE

The move command allows the user to move a cell or range of cells to another location.

FILE

The file command is the file management system of the spreadsheet. The user can retrieve a worksheet from a file, save a worksheet to a file, erase a file, copy a file, move a file, or combine two different files.

PRINT

The print command allows the user to print the spreadsheet. The user can specify the type of printer and range of cells to be printed. Certain columns and/or rows can be specified as borders for worksheets that span multiple pages when printed.

One option the user has is to print the spreadsheet to a disk in the form of an ASCII file. This is an important feature because the resulting ASCII file can be used in a variety of ways. When designating the filename to be printed to, the user should be careful not to use the same filename as the original worksheet, as it will save the ASCII file over the spreadsheet file. The user should use an extension, such as TXT or ASC, to indicate that the file is an ASCII file and not a spreadsheet file.

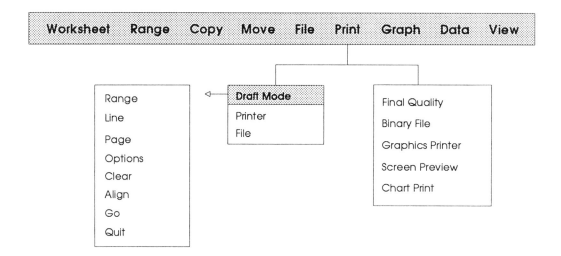

Figure 20-8. An abbreviated tree of the print command menu and printer submenus.

ADVANCED SPREADSHEET COMMANDS

While the standard features are similar on almost all spreadsheet programs, the more powerful programs include more options (submenus) under some of the standard commands and may also include more commands on the command line. Some of the more frequently used advanced commands are describe below.

WORKSHEET

In addition to the standard features of the worksheet command, some programs include advanced subcommands. The macros command allows the user to define and run macros to save time. (For a more detailed description of macros, see Chapter 19.)

RANGE

Advanced subcommands under the range command include the option to protect a range of cells and the ability to search for specific data in cells.

FILE

Although most spreadsheets have basic file management capabilities, some spreadsheets go a step further. An advanced subcommand under the file command gives the ability to import a file created by another application. Several spreadsheets can import files from popular database management programs such as DBase and Paradox. One spreadsheet, InstaCalc, can import files from Quicken, an accounting package discussed in the next section.

PRINTER

In addition to the print capabilities, some spreadsheets offer the view subcommand. View allows the user to see what the printout of a worksheet or graphic would look like without actually having to print it.

GRAPH

Early spreadsheets required *companion programs* to produce graphs from data entered into the spreadsheet. The ability to provide presentation-quality graphics is now a must for many spreadsheet users. Most spreadsheets have extensive graphics capabilities. Because of this, the graph command is often one of the commands on the main command line.

The graph command asks the user to select a graph type and indicate a range of cells to include in the graph. Another choice is for the user to enter plot values from the number pad or keyboard. The user can view the graph on screen without printing, and may be able to incorporate it into a presentation. Many options exist for customizing the colors and patterns of the graphs.

DATA

The data command assists the user in entering and sorting data. It includes a fill subcommand, which fills in between two cells with sequential data. For example, if the user indicates 100 for cell C1 and 1000 for cell C10, the program will fill in cells C2 through C9 with 200, 300, 400, etc.

Users can also use the data command to sort data and put it in table form for printing. Some programs include advanced statistics calculation as part of the data command.

VIEW

With the growth of GUIs, many DOS spreadsheets have been adjusted to make the interface of their programs more user-friendly. One of the newer features is the view command, which allows the user to change worksheet sizes, open multiple worksheets in individual windows, stack worksheets, and many other functions previously reserved for Macintosh or Windows users.

ACCOUNTING SOFTWARE

Users who do not wish to get involved in creating a spreadsheet system of recordkeeping may want to try accounting software. *Accounting software* is designed to be an easy-to-use alternative to electronic spreadsheets. Instead of setting up labels, titles, and formulas, the accounting package comes with a built-in set of accounts and the user enters only data into the existing framework.

The most popular accounting software package is Quicken from Intuit. Quicken comes with five basic accounts to let a person or business keep track of finances. The accounts are (1) cash, (2) checking, (3) credit cards, (4) assets and (5) liabilities. These accounts are functional but limited in scope.

Accounting packages do not have the flexibility of spreadsheet applications, but they work hard to provide customers with features that are commonly used in business in a format that is very user-friendly. For example, Quicken allows the user to write checks from the computer (using special checks available from Intuit) or make electronic payments using telephone hookups. Also, some of the more common financial analysis records, such as a cash flow statement or a net worth statement, are

Figure 20-9. Quicken, a popular
accounting
software package
developed by Intuit.

computed and printed easily, whereas with a spreadsheet the user must set up these statements and write formulas to compute them.

Although accounting software is popular with some users, most agribusinesses with more than five employees will need to use a more flexible spreadsheet for keeping records. Larger agribusinesses may use software designed especially for their business by a computer programmer or obtain their software from their corporate offices.

CHAPTER QUESTIONS

1. What is the most popular spreadsheet program in use today?

2. What tool is the electronic spreadsheet based on? How are they alike? Different?

3. Define the following terms as they relate to electronic spreadsheets:

> Cell
> Address
> Worksheet
> Formula
> Value
> Label
> Variable

4. Describe a good computer hardware system for operating a spreadsheet like Lotus 1-2-3 or Quattro Pro.

5. Briefly describe the five major functions of electronic spreadsheets.

6. Describe four standard spreadsheet commands.

7. Describe four advanced spreadsheet commands.

8. How are accounting software packages different from spreadsheets?

Chapter 21

DATABASE MANAGEMENT

Database management systems are probably the most flexible and powerful applications used on personal computers. The distinguishing characteristic of database management systems is the ability of the software to organize and manage both text and numerical data.

Agribusinesses use database management systems to perform a variety of tasks. Two important uses are inventory control and customer records.

Many people think database management systems are too difficult for novice computer users to operate. While it is true that these programs have many features, some complex and extensive, there are varieties of database software for all levels of users.

This chapter describes the basic concepts of database management. A look at some of the functions and features of the desktop versions of these powerful programs is provided.

OBJECTIVES

1. Define database management.

2. Identify functions of database management systems.

3. Describe database software and hardware requirements.

4. Discuss basic concepts associated with database management systems.

5. Describe features of database management programs.

DATABASE MANAGEMENT
AS A BUSINESS APPLICATION

In general, a database is a collection of information called data. Database management is the use of the computer for maintenance, organization, and analysis of data.

Database management systems—database managers for short—are the software applications that allow users to manage data. Sizes of databases and programs vary greatly. Some commercial databases contain several gigabytes of information and have computer networks built around them. Others may be as small as a database of addresses and other information on 100 or fewer customers of a local feed store. This chapter focuses on the smaller databases that can be managed with desktop or personal computers.

FUNCTIONS

Database managers may be used for a variety of functions in an agribusiness. These flexible systems can be used to:

1. Generate mailing lists and labels

2. Generate directories of addresses

3. Maintain inventory control

4. Generate orders for supplies and other goods

5. Keep customer information on record

6. Maintain and analyze tax records

7. Generate work schedules

8. Organize and analyze production data

SOFTWARE

Database management software can be divided into two categories: single-purpose and general-purpose.

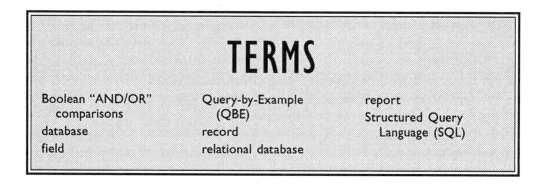

TERMS

Boolean "AND/OR" comparisons	Query-by-Example (QBE)	report
database	record	Structured Query Language (SQL)
field	relational database	

Single-purpose database managers are designed to manage a specific database with specific types of data. These programs are generally easy to use but not very flexible. They can be large or small, and expensive or inexpensive. For example, shareware programs that organize mailing lists and fit on one 360K disk are available for a registration fee of $50 or less, while the database program used by the Dairy Herd Improvement Association is a very large (and probably very expensive) program.

The two types of general-purpose database software are further divided as programmable database managers and flatfile database managers. Both types are characterized by their flexibility that allows the user to customize the database and its management, but they vary by features and the amount of training necessary to operate the software. As a general rule, the more powerful the program, the more training required to familiarize the user with the many capabilities of the software. Most users agree that the amount of training is worth the time and expense because the operator is able to use the software properly.

Table 21-1
POPULAR DATABASE MANAGEMENT SYSTEM APPLICATION SOFTWARE

PACKAGE	MS-DOS	WINDOWS	MACINTOSH
dBASE	Yes	No	No
Paradox	Yes	Yes	No
FoxPro	Yes	Yes	No
PC File	Yes	No	No
Alpha Four	Yes	No	No
Q and A	Yes	No	No
PFS: File	Yes	No	No
R:BASE	Yes	No	No
Superbase	Yes	Yes	No
Omnis	Yes	Yes	Yes
Ingris	Yes	Yes	Yes

The most popular database manager program in use today is dBASE—a general-purpose, programmable database manager. Newer versions of programmable database managers such as dBASE, Paradox, and FoxPro have improved their interfaces in an effort to become more user-friendly, but have so many features that some training is commonly required before they can be used to their full potential.

Flatfile database managers are typically easier to operate but don't have as many features as programmable database managers. These programs still require the user to set up, or design the database, allowing for maximum flexibility in how the information is organized. Popular flatfile database managers include Alpha Four, Q and A, PFS:File, and PC File.

HARDWARE

The primary hardware concern associated with database managers is the amount of disk storage space and RAM they require. The minimum storage and RAM are determined by the size of the databases (the information) that need to be managed by the system. A hard disk drive is necessary to run the popular database managers. Most of the popular programs will run with 1MB of RAM, but more may be necessary, depending on the size of the database to be managed.

DATABASE MANAGEMENT CONCEPTS

Database managers organize information into two categories: fields and records. A *field* is a category of information such as name, account number, or zip code. A *record* is a collection of all fields for a subject, business or individual. Some database managers come with templates (pre-designed formats for recording information) for specific uses, such as customer or employee records.

A *database* is a collection of all the individual records which are kept in a file. This information may be printed to the screen, a printer, or to a disk file in the form of a *report*.

A *relational database* is a database with common data between fields and records. In other words, all records contain the same fields and all fields are located in all records. These fields may be linked to fields in another database. Linking means that updating the information in one database automatically updates the information in the related database.

The most powerful database managers use *Structured Query Language (SQL)*, a totally relational database language. Most of the popular programmable database managers used on personal computers use *Query-by Example (QBE)*, which has some relational characteristics. The low-end, flat file databases do not use a query language, but rely on menus and key words to search for specified fields and records.

SUMMARY OF
DATABASE MANAGEMENT
FEATURES

All database managers have the following in common:

1. The process involves keeping the same type of information on multiple units (also called subjects or individuals)

2. With a large number of units, the information can be managed more easily and efficiently using the computer than by hand

3. The database management system allows for updating, editing, and sorting the data contained in the database

Database managers differ in the number of features they offer the user and in the commands which access these features. Some of the more commonly used features of database managers are described below.

CREATING

Creating involves three processes. The first is designing the database—deciding what information the user wishes to maintain about each unit to be included in the database, how much space will be needed for each field, the type of field needed, and the organization of the fields in a record. The second step is defining the database—entering the design into the computer. The third step is entering the data into the database for each individual unit.

Field Names

For most database managers, field names must be 10 characters or less in length. A good rule of thumb is to keep the field name as short or shorter than the number of characters allocated to the data in the field. This keeps the field name from taking up more space in a listing than the data.

An example is the field "state," referring to the state in which a person lives, such as Ohio or Mississippi. State names can be long or short, but each state has a two-letter postal abbreviation. Since mailing labels require this abbreviation anyway, it is a good idea to keep it in the database in that form. Of course, a database field name of "STATE" would be longer than the postal abbreviation. Most users shorten the name of this field to "ST."

Types of Fields

In order to do a better job of managing data, some database managers require the user to define the field types when defining a database. A brief description of the field types follows. These descriptions show why defining field types can be useful.

Character fields. Character fields are used to store any characters such as letters and numbers.

Date fields. Date fields are used to store dates. The format is usually MM/DD/YY, requiring a field eight characters in length.

Numeric fields. Numeric fields store numbers. The numbers may contain a decimal point or a negative sign. If a field is to be used in a calculation, it must be defined as numeric.

Logical fields. Logical fields refer to fields that answer a question. Logical fields contain only one space and must be in the form of Y for yes, N for no, T for true, or F for False.

Memo fields. Memo fields are used to store large blocks of text and generally are not used to search or sort records. Some programs refer to these fields as global fields. These can be the largest fields in the database—some programs allow these files to be several thousand characters in length.

A Database Definition Example

The manager of a local farm supply business may determine that the following fields are needed for a customer database: last name, first name, farm name, address, city, state, zip, telephone, crops/livestock grown (beef, corn, cotton, etc.), sales, account number, account balance, credit rating, and comments about the customer. Table 21-2 contains a possible organization of these fields, their type, and their widths.

SORTING

One requirement of database management is the ability to sort the

Table 21-2
POSSIBLE FIELDS AND CHARACTERISTICS FOR A CUSTOMER DATABASE.

DESCRIPTION	NAME	TYPE	WIDTH
Last name	LNAME	Character	15
First name	FNAME	Character	15
Farm name	FARMNAME	Character	30
Mailing Address	MADDRESS	Character	30
Delivery Address	DADDRESS	Character	30
City	CITY	Character	16
State	ST	Character	2
Zip Code + 4	ZIP	Character	10
Telephone	PHONE	Character	12
Account Number	ACCTNUMBER	Character	10
Account Balance	ACCTBAL	Numeric	10
Last year's sales	SALES	Numeric	10
Current credit rating	CREDRATE	Numeric	10
Produce beef cattle	BEEF	Logical	1
Produce catfish	CATFISH	Logical	1
Produce corn	CORN	Logical	1
Produce cotton	COTTON	Logical	1
Produce dairy	DAIRY	Logical	1
Produce grain sorghum	GRAINSORG	Logical	1
Produce soybeans	SOYBEAN	Logical	1
Produce sheep	SHEEP	Logical	1
Produce swine	SWINE	Logical	1
Customer Comments	COMMENTS	Memo	800

Note that some fields contain numbers but are not listed as character fields. This is because those fields will not be used in any calculations.

information into almost any sequence. This is generally accomplished by specifying a field or fields by which to sort. The primary option is choosing ascending or descending order for the sort.

SEARCHING

Searching involves locating a record or records based on the information contained in a field or combination of fields. For example, the manager of the local farm supply business mentioned in Table 21-2 may want to send information about a new cotton growth regulator to customers who are cotton farmers. A search of the COTTON field in the customer database will let the manager know which of the customers grow cotton, then select these records and print their addresses.

Most database managers allow users to search for and select records by field contents using *Boolean "AND/OR" comparisons.* The Boolean "AND" means that the search will include every unit with a certain value in one field **and** a certain value in another field. The Boolean "OR" means that the search will include every unit with a certain value in one field **or** a certain value in another field. The "OR" comparison will yield more total units using the same fields and values.

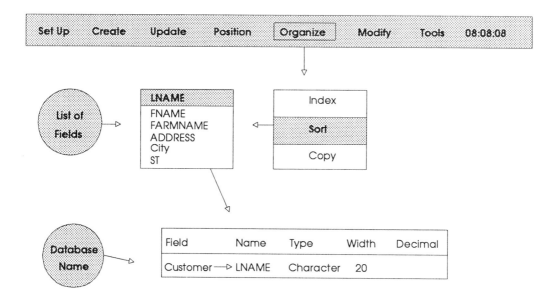

Figure 21-1. An abbreviated menu tree from dBASE III showing selected options under the organize command. The file is the CUSTOMER database defined in Table 21-2.

REPORTING

Reporting involves printing the information from all or selected fields in the database. Options include printing to the disk, printer or screen. The user may use pre-defined report formats that are included with the program or define his or her own report format. Defining a report format includes selecting the fields to be printed, selecting the records to be printed, and determining the organization of the selected records.

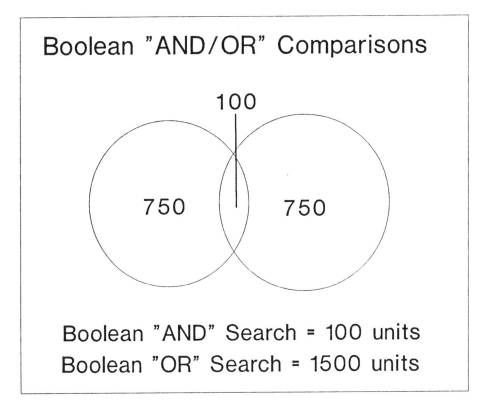

Figure 21-2. A diagram showing the effects of Boolean "AND/OR" comparisons. 1,500 units meet one of the two search criteria values, but only 100 meet both.

UPDATING

Updating means changing the data in a database. This may involve changing data for existing records (either all or selected) in certain fields. It may also involve adding records to the database, deleting obsolete records, or undeleting deleted records.

CALCULATING

Most databases give the user the option of performing arithmetic calculations on fields with numerical data. These calculations may include summing data fields, computing an average of the fields, and counting the number of records with particular information. Most programs will also give subtotals of numerical fields based on classifications by a user-selected field.

B: Customer 150 records, disk can hold approximately 275 more

F1 ADD - Add a record	(ALT) F1 BIN - Set binary search on/off
F2 MOD - Modify a record	(ALT) F2 GLO - Global update or delete
F3 DEL - Delete a record	(ALT) F3 KEY - Set up the smart keys
F4 DIS - Display a record	(ALT) F4 NAM - Alter field name or mask
F5 FIN - Find a record	
F6 LIS - List or clone	
F7 SOR - Sort the Index	
F8 UTI - Utilities	
F9 MEN - Show Smart Key Menu	(ALT) F9 END - Quit or change database

Please press the appropriate function key, or supply one of the 3-character commands ▶ _ ◀

Figure 21-3. **Easy to use! The menu screen from PC File, originally a shareware program from Buttonware that has become commercial software. It is a very popular, inexpensive database manager.**

MERGING/COPYING

The ability to merge databases or copy records from one database to another can save the user time and trouble. Time is saved because the data for each individual does not have to be entered again. Trouble is saved by avoiding keystroking errors that inevitably occur when entering data. This feature is sometimes called "cloning."

INDEXING

Indexing involves marking selected words in records and saving those words in an index file. The index file contains a list of the words and the number of each record that contains the words. The user can search using the indexed words to determine which records to select for an operation.

PROGRAMMING

With some database managers, programming refers to the creation of programs that act as macros do in word processors or spreadsheet applications. The programs are used to save the user time by combining a series of frequently used command sequences into one program that can be run using just one or two commands. Database programs vary greatly in this capability. Some programs offer basically no programming or macro capabilities; others, such as dBASE and Paradox, have their own programming languages, used for application development.

CHAPTER QUESTIONS

1. Select an agribusiness in your community and describe how that agribusiness might use a database management system.

2. What is the difference between a single-purpose database manager and a general-purpose database manager?

3. Define the following terms as they relate to database management:

   database
   field
   record
   relational database
   report

4. What is the difference between a Boolean "AND" search and a Boolean "OR" search?

5. Select five features of a database management system and describe what they do.

Chapter 22

GRAPHICS

The ability of users to generate graphics images using computers has increased dramatically in the last few years. Faster computers, better-quality monitors, and improvements in software have made it easy to produce quality graphics from personal computers. Items that had required the services of graphic artists and professional typographers are now being produced in-house by many agribusinesses.

The result of these new capabilities has been to allow agribusinesses to gain more outputs with the same personnel. The new packages are easy-to-use and require a minimal amount of training time and money. Most DOS graphics programs are menu-driven; programs designed for use under Microsoft Windows or on the Macintosh take advantage of the graphical orientation of their environments.

This chapter looks at the five major types of software used to produce graphics output. The features of each are described, with the primary focus given to presentation graphics programs, the ones that can do almost anything graphical.

OBJECTIVES

1. Describe the use of computer graphics in business.

2. Describe the different types of graphics software.

3. Describe the capabilities of presentation graphics software.

4. Discuss hardware requirements for various graphics functions.

COMPUTER GRAPHICS IN BUSINESS

Information that is presented in the form of a chart, graph, *line art*, or photograph is referred to as graphics. The term *business graphics* refers to using these graphics to convey this information to clients, management, shareholders, and others in a meaningful way. The use of computer software to generate business graphics with special effects designed to impress the viewer is referred to as *presentation graphics*. Presentation graphics include the special effects of color, patterns, and illustrations designed to "spruce up" a presentation.

The five most common types of graphs/charts produced in the business world are *pie graphs, line graphs, bar graphs,* line art/drawings, and pictures. Pie graphs, line graphs, and bar graphs are usually constructed by the software package after the user enters the data for the different parts of the graph, but the data may also be imported from a spreadsheet or database file. Line art can be drawn by the user or loaded into the software package from a file on a disk. Pictures may be loaded from files on a disk, from a CD-ROM disk, or from a paper copy using a scanner and scanning software.

Several standards have been developed for graphics files, especially for line art and illustration files. Users can buy floppy disks or CD-ROM disks filled with images produced in these *standard graphics file formats* for use with their software. Some of these standard graphics formats include: .PCX, .PIC, .DRW, .DXF, CGM and TIFF formats. Other formats have been developed to work with particular software and/or hardware. These include: .WPG (for use with WordPerfect), WMF (Windows Metafile), PICT (for use with MacDraw), HPGL (for use with the Hewlett Packard Graphics Language for HP printers).

TERMS

bar graph	floating-point calculations	portrait orientation
bullets	graphics drivers	presentation graphics
business graphics	landscape orientation	scale
computer aided design (CAD)	line art	screenshow
film recorder	line graph	standard graphics file format
	pie graph	

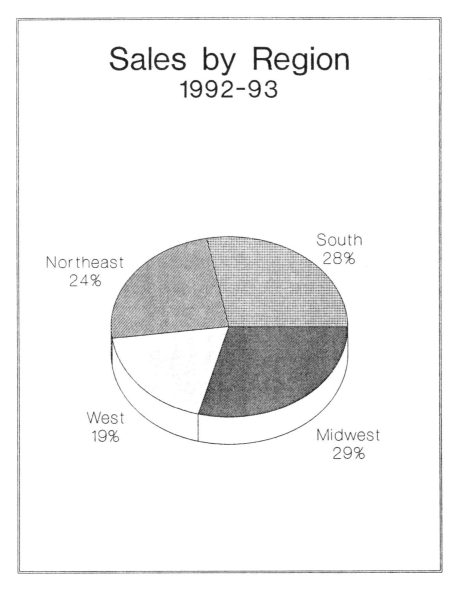

Figure 22-1.   An example of a pie chart (from Harvard Graphics).

TYPES OF
GRAPHICS SOFTWARE

Many different types of graphics programs are available. These programs are usually grouped by their primary function, although many have other capabilities as well. The five major types of graphics software are painting programs, drawing/drafting programs, canned graphics programs, presentation graphics programs, and other programs that incorporate graphics functions as an additional feature. Each of these types of programs are described briefly below. In the next section, the features of presentation graphics programs are discussed in more detail.

Figure 22-2. Good documentation is very important to the successful use of software. One argument for buying popular software is that easy-to-understand books are often available to supplement the user's manual.

PAINTING/DRAWING PROGRAMS

Painting/drawing programs are primarily designed for people with some artistic ability, although almost anyone can produce a decent looking product using these programs. These programs are characterized by their use of a mouse and icons representing different drawing tools, such as geometric shapes, pens, erasers, and paintbrushes. The user selects a pattern and color from the menu to fill in the designs. Text can be incorporated into the drawing as well. Once the user enters the text, it can be placed anywhere on the drawing screen.

Painting/drawing programs often allow the user to import line art or illustrations in one or more of the standard formats. The user can then make changes as desired. The output of these programs is often incorporated into other documents using one of the other types of graphics packages. Some programs can export files to make color 35mm slides on a *film recorder*.

Examples of popular painting/drawing programs include MacPaint, CorelDRAW, PaintShow, and Paintbrush. Programs that operate in Microsoft Windows or on a Macintosh are generally considered easier to use and usually interact with peripherals better because of the advanced *graphics drivers* in these programs.

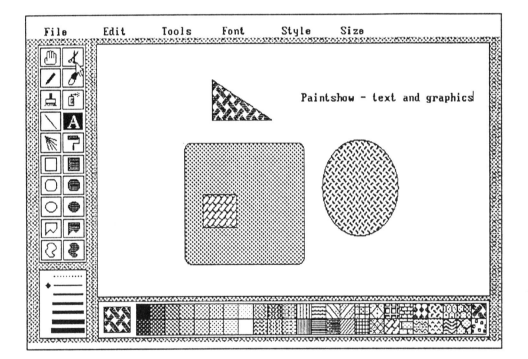

Figure 22-3. The Paintshow program with some examples of shapes and patterns. Note the icons for drawing tools on the left and for colors and patterns on the bottom. The pull down menu bar at the top makes the program easy to use.

CAD PROGRAMS

CAD programs are used to create original technical drawings. CAD stands for computer aided design. These programs are commonly used by

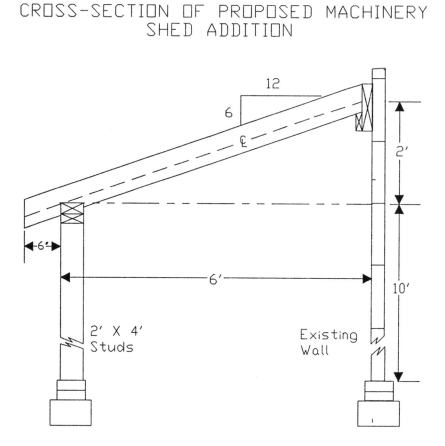

Figure 22-4. A drawing completed using a CAD program. (Courtesy, Donald M. Johnson, Mississippi State University)

interior designers, architects, landscape architects, engineering designers, and others.

These programs use mathematical formulas to draw blueprints and schematics, and diagrams to *scale*. The designs are saved to a disk, making revisions much more easily accomplished than with hand-drawn designs. Design databases are created so designers can easily search for designs to fit specific situations.

An important feature of CAD programs is the ability to include 3-D views, reverse angles, measurements, and other features without having to draw the designs separately. Some firms report a time savings of over 50 percent per designer when using CAD programs.

AutoCAD is the most popular CAD program. Other popular programs

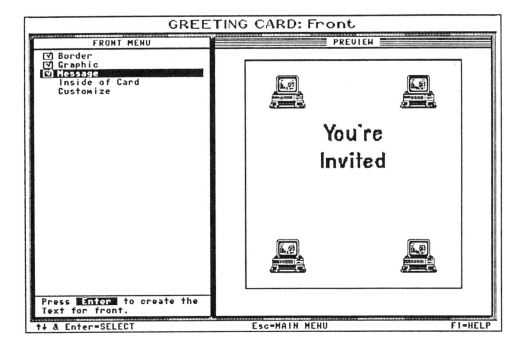

Figure 22-5. The greeting card production screen from Printshop, a canned graphics program.

include Generic CADD, MicroStation PC, VersaCAD, EasyCAD, AutoSketch, and FastCAD.

CANNED GRAPHICS PROGRAMS

Canned graphics programs feature an easy-to-use interface with a limited number of output capabilities. Line art can be imported into the program from disk files to improve the looks of the documents produced. Text and graphics can be incorporated into the same document.

Common outputs of canned graphics programs include banners, letterhead, posters, and cards (printed on one sheet and then folded by the user). Printshop, Print Master Plus, and PrintPARTNER are popular programs.

PRESENTATION GRAPHICS PACKAGES

Presentation graphics packages include several features in one graphics program. Most allow the user to draw figures, create various graphs using text and/or data, produce screen shows and 35mm slides, and much more.

Popular DOS versions of presentation graphics packages include Harvard Graphics, Freelance Graphics for DOS, DrawPerfect, and Applause II. Popular Windows versions include Microsoft PowerPoint, CA-Cricket Presents, Persuasion, and CorelCHART. For Macintosh computers, MacDraw and PowerPoint are popular packages.

OTHER GRAPHICAL PROGRAMS

Many other programs have the capability of including graphics in their regular outputs. The three primary types of software that can do this are desktop publishing packages, spreadsheets, and word processors.

Desktop publishing packages are designed to produce professional quality documents on a personal computer. These packages incorporate text and graphics into high-quality newsletters, brochures, and other documents that otherwise would be taken to a printing company. The quality of the printer and other output devices affects the quality of work that can be produced with these packages.

Spreadsheets that can produce graphics are rapidly becoming a standard in the business world. Quattro Pro was the first spreadsheet to incorporate the ability to produce presentation-quality graphics as part of the standard spreadsheet package. Windows-based spreadsheets have the ability to produce graphics that are comparable to those produced by the presentation graphics programs mentioned earlier.

Some of the high-end word processors, like Microsoft Word for Windows, Ami Professional, and WordPerfect, have included graphics support that allows them to function almost like desktop publishing packages. These programs include a standard library of line art that can be called up from a disk. Many painting/drawing packages and scanning software packages also have the capability of producing graphics that can be used by these programs.

FEATURES OF
PRESENTATION GRAPHICS
SOFTWARE

As mentioned earlier, presentation graphics software packages have numerous features. Some of the most important features are graph production, text charts, page orientation, drawing, importing graphics files, importing data files, screenshow building, and output choices. Each of these features is described below.

GRAPH PRODUCTION

Graph production refers to the package's ability to produce the three common types of graphs: pie graphs, line graphs, and bar graphs. The most

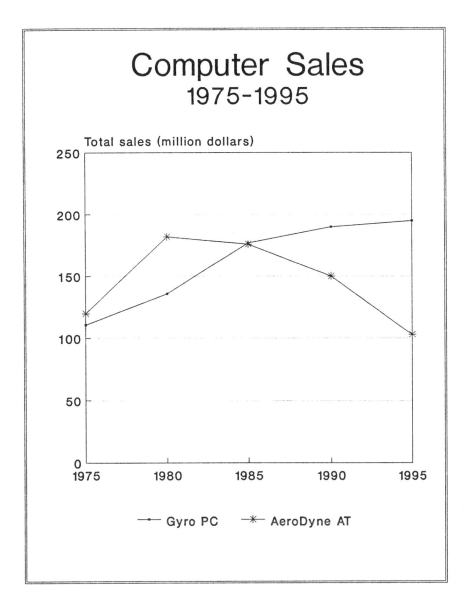

Figure 22-6. An example of a line graph (from Harvard Graphics).

standard way these are produced is for the user to specify titles and labels and then enter the data. Another way is to import data from a file on disk.

Pie charts are used to show parts of a whole and to make simple comparisons. Pie chart options include use of colors, patterns, comparison pies (two on the same chart), 3-D views, and breaking out of one or more pieces of the pie. Line charts are used to show trends and make simple comparisons. Bar charts are used to show trends, make simple comparisons,

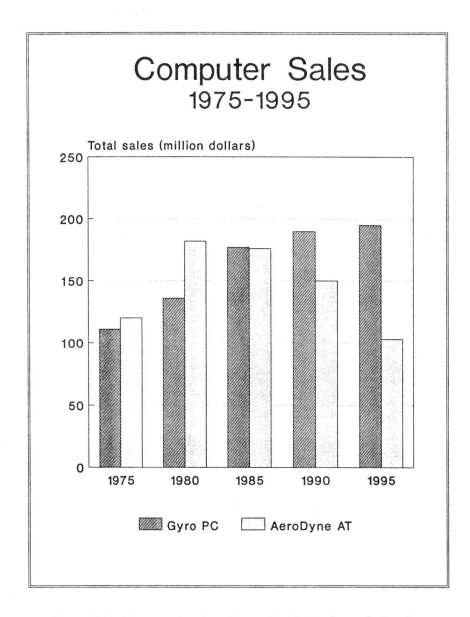

Figure 22-7. The same data from Figure 22-6 in the form of a bar chart.

and make multiple comparisons. Bar and line chart options include colors, patterns, spacing (for bar charts), labels for series, and labels for the x axis and y axis.

TEXT CHARTS

Every presentation graphics program has the capability of producing text only charts that can be shown on the screen or used as a master for an overhead transparency. Most of these programs allow the use of different typestyles in almost unlimited sizes. Text may also be incorporated into drawn charts and graphs. *Bullets* can also be incorporated into these charts.

PAGE ORIENTATION

Page orientation may be either portrait or landscape. *Portrait orientation* means that standard paper is viewed as 8.5 inches wide and 11 inches high. *Landscape orientation* means that standard paper is 11 inches wide and 8.5 inches high. These programs allow the user to switch back and forth between the two orientations.

DRAWING

Most presentation graphics packages have drawing capabilities similar to the drawing programs mentioned earlier. The user can draw and place geometric shapes, lines, and text. This feature is also used to edit imported line art and/or photographs.

IMPORTING GRAPHICS FILES

Most of these programs include a fairly extensive selection of line art files. These can be imported using the drawing screen. Many also can import files saved in one or more of the standard graphics formats.

IMPORTING DATA FILES

Data files usually contain numerical information used to create pie, bar, or line graphs. The data may be imported from an ASCII file, a spreadsheet file, or a database file. Once the data file is imported, the user

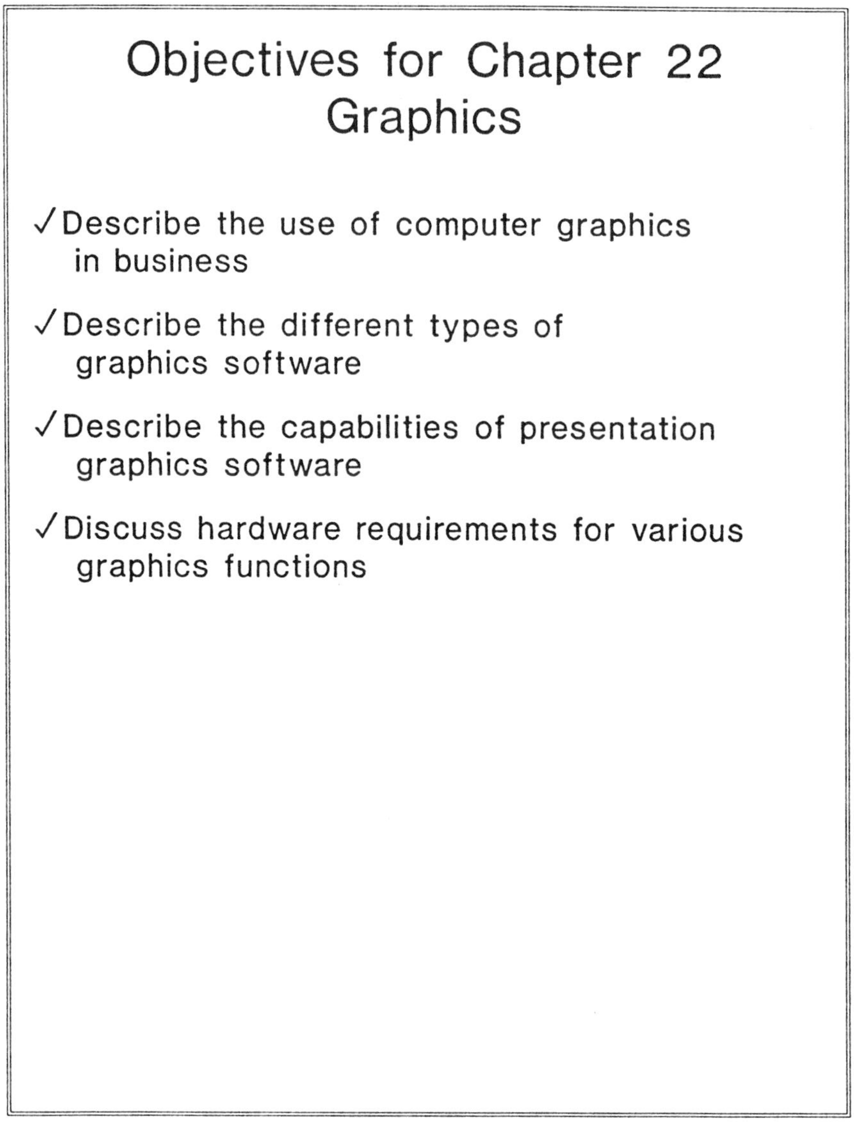

Objectives for Chapter 22
Graphics

✓ Describe the use of computer graphics
in business

✓ Describe the different types of
graphics software

✓ Describe the capabilities of presentation
graphics software

✓ Discuss hardware requirements for various
graphics functions

Figure 22-8. An example of a chart with bullet statements.

selects the type of graph and options and the chart is complete. Because the data is not re-entered, many possible mistakes are eliminated.

SCREENSHOW BUILDING

When a user has completed a file, he or she can save the file to a disk.

When this is done, the user has the option of adding it to the current screenshow. A *screenshow* consists of a group of chart files on a disk that have been specified for presentation as a group. Screenshows can be edited to add or delete files from the lineup. The user can customize the screenshow by specifying how one chart replaces the other on the screen and how the user indicates that it is time for the next chart to appear. Replacement of chart options include scrolling, replacing, fading and wiping. The user can select a timed presentation, where one chart automatically replaces the next after a specified time, or a key can be pressed to make the next chart appear.

OUTPUT CHOICES

One of the major features of presentation graphics programs is the different possible outputs that can be generated. Output may go to the screen or other viewing device, be sent to a printer, be sent to a plotter, recorded in a file for processing into a 35mm slide by a film recorder, or saved in a standard graphics format for use by another program.

Screen Viewing

In addition to viewing on the regular monitor, the computer can be hooked up to a projector which projects the images on a wall screen, or to a viewer that is placed on an overhead projector for viewing on a wall screen. The screenshow feature is often used in one of these ways.

Printing

Presentation graphics packages support a wide variety of dot matrix, laser, and inkjet printers. The resulting documents may be used in a portfolio or other document, or they may be used to make overhead transparencies. Most of the packages will allow the user to select the print quality (draft for first looks at a printout, high-quality for finished products). Of course, laser or inkjet printers with color printing capability are supported by these packages as well.

Plotting

A plotter is an output device that makes use of colored pens to draw

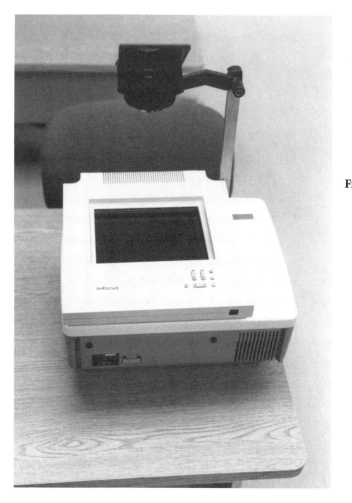

Figure 22-9. This viewer allows the user to send the output that normally goes to the monitor to an overhead projector for displaying on a wall screen.

graphs and line drawings on paper or transparency film. Most presentation graphics packages have drivers to support plotting of pie, bar, and line graphs. The result is a high-quality document that might be included in a report or shown as an overhead transparency.

35mm Slides

Most presentation graphics packages give users the option of saving files into a format to be made into 35mm slides by a film recorder. The slides may be produced in-house or sent to a custom slide service bureau such as Autographix or MagiCorp. These companies will develop the slide from a floppy disk.

HARDWARE REQUIREMENTS FOR COMPUTER GRAPHICS

To get the maximum benefit from a graphics program, a user must have a computer system that supports the software adequately. The most popular personal computer operating system for production of graphics has been the Macintosh system. If a business plans to produce almost exclusively graphics, a Macintosh is recommended. With IBM-compatible computers, the Microsoft Windows or OS/2 environments are generally preferred over DOS.

Graphics files that are bitmapped require a large amount of storage space. If the business plans to do a lot of graphics work, a hard disk in the 200MB range is recommended. A CD-ROM disk is also a good investment,

Figure 22-10. This scanner will create a graphics file containing an image of a page that it has scanned. It will use one of the standard graphics file formats such as .PCX or TIFF.

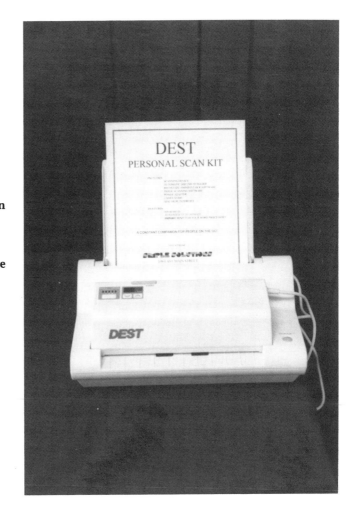

as many packages are starting to provide extensive graphics libraries on CD-ROM. For the same reason, the computer for graphics programs should have adequate memory—at least 4MB of RAM.

A scanner can save a lot of time by scanning graphics images (and text) from paper copies without having to redraw or retype them. The user should be sure that the scanning software will save scanned files in a standard graphics format that can be used with other applications.

CAD users will probably want to invest in a math coprocessor. The CAD software uses *floating-point calculations* for production of the designs and different views shown. A math coprocessor will cut the processing time almost in half for these programs.

A monitor for graphics production must be a color monitor. The Super-VGA standard is preferred because it will produce the sharpest images. Another consideration is the size of the monitor; at least a 14-inch monitor is recommended. Desktop publishing users often select a 17-inch monitor, so the entire page of a document can be seen in WYSIWYG format without scrolling.

The capability of the output device is often a limiting factor in the

Figure 22-11. A portable computer running Harvard Graphics. This computer is a wise choice for users who need to travel to different places and make presentations on a regular basis.

production of quality graphics. A laser printer will serve as a good general-purpose printer and also produce good graphics. Users should be aware of the memory available when purchasing a laser printer for graphics. Most laser printers come with 1MB of memory standard, not enough to produce high quality graphics using the presentation graphics packages. A minimum of 2MB of printer memory is recommended. Plotters and color printers should be considered by users who expect to produce a large quantity of graphics.

A film recorder is usually not necessary for most businesses. Slide services will produce high-quality slides, usually in less than two weeks.

One option that users may want to consider is buying a portable or notebook computer. For those users who have to travel and make presentations, a notebook computer combined with a viewer for an overhead projector works well. Newer notebook computers come with VGA monitors, docking stations with extra storage space, and CRT monitors.

CHAPTER QUESTIONS

1. What are presentation graphics?

2. Briefly describe the five major types of charts/graphs.

3. What is a standard graphics file format?

4. Briefly describe the five major types of graphics software.

5. Briefly describe five features of presentation graphics software.

6. What operating system(s) are considered the best for users who will be doing primarily graphics work?

7. Why do CAD programs run faster with a math coprocessor?

8. What type of user would benefit most from buying a portable computer?

Chapter 23

COMMUNICATIONS/NETWORKING

The combination of computer technology and communications technology has created an environment in which almost anyone can get information from almost anywhere. A farmer can check the current market prices of commodities using a computer and a database network such as AgriData. A tractor dealer can order replacement parts by punching a few buttons on a computer. A manufacturer in the United States can send a question to a supplier in Australia and have the answer back in seconds. Never before has the world been as connected as it is in the 1990s.

This chapter discusses some of the concepts that are important to computer communications and networking. Types of networks, requirements, operating systems, and communications software are presented.

OBJECTIVES

1. Define networking and data communications.

2. Describe components of a data communications system.

3. Describe the functions of networks.

4. Identify the types of networks.

5. Describe the configurations of local area networks.

6. Identify UNIX operating system functions and commands.

USING THE COMPUTER
AS A COMMUNICATIONS
NETWORKING TOOL

Data communications is the transfer of information from one computer to another over a communications channel. The primary method is by telephone lines, although use of other methods is increasing.

A computer *network* is a group of computers or terminals that are connected for the purpose of communicating. The primary purpose of networking is to share information—data files, software, messages—without having to physically carry disks or play "telephone tag" and to share hardware, such as storage space, printers, or microprocessors.

A single communications line directly connecting one computer to another is called a point-to-point line. If more than one computer is connected, it is referred to as a multi-drop line.

COMPONENTS OF A DATA COMMUNICATIONS SYSTEM

A data communications system has four major components: the computers, the transmission channel, the communications hardware, and the communications software. Computers have been discussed in previous chapters. The other three components are described below.

COMMUNICATIONS CHANNEL

The *communications channel*, also called a link, is the means or path by which the data gets from one computer to another. The three most

TERMS

analog signals	electronic mail	node
baud rate	Ethernet	protocol
bits per second (bps)	fiber optic cable	ring network
bus network	Internet	server
coaxial cable	local area network	star network
communications channel	(LAN)	terminal emulation
data communications	modem	twisted pair wire
digital signals	network	

common types of communications channels are twisted pair wire, coaxial cable, and fiber optic cable.

Twisted Pair Wire

Twisted pair wire is the type of wire used for telephone lines. Telephone lines are the most common communications channel used in data communications systems. This method of communicating is inexpensive, but data can be adversely affected by electrical interference, called noise.

Coaxial Cable

Coaxial cable is a high quality wire commonly used in cable television systems. This cable is not susceptible to interference and can transmit data faster than a twisted pair wire.

Fiber Optic Cable

Fiber optic cable is made of thin strands of glass, not copper wire like twisted pair wire and coaxial cable. The cable is light, inexpensive and does not have to be protected from moisture because it does not rust. Data transmission is very fast with no interference. Most data communications systems developed will use fiber optics. It is already replacing twisted pair wire in many locations.

Other Communications Channels

In addition to the three most common channels, three others are sometimes used in data communications systems. Microwave transmission will transmit voice and data signals over radio waves, but only in line of sight transmission. Satellite transmissions are used to transmit data in some instances, usually when long distances are involved. Wireless transmission uses radio waves or light beams. Some wireless transmissions work like a cellular telephone, while others use existing electrical wiring to transfer the radio signals.

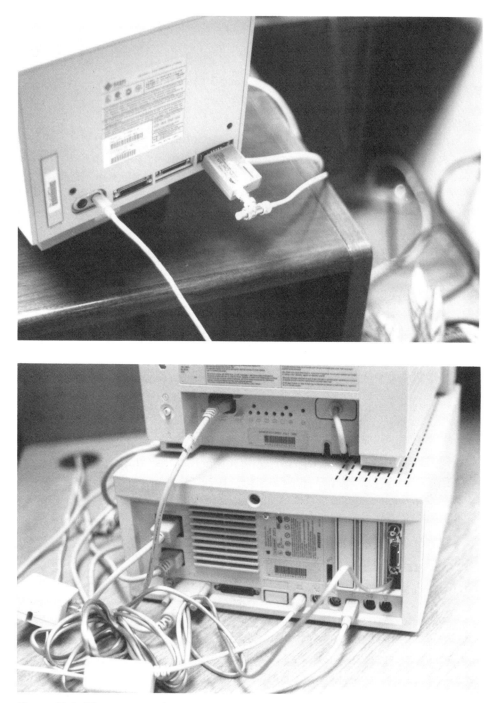

Figure 23-1. These two machines are both connected to a network. Above is a terminal
           connected to a mainframe with coaxial cable. Below is a Macintosh
           which is connected to a LAN by use of the twisted pair telephone wire
           (last connection on the right).

COMMUNICATIONS HARDWARE

Within short distances, up to approximately 1,000 feet, computers can be connected by wires from serial port to serial port. For further distances, special equipment must be used to convert the computer signal to a communications signal and then convert it back to a computer signal when it reaches its destination. A *modem* is the device used to do this.

The name modem is derived from the terms *mod*ulate-*dem*odulate. A computer communicates by sending *digital signals*, distinct electrical impulses. A communications channel, such as twisted pair wire or fiber-optics cable, transmits *analog signals*, electrical waves. The modem modulates (converts the digital signal to an analog signal) data going out of the computer. It demodulates (converts an analog signal to a digital signal) data coming into a computer. For two computers to communicate at long distances, both must have a modem.

Modems can be described in several ways: type of hookup to the computer, data transmission rate, and method of transmission.

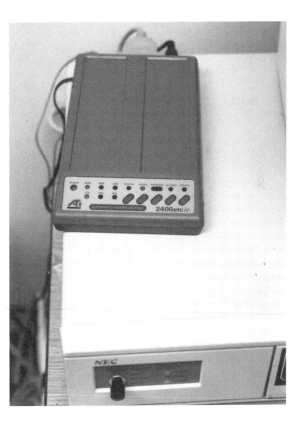

Figure 23-2. An external modem.

Modem Hookups

Modems are classified as either internal or external. Internal modems usually occupy an expansion slot in the computer and the communications lines plug directly into the back of the computer. External modems connect to the serial port of the computer. The advantage of external modems is that they can be disconnected easily and transferred for use with another computer. The disadvantage is that they take up room on the desktop and may get knocked off and damaged.

Data Transmission Rate

The data transmission rate of modems is expressed in either *bits per second (bps)* or *baud rate*. Bits per second is the number of bits per second that can be transmitted. Common speeds are 1200 and 2400 bps. The baud rate is the number of times the signal changes per second. One or more bits may be transmitted each time the signal changes. This means that the actual bits per second will be higher than the baud rate. A modem with a baud rate of 4800 may have a bps of 9600 or more.

Method of Transmission

The three methods of transmission of data are simplex, half-duplex, and full duplex. Simplex refers to transmission in only one direction. It is almost never used. Half duplex means that transmissions can occur in both directions, but not at the same time. Full duplex means that transmissions can occur in both directions at the same time.

COMMUNICATIONS SOFTWARE

Communications software provides the link between the user and the data being transferred. The three primary functions are telephone dialing, file transfer, and terminal emulation.

Telephone dialing simply means that the software is dialing the telephone number of the computer to be connected. Most software systems provide a dialing directory which the user can customize with commonly used numbers.

File transfer is the ability of the software to send and receive files over the communications channel. The software uses a standard *protocol* so both

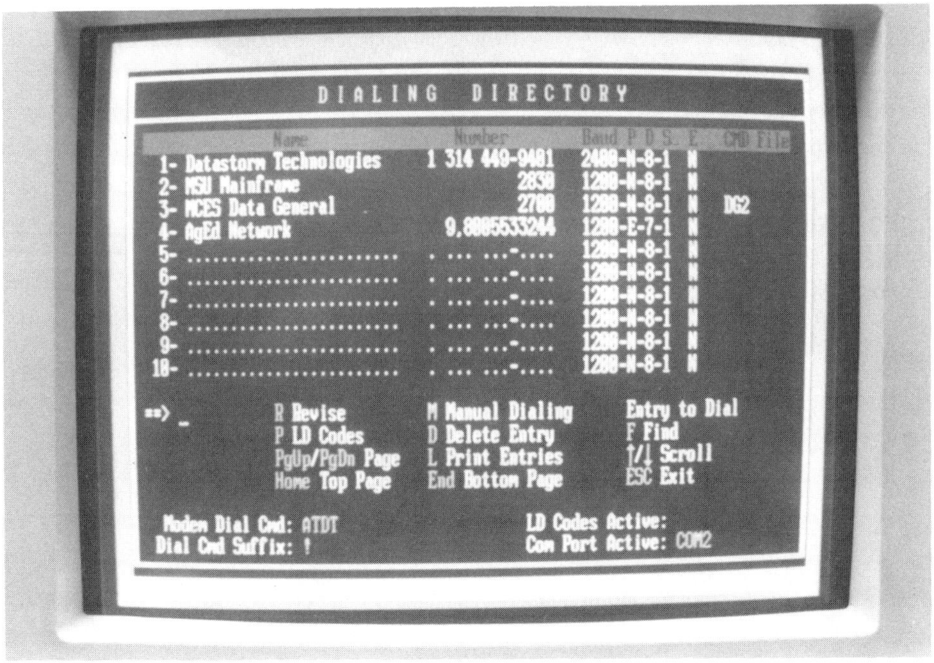

Figure 23-3. A dialing directory from the ProComm communications program.

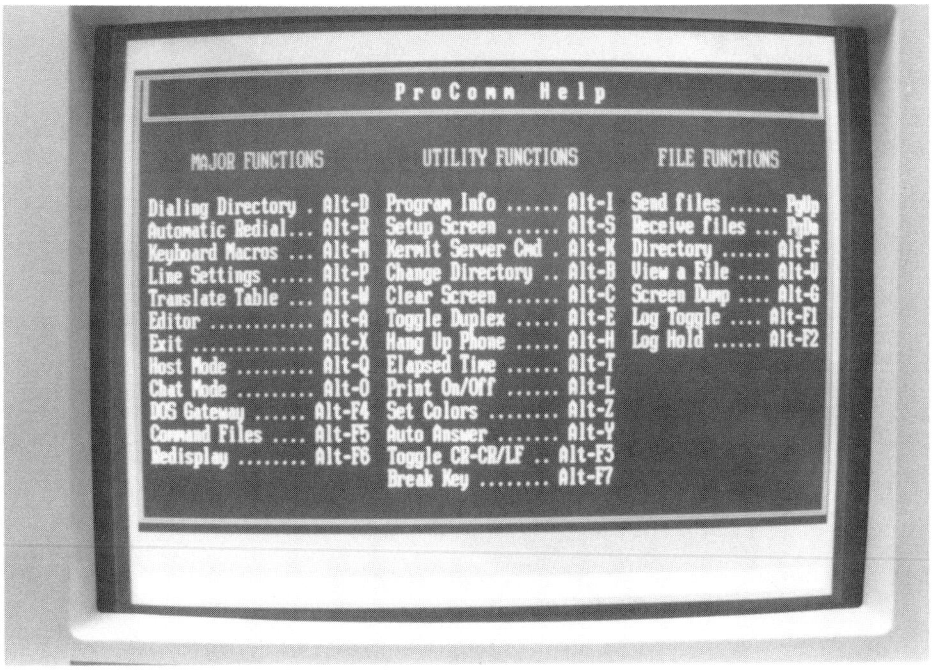

Figure 23-4. The help screen in ProComm. This feature makes the software package user friendly.

computers can interpret the file being transferred. Standard protocols for file transfer include Kermit, Xmodem, Ymodem, Zmodem and several variations of each.

When connected with some network computers, the personal computer may have to emulate a specific type of terminal in order to communicate. *Terminal emulation* is provided by the communications software. Some popular communications programs include ProComm, Telix, Smartcom, Qmodem, HyperAccess and Crosstalk.

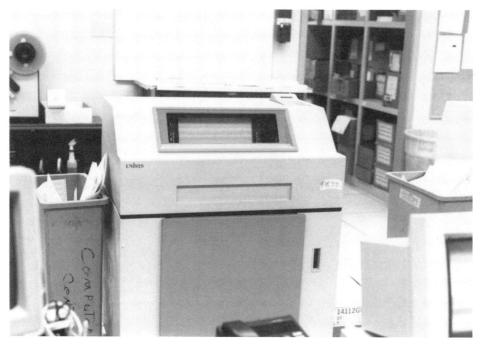

Figure 23-5. Many networks have a line printer, a heavy duty printer designed to handle the large printing loads of a network.

TYPES OF NETWORKS

Any time two or more computers are connected, they are considered to be networked. The two commonly used descriptions of networks are local area networks (LAN) and wide area networks (WAN).

LOCAL AREA
NETWORKS (LAN)

A *LAN* is a network of computers located in close proximity to each other. These networks usually are located in an office, building, or group of buildings. LANs are privately owned networks, usually with a series of personal computers connected via a communications channel, such as an *Ethernet* cable or telephone cord.

The functions of a LAN include sharing data files, sharing applications software, messaging (electronic mail), and sharing resources. The resources might include a network printer, usually a laser or a line printer, or a gateway. The gateway is a means of communicating with a different type of network outside the LAN.

Some LANs have a computer designated as a *server*. The server may be one of the personal computers or a minicomputer. A file server is used mostly for handling files and routing requests. A client server performs most of the processing for the computers on the network. The server must be operating for the system to work. It is important for the system administrator to keep a current backup of the disk storage on the server so system failure does not cause users to lose data.

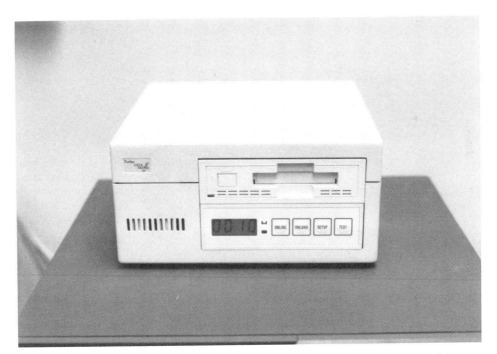

Figure 23-6.   This tape drive is used to back up files from the server every night.

WIDE AREA
NETWORKS (WAN)

A *WAN* is different from a LAN in two ways. It is spread out more geographically and it uses telephone lines or satellite transmission to communicate between computers.

WANs include commercial database networks that provide a variety of services for their users: CompuServe, Prodigy, America Online, GEnie, and Delphi are large commercial networks. These networks serve as information clearing houses and provide *electronic mail* services, catalog shopping, weather updates, and much more information. Users pay a monthly subscription fee and may have to pay more for special services.

Agribusinesses may benefit from subscribing to the AgriData Network, which provides agricultural market updates, agricultural news, and other services. Other on-line sources of agricultural information include the National Agricultural Library, USDA, and Doane's Agricultural Computing network.

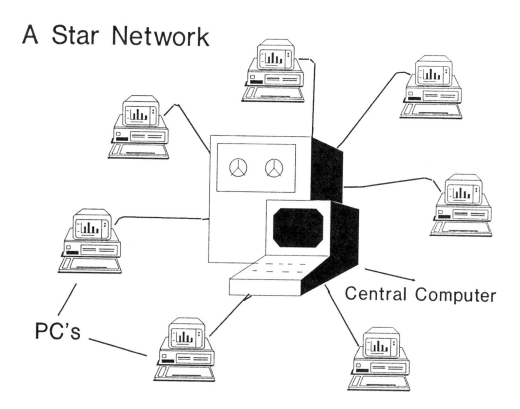

Figure 23-7.   Diagram of a star network.

CONFIGURATIONS
OF NETWORKS

Networks may be configured in a number of different ways. A *star network* has a central computer with various personal computers and/or terminals attached. This is an efficient configuration, but problems with the central computer shut down the entire system.

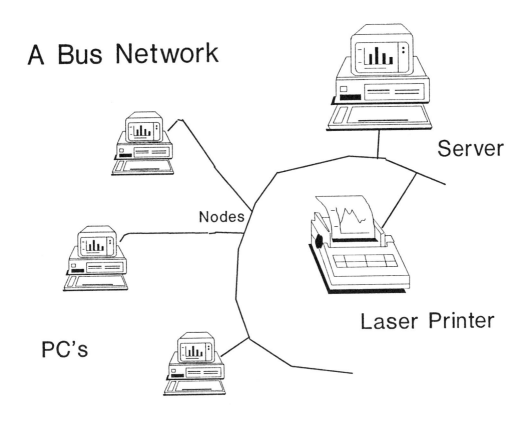

Figure 23-8. Diagram of a bus network.

A *bus network* has several computers connected on a single communications line. The duties of network management may be shared or one machine may be used as a server. Peripherals can be attached or removed without hurting the system. When one computer goes down, the rest are usually not affected. The majority of LANs use a bus configuration with an Ethernet networking system and high speed cable.

A *ring network* does not use a central computer or server. Data passes

A Ring Network

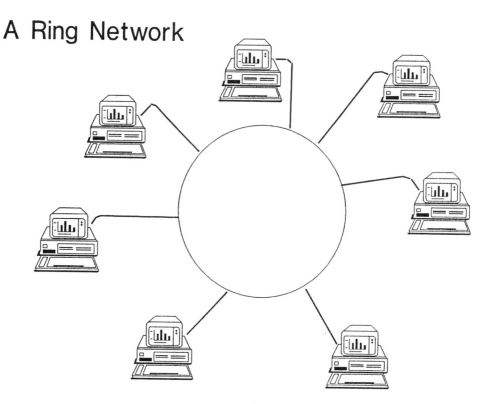

Figure 23-9. Diagram of a ring network.

around the ring through each *node* (computer) on the network. If one computer breaks down, the entire network is down.

THE UNIX OPERATING SYSTEM

As mentioned in Chapter 17, UNIX is a multitasking, multiuser operating system. As such, it provides password protection for users' files. These characteristics make UNIX a very popular operating system for networks.

When using UNIX, users should remember that it is case-sensitive, unlike DOS. UNIX commands are entered in lower case. Table 23-1 contains a summary of UNIX commands and the similar DOS commands as quick reference.

UNIX has three significant capabilities that make it popular for data communications: electronic mail, file transfer protocol, and telnet.

ELECTRONIC MAIL

The electronic mail function in UNIX allows the user to send messages to all other users of the network. If the host computer is connected to other computer networks, such as the *Internet* or Bitnet, then the electronic mail function in UNIX will allow the user access to these networks as well. Each user is assigned a network address, usually the same as their login code.

Table 23-1
A COMPARISON OF UNIX AND MS-DOS COMMANDS

Function	UNIX Command	MS-DOS Command
Directory listing	ls	DIR
Copy a file	cp	COPY
Delete a file	rm	DEL
Change directory	chdir	CHDIR
Create a subdirectory	mkdir	MKDIR
Remove a subdirectory	rmdir	RMDIR
Print a filel	pr	PRINT
Display a file on screen	cat, more	TYPE, MORE
Online help	man	HELP
Send and receive mail	mail	
Obtain info about other users	finger	
Chat with other user	talk	
Write a message to a user	write	
List active users	who	
Remote terminal login	telnet	
Remote file transfer	ftp	

A user's Internet address is his or her network address, followed by an @ symbol, followed by the address of the host computer. The host computer address is divided into three parts: the computer name, the location, and a suffix indicating the type of institution, all separated by a period. For example, John Doe at AT&T may have the following address:

jdoe@computer1.att.com

The com suffix means that he is at a company. An edu suffix refers to an educational institution and a gov suffix refers to a government agency.

FILE TRANSFER PROTOCOL (FTP)

File transfer protocol is the means by which UNIX allows users to transfer files from computers at which they have a password. Anonymous ftp allows the user to transfer files which have been left open by the person at the remote site.

Anonymous ftp is used by accessing the remote computer using the ftp command. The user types anonymous at the login and his or her full address at the password prompt. Only certain directories and files on the remote computer system will be available.

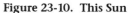

Figure 23-10. This Sun SparcServer functions as the central computer in a network at Mississippi State University. Note that it is connected to the Internet—the host address is isis.msstate.edu.

TELNET

The telnet command allows the user to login to a remote computer using a different operating system or a different version of UNIX. Some systems allow users to login and access bulletin boards, etc. Many educational and extension networks allow remote users to login to their systems and share or access information.

CHAPTER QUESTIONS

1. What is data communications?

2. What is networking?

3. What are the four components of a data communications system? Briefly describe each.

4. What does a modem do?

5. Which type of communications channel is the best?

6. What are the three ways of classifying modems? Briefly describe each.

7. What is communications software? What functions does it perform?

8. What are the two primary types of networks?

9. What are the three major configurations of networks?

10. Briefly describe the three major features of UNIX as a communications operating system.

Glossary

Account–a record of financial data pertaining to a specific asset, liability, income, expense, or net worth item

Accountant–a person whose work is to inspect, keep, or adjust accounts

Accounting–the practice of systematically recording, presenting, and interpreting financial accounts

Accounting procedures–the rules followed by an accountant or bookkeeper

Accounting software–ready to use recording system based on general accounting practices

Accounting system–a system assuring the availability of data required by management in reporting to owners, creditors, and other interested parties

Accounts payable–the money owed outside the business for purchases made on credit

Accounts receivable–the money claims due the business by others

Accrual basis–a tax reporting method recognizing income and expenses as incurred without regard for payment dates

Accumulated–the collective amount from all prior periods

Address–the relative or actual location of data

Administrative expenses–expenses incurred in the general operations of a business

Advertise–the presentation of the merits of products or services publicly

Advertising agency–a service organization specializing in preparing advertisements and advertising campaigns for others

Advertising campaign–a planned advertising program

Advertising copy–the words of an advertisement

Age Discrimination in Employment Act (1967)–prohibits discrimination because of age

Agent–a person or firm empowered to act for another

Aggregate—a group of insurance claims considered as a total, one

Agribusiness—those businesses that sell items to farmers for production; provide services to the agricultural sector of the economy; and businesses engaged in marketing, transportation, processing, and distribution of agricultural products

Alternate price—a different price for the same item or service

Americans with Disabilities Act (1992) and (1994)—prohibits discrimination in employment based on physical or mental handicaps

Amortized—to put money aside at intervals for gradual payment

Analog signal—electrical waves

Anticipated sales—expected sales

Application—a computer program used for a particular kind of work, such as word processing or database management; synonymous with computer program

Appraisal—the setting of a price or deciding the value officially

Arbitration—the settlement of a dispute by a person chosen to hear both sides and come to a decision

Artificial intelligence—simulated ability to acquire and retain knowledge

ASCII files—files organized using characters represented by American Standard Code for Information Interchange

Assess—to set an estimated value on property for taxation

Assets—all entries, tangible or intangible, on the balance sheet showing the entire resources of a business; properties owned by a business

Attitude—the posture assumed by the whole, good or bad feelings

Audit—a CPAs formal examination and checking of accounts or financial records to verify their correctness

Auditors—ones who examines or checks financial records

Audit trail—the controls used to prove accounts and balances

AUTOEXEC.BAT—a user created program containing a list of commands which are executed at setup

Back order—an order not yet filled

Backup—to make a spare copy of a file or disk ensuring that the information won't be lost if the original is lost or damaged

Bad debts—operating expenses incurred because of failure to collect a receivable

Balancing—finding any differences which may exist between the debit and credit side of accounts

Balance sheet—a financial statement summarizing assets, liabilities, and net worth

Bankrupt—legally declared unable to pay debts

Bar graph—a graph that shows numeric data as a set of evenly spaced bars

Basic coverage—the required coverage, such as liability and property damage

Baud rate—the transfer rate of data over a serial interface

Beneficiary—the designated recipient of the benefits of an insurance policy

Benefits—the amount payable by an insurance company to a claimant, assignee, or beneficiary

Binary logic—binary, meaning two, is the number of distinctions the computer can make on the signals it receives

Binding agreement—an agreement that holds one to a contract

Bit—short for binary digit, one signal represents open or closed (off or on)

Bitmapped font—each character is described as a pattern of dots in a specific point size

Bitmapping—the process of using pixels to generate a graphic of an image as a digital image

Bits per second (bps)—an expression of data transmission rate

Blocking—marking a section of text

Board of directors—a group of persons who manage or control a business

Bond—a certificate for a specific amount of money to be repaid on a specific date

Bonding—an agency guaranteeing payment of a specified sum to an employer through an insurance contract in the event of a financial loss caused by the act of a specified employee or by some contingency over which the payee has no control

Bookkeeping—the work of maintaining a systematic record of business transactions

Boolean "AND/OR" comparisons—"AND" means that the search will include every unit with a certain value in one field and a certain value in another, "OR" means that the search will include every unit with a certain value in one field or a certain value in another field

Booted—the procedure of what the computer does when started up

Break-even analysis—a level of sales at which revenues and costs are equals

Broker—a person hired to act as an agent in making contracts or sales

Budget—a formal written statement of plans for the future, expressed in financial terms

Budgetary constraints—limitations of planned financial commitment

Buffer—part of RAM used for temporary storage of data for input or output functions

Building permits—legal permission to build, renovate, or demolish a structure

Bullets—graphic symbols variable in size and used to highlight text

Business expansion—growth and enlargement in marketplace

Business graphics—using graphics to convey information to clients, management, shareholders, etc.

Business plan—a detailed method, formulated beforehand, for objectives and goals of the business

Business referral—a customer directed to a business by another

Business transaction—the occurrence of an event or a condition that must be recorded

Business venture—a business enterprise where there is danger of loss as well as a chance for profit

Bus network—several computers connected on a single communications line

Byte—collectively eight bits with 256 possible on or off combinations used to represent all of the characters

Cancellation penalty—the cost of invalidating a contract before it has terminated

Capital—the term applied to owner's equity in a business —assets owned and borrowed monies

Capitalism—an economic system in which all or most of the factors of production and distribution are privately owned and operated for profit

Cash basis—a tax reporting method recognizing income and expense when cash payments are made and cash receipts received

Cash disbursement—the money paid out of the business

Cash discount—a discount from the purchase price allowed a purchaser paying within a specified period

Cash flow—the way money flows in and out of a business

Cash flow problem—more money is being paid out than is being received by the business

Cash flow projections—estimates of cash receipts and cash payments for a specific period

Cash payment—money paid out of the business

Cash receipts—the money received by the business

Cash settlement—the money paid to settle an insurance claim

Catastrophic loss—any great and sudden disastrous loss

Cathode ray tube (CRT)—the most common type of monitor for personal computers

Cell—a unit of a spreadsheet formed by the intersection of a column and row that stores data

Cell address—the column and row label intersection

Chamber of Commerce—an organization established to further business interests

Characters per inch (cpi)—the number of vertical characters in an inch for a printer

Chart of accounts—the listing of financial accounts maintained by a specific enterprise

Chattel—a movable item of personal property

Chief executive officer—an administrative executive or general manager

Chief operational officer—an operating or managing officer

City zoning ordinance–a law that divides a city into areas where certain types of businesses may be located

Civic activities–actions for the good of the city or community

Civil Rights Act, Title VII (1964) & (1991)–prohibits discrimination based on race, sex, religion, or national origin

Claim–a demand to the insurer for payment of benefits under an insurance contract

Clients–customers or patrons

Coaxial cable–a connecting cable consisting of two insulating layers and two conductors

Code–command or function, as opposed to text

Coinsurance–a policy provision by which the insured and the insurer share the covered loss

Collateral–pledged assets to secure a loan

Collection agency–a business that specializes in collecting money due others for a fee

Command economy–an economic system in which most of the means of production and distribution are regulated or controlled by a centralized decision-making structure

Command files–files used by the operating system and utilities

Commercial software–software copyrighted by the owner and illegal to copy, other than to make backup copies for personal use

Commission–the pay based on a percentage of sales

Common stock–the ownership in a corporation which may receive dividends and allows a vote

Communications channel–a data communication path that allows data transmission to travel from its origin to its destination

Companion programs–associated programs required for certain functions

Company benefits–compensation in addition to salary, commission, or wages

Company policy–a principle, plan, or course of action followed by a business

Compensation–wages or remuneration

Competition–rivalry in business, as for customers or markets

Competitive pricing–charging the same or almost the same price for a product or service as competitors

Compilation–a gathering and putting together in an orderly form

Computer aided design (CAD)–software used to create original technical drawings

Concordance file–a list of important words

CONFIG.SYS–a file created when DOS is installed specifying buffers, location of files, etc. which can be user modified

Conglomerate–a business involved in a number of different and frequently unrelated activities as a means of spreading risk and being able to enter additional markets

Conservative–tending to preserve established tradition and to resist or oppose change

Consumers–those who buy goods or services

Contact person–a person who knows a business well enough to provide useful information

Contingent liability–a potential obligation that will materialize only if a certain event occurs

Conventional memory–the first 640K of RAM memory in a DOS based system

Conversion privilege–an opportunity to convert to a different insurance plan without providing evidence of insurability

Cooperative–a business owned and operated by and for the benefit of its members

Copyrighted–protected by an exclusive right to publication, production, or sale of the right of a work

Corporation–a business that is treated as a single entity (legal person) owned by shareholders

Cost–the amount spent in producing or manufacturing a commodity

Cost benefit–a comparison of cost to revenue

Cost-of-goods sold–the variable costs directly assigned to products sold

Covenant–a binding agreement made by two or more parties

Credit—the obtaining of goods or services with the agreement that payment will be made at a future date

Credit application—a form used to gather information in order to evaluate extending credit

Credit bureau—an agency that collects credit information for dissemination to members or subscribers upon request

Credit life insurance—term life insurance issued through a lender to cover payment of a loan or other obligation in case of death

Credit limit—the maximum amount of credit available per credit agreement or policy

Credit policy—the plan set forth in determining the availability of credit

Credit rating—a rating given based on past debt repayment and financial status

Credit terms—arrangements agreed upon as to when payments are to be made

Criteria—a standard, rule, or test by which something can be judged

Cursor—the pointer on the computer screen that indicates current location

Cursor control keys—arrow keys and others used to move the cursor around the computer screen

Customer relations—dealings to effectively meet the requirement of clients or patrons

Database—an organized collection of related information

Data files—files created within an application program

Daisy wheel printer—an impact printer based on technology available in many typewriters

Data—facts or figures from which conclusions can be inferred, information

Data communications—the transfer of information from one computer to another over a communications channel

Debentures—vouchers or certificates acknowledging that a debt is owed by the signer

Debts—obligations or liabilities to pay or return something

Debt service—the money needed to repay an obligation

Deductible—the amount of covered charges incurred by the insured that must be assumed by the insured before benefits from the insurance company become payable

Delegation—the appointing or assigning someone else to be responsible

Demand—the desire for a commodity or willingness to buy

Demographics—statistics dealing with distribution, density, vital statistics, etc. of populations

Depreciation—the reduction in potential usefulness of a fixed asset due to wear and tear or the passage of time

Device drivers—the software that interfaces a particular peripheral to the microprocessor

Dialog box—a window which appears temporarily to request information

Digital signals—distinct electrical impulses

Direct mail—mail sent directly to customers or potential customers, advertising or promoting a product or service, and soliciting orders

Directory—a computer index of files, programs, or other directories on a disk

Disability—a physical or mental impairment resulting from sickness or injury

Disclosure—a revelation or fact made known

Discount—a reduction from a usual or list price

Discrimination—dividing or distinguishing; to differentiate

Disk drive—a device used for recording and retrieving information on disks

Diversification—a business expansion by increasing the variety of things produced or undertaken

Dividends—sums or quantities, usually of money, to be divided among stockholders, members of a cooperative, etc.

Document—grouping of words, sentences, paragraphs, and pages

Documentation—supporting references

Document layout—positioning text or graphics in certain ways in a document

Dot matrix printer—prints characters composed of dots by pressing wires against an ink ribbon and onto the paper

Dot pitch—the physical size of the pixel on a monitor

Down payment—the money put down at time of purchase, with the balance to be paid later

Earnings—money made by an investment or enterprise; profits

Easement—a right or privilege that one may have in another's land

Economic downturn—a financial decrease in the economy

Economic risk—a chance for financial gain or loss

Economics—the science that deals with the production, distribution, and consumption of wealth

Economist—a specialist in economics

Economy—a system of producing, distributing, and consuming wealth

Editing—making changes in an existing document

Elastic demand—a sale that is sensitive to changes in price

Electronic mail—the ability to send personalized messages via personal computers from one to another

Emotional—appealing to one's emotions; feelings

Empathy—the capacity for participation in another's emotions or feelings

Employee incentive—a stimulating of employees to take action, work harder; motivation

Employee Retirement Income Security Act (1974) & (1982)—assures continuition of defined company benefits for employees

Entity—something that is separate and exists independently

Entrepreneur—a person who organizes and manages a business, assuming the risk for the sake of the profit

Entrepreneurship—assuming the risks of owning your own business

Enterprise—a business venture or company

Equal employment opportunities—employment without prejudicial discrimination including recruitment; hiring; termination; promotion; training; salary, benefits, and privileges; and working conditions

Equal Pay Act (1986)—a law that requires equal pay to women who perform the same tasks as men

Equity—the value of property beyond the total amount owed on it

Estate—assets and liability of deceased or bankrupt person

Estimate—to calculate approximately

Ethernet—a type of connection for a LAN communication channel

Ethical—conforming to the standards of conduct of a given profession or group

Excise taxes—taxes on manufacture, sale, or consumption of a commodity

Exclusions—specific conditions or circumstances listed in a policy for which the policy will not provide benefit payments

Executive Order 11246—a federal law that requires no discrimination in employment practices on basis of race, sex, color, or religion

Expenses—costs that have been consumed in the process of producing revenue

Expertise—the skill, knowledge, judgement, etc. of an expert

Extension—up to three characters in length preceded by a period (.) following the filename

External commands—commands not part of the operating system kernel and each has its own filename as a part of DOS files

Extrovert—a person whose interests are more in one's own environment and in others than in oneself

Facilities—buildings, special rooms, etc. that make possible some activity

Factory overhead—operating costs not associated with production

Family and Medical Leave Act (1993)—provides up to 12 weeks of unpaid leave per year for eligible employees

Family living costs—the money needed to sustain a family and pay their bills

Fiber optic cable—cable made of thin strands of glass which allows light to pass through

Field—a defined area which contains one kind of information, a labeled column

FIFO—first-in, first-out; a method of costing inventory based on the assumption that costs should be charged against revenue in the order in which they were incurred

File allocation table (FAT)—the address location of a file on disk recorded in table format

File—a collection of information that has been given a name and stored on a disk

File management—the techniques of organizing and maintaining data

Filename—the name assigned to a computer file

Film recorder—an output device to make 35mm slides from an exported graphics file

Finance charge—interest expense associated with credit

Financial accounting—preparation of reports of financial history

Financial restrictions—limitations placed on capital or assets

Financial statement—a balance sheet and income and expense summary for one point in time

Finished goods—goods in the state in which they are to be sold

Fiscal year—a 12 month defined business year for tax and financial reporting

Fixed costs—operating expenses that are not directly attributable to production

Fixed interest rate—an interest rate that cannot change during a specific period

Fixed-pitch font—uses the same space on a page for each character

Floating-point calculations—a system of arithmetic involving having the numbers expressed in scientific notation for calculations, e.g. .0005 becomes 5×10^{-4}

Floppy disk—a disk that can be inserted in and removed from a floppy disk drive; usually $3\frac{1}{2}$" or $5\frac{1}{4}$"

Font—a complete alphabet of a typestyle in one size

Font renderer—a scheme to interpret the mathematical formula of a scalable font in a printable character

Footers—printed at the bottom of each page

Forced sale—a sale of a business caused by a factor other than the owner's choice

Forecasting—estimating or calculating in advance; predict

Formula–a mathematical expression or calculation entered into the cell of a worksheet

FORTRAN–an acronym for Formula Translation, the first computer programming language to use English commands

Founder–the person who established a business

Franchise–the right to market a product or provide a service as granted by the owner

Freeware–freely-distributed software that has been placed in the public domain

Fringe benefits–compensation other than wages or salary made to an employee

Function keys–10 to 12 keys on a computer keyboard that perform specific actions in application programs

Funded–financed by a sum of money set aside

General ledger–the principal ledger, which contains all of the balance sheet and income statement accounts

General manager–a person that carries out the policies adopted by the board of directors and reports to them on the operations of the business

Gigabyte (GB)–1,024MB or 2^{30}

Goals–ends that one strives to attain

Good will–the value of a business in patronage, reputation, etc., over and beyond its tangible assets

Grammar checker–software designed to accomplish the editing and proofreading function

Graphical user interface (GUI)–a computer interface characterized by the use of a mouse to access its pull-down menus and icons

Graphics–the ability of the computer to display images

Graphics drivers–a program that translates operating system requests into a format that is recognizable by specific hardware

Grievances–complaints against a real or imagined wrong

Group insurance plan–the insurance provided, usually by an employer, on a group of people under a master policy

Hard disk—a magnetic storage medium, usually much larger than floppy disks, used to store files and software

Hardware—the equipment that makes up a computer; such as the keyboard, printer, monitor, mouse, disk drive, etc.

Headers—printed at the top of each page

Heir—a person who inherits or is legally entitled to inherit another's property

Horizontal integration—many individual business units involved, in which each one performs approximately the same type of marketing function over a relatively wide area

House organ—a periodical published by a business firm for distribution among its employees, affliates, etc.

IBM compatible computer—IBM clones, computers that use the DOS operating system

Icons—symbols representing computer commands

Image—the visual impression

Income and expense summary—Profit and loss statement-a summary of the revenue and expenses of an entity for a specific period of time

Independent agent—one who represents a number of insurance companies

Inelastic demand—a sale which is comparatively insensitive to changes in price

Inflation—an increase in the volume of money and credit relative to the supply of available goods, resulting in a rise in the general price level

Inheritance tax—a tax levied upon the right of beneficiaries to receive property

Inkjet printer—a printer using a spray nozzle to spray ink on the paper to produce a character or graphic

Input device—any computer peripheral that sends information to the computer's microprocessor

Insider information—secret or confidential facts known to only a few people

Installment purchase—a purchase made with all or part of the payment made at regular times over a specified period

Installment sale—a sale of property for which a series of payments is made over a period of time

Insurability—the acceptability by the insurance company of an applicant for insurance

Insurance—the protection by written contract against whole or part of a financial loss based on the happenings of specific events

Integrated software—several software applications packaged together and sold at one price

Integrity—the quality or state of being of sound moral principle

Interest expense—the extra cost involved when an item is purchased on credit or on money borrowed

Internal commands—those commands most commonly used by users and application programs which are loaded in RAM when the system is booted

Internet—a computer connected to other networks allowing the user access to these networks as well

Interpersonal relationship—of or involving relations between persons

Introvert—a person who directs interest or attention upon oneself

Inventory—any merchandise held for sale and materials used in the process of production

Inventory reconciliation—the verification of physical inventory counts and adjusting inventory records

Invoice—an itemized list of goods shipped or of services rendered

Job description—a listing of duties and responsibilities of an employee

Joint venture—a single undertaking of short duration similar to a partnership

Journal—a book of original entry for recording all transactions with an indication of the special accounts to which they belong

Kernel—the central core of information of the operating system resident in RAM memory

Kilobyte (K)—1,024 bytes

Label—descriptive text in a worksheet

Landscape orientation—printing across the page length

Laser printer—a computer printer using laser technology producing a page at a time

Leave of absence—permission to be absent from work for an extended period of time granted

Legal compliance—the complying with federal, state, and local laws

Lessee-one to whom property is leased

Lessor—the owner or landlord of a leased property

Leverage—an indication of the amount of total capital a business has access to in relation to the amount of equity or risk capital involved

Liability—a debt owed to outsiders

License fee—the money paid for the formal permission to do something

LIFO—last-in, first-out; a method of costing inventory based on the assumption that the most recent costs incurred should be charged against revenue

Limited Partnership—a partnership where one or more partners shares in financing but not in managing a business

Line art—artwork composed of line drawings

Line graph—a graph that represents numeric data as a set of points along a line

Line of credit—the maximum amount of credit to be extended, as to a borrower by a bank

Liquidated—closed one's business by collecting assets and settling all debts

Liquid crystal display (LCD)—images displayed by using a liquid crystal material between two pieces of glass

Liquidity—assets readily convertible into cash

Loan committee—the committee in a lending institution that recommends that loans be granted or denied

Local area network (LAN)—a series of personal computers connected via a communications channel which are located in close proximity to each other

Location—the position in space where a business is situated

Login—the process of signing on an on-line computer network

Logo—a unique symbol providing immediate recognition

Logout—the process of signing off an on-line computer network

Long-term liabilities—debts that will not be due for more than one year

Loss frequency—the number of times a loss occurs in a given time

Loss leader pricing—a technique used in retailing; an item is sold at or below cost to attract customers

Loss severity—the intensity or gravity of damage

Lower margin—the difference between selling price and cost where there is less profit than normal markup percentages

Machine language—the actual binary language the computer uses to function

Macro—one instruction which produces a series of action to be accomplished

Management—the person or persons controlling a business

Margin—the difference between cost and selling price

Margins—top, bottom, left and right blank area of page

Markdown—the reduction from the original selling price of an item

Market areas—areas from which a business hopes to attract customers

Market economy—an economic system based on private ownership of property and free enterprise principles

Marketing—a major specialized activity including physical distribution, pricing, advertising, or related activities

Marketing plan—a program for achieving your sales forecast

Market niche—a place or position in the market particularly suitable

Market penetration—the strength in a given market area or segment

Market pricing—establishing a price at which goods will change hands

Market research—the systematic gathering, recording, and analyzing data related to marketing

Market segments—classifications of customers into categories according to similar characteristics

Market share—that portion of the market area controlled or allotted to a business

Markup—the amount of increase in price over cost to provide a profit

Math coprocessor—a chip in conjunction with the microprocessor which may double its processing speed with math-intensive software

Megabyte (MB or Meg)—1,048,576 bytes or 2^{20}

Memory—the part of computer storage directly accessible to the microprocessor; usually synonymous with random access memory (RAM)

Menu—a list of choices presented by a computer program

Merging documents—the combining of two or more separate documents

Meticulous—extremely careful about details

Microchip—highly miniaturized integrated electronic circuits on a silicon chip often smaller than a dime

Microprocessor—the integrated circuit "chip" component within the computer that directly executes instructions

Microsoft Windows—an operating environment used with MS-DOS that is a graphical user interface with multitasking capabilities

Millions of instructions per second (MIPS)—term used to express microprocessor speed

Modem—a communication device that enables a computer to transmit over a telephone line

Mouse—a small hand-held device used to control a pointer on the computer monitor

Multimedia—a combination of various media; such as sound, graphics, animation, and video

Multitasking—an operating system's ability to concurrently execute more than one application

Near letter quality—a mode of operation in a dot matrix printer which prints each line two times making it close to letter quality

Negligence—failure to use a reasonable amount of care when such failure results in injury or damage to another

Nepotism—favoritism shown to relatives

Net income - Net loss—the net increase or decrease in capital resulting from profit-making activities

Network—two or more computers connected by cables or other means and using software that enables them to share equipment and exchange information

Net worth—equity, the difference between assets and liabilities

Node—any network station

Nonverbal communication—a message carried out by means other than verbal; body language

Numeric keypad—a separate area on the keyboard with the numeric keys arranged similar to a calculator keypad

Objective—something aimed at or striven for

Obsolete equipment—out-of-date equipment that is no longer useful

On-line time—the actual amount of time a user is signed on a computer network

Open account—the purchasing on credit

Open house—an informal reception to attract visitors to your business

Operating—conducting or directing the affairs of a business

Operating loan—a working line of credit to conduct or direct the affairs of a business

Operating system—the system program which controls the hardware and interfaces with user software programs

Optimist—a person who tends to take the most hopeful view of matters or expects the best outcome

Option—the right, acquired for a consideration, to buy, sell, lease, sign, etc., something within a specified period

Ordinances—governmental statutes or regulations

Organizational chart—a conceptual presentation of the areas of responsibility of the various people in the organization and the channels of communication

Organizing—grouping activities and people in the best possible relationship to get a job done effectively and economically

OSHA—Occupational Safety and Health Agency; federal agency that regulates safety in the work place

Output device–any computer peripheral that receives information from the computer's microprocessor

Overhead–the general continuing costs involved in running a business

Page description languages–programming languages that describe the placement and appearance of text and graphics on a page

Paid-in capital–the money invested in the business by owners

Parameter–value following a DOS command which tells the command where to perform its function

Partnership–an association two or more persons as co-owners of a business for profit

Par value–the nominal value of a stock, bond, etc. fixed at the time of its issue

Patented–granted a certain right or privilege through an official document

Patronage–regular customers

Peer–a person of the same rank, value, quality, or ability, etc.; an equal

Perils–exposures to harm or injury

Peripherals–input or output devices that connect to the computer's microprocessor

Permanent records–records lasting or intended to last indefinitely without change

Perseverance–persistence in doing something in spite of difficulties or obstacles

Pessimist–an individual who expects misfortune or the worst outcome in any circumstances

Petty cash–a small available cash fund for the payment of relatively minor purchases

Philosophy–the principles underlying conduct, thought, and knowledge

Physical distribution–transportation and storage function

Pie graph–a graph that compares parts to the whole

Pixel–the dots that can be illuminated on a monitor or printed creating a graphic or text

Planning–forward thinking about courses of action

Pledging—to present as security or guarantee

Point-and-click—a user interacting with a computer interface characterized by use of a mouse to access icons and pull-down menus

Policies—guidelines of principles, plans, and courses of action

Portrait orientation—printing across the page width

Posting—transferring to the ledger

Potential—that can, but has not yet, be possible

Precedent—a prior act, decision, or legal judgement that serves as a basis for justification of future decisions

Preferred stock—ownership in a corporation which guarantees a share in the profits and redemption privileges but without voting privilege

Premium—the amount payable or paid for an insurance policy

Preplanning—preparation in advance for doing, making, or arranging

Presentation graphics—includes the special effects of color, patters, illustrations, etc.

Present market value—a realistic selling price in today's marketplace

Preservation—the maintaining of and protection

Price—the amount in terms of money

Price sensitivity—a market demand easily affected by price

Prime interest rate—the most favorable rate of interest available on loans from banks

Priorities—rights to precedence over others

Probationary period—the time frame allowed testing or trial, as of a person's character, ability to meet requirements, etc.

Procedures—particular courses of action or ways of doing something

Procrastinate—to put off doing until a future time

Production—a series of activities guided by a set of procedures that result in a product or service

Program—a detailed set of instructions written by a computer programmer

Program file—a file used to operate an application program

Programmer—one who writes the detailed set of instructions for the computer to execute

Profits—sums remaining after all costs are deducted from the income of a business

Profitability—the kinds and amount of profit possible

Profit and loss statement—(see income and expense summary)

Promissory note—a promise to pay a specific amount of money and interest by a specified date

Prompt—where the computer user gives commands by typing them in

Prompt area—display area for the command line and entry/status line for an electronic spreadsheet

Property tax—a tax based on the value of real estate or other personal property

Proportionally-spaced font—varies the space given to each letter based on the width of the letter

Prospective—expected, likely

Protocol—a standard method for determining how and when to format and send data

Prudent—capable of using sound judgment in practical matters

Publicity—any information, promotional material, etc. which brings a person, place, product, or cause to the attention of the public

Public relations—the promotion of good will toward a business to create a positive image

Pull-down menu—a graphical user interface of commands or options which may be accessed with a mouse

Purchase order—the customer authorization to deliver the items listed or perform a specified service at the prices specified

Qualifying—determining if a prospect is really a potential customer

Quality—the degree of excellence a product or service possesses

Quantity discount—a reduction in the unit price of an item based on the number of units purchased

Query-by-Example—a technique relying on names and key words with some national characteristics used by most of the popular programmable database managers

Random access memory (RAM)—memory used by applications to perform necessary tasks while the computer is turned on. When turned off, RAM is cleared

Range—a cell or contiguous group of cells

Ratio—a fixed relationship between two similar things

Raw materials—unprocessed materials used in the manufacturing of other goods

Read only memory (ROM)—memory which can be read, but not modified

Realistic—tending to face facts

Record—a collection of the information for all fields on a single subject

Records—permanent or official notes

Regulations—rules, ordinance, or law by which conduct is regulated

Relational database—a database with common data between fields and records

Relocate—to move to a new location

Remitting—sending money in payment

Replacement cost—the cost of providing an item of equal or better value when replacing damaged property

Report—a collection of individual records in printed form

Reputation—character in the view of the public

Reserve—asset readily turned into cash, held out of use to meet expected or unexpected demands

Residual—the remainder left over after part or most is taken away

Resolution—the number of dots that make up an image on a monitor or scanner

Resources—something that lies ready for use or that can be drawn upon

Résumés—statements of a job applicant's previous employment experience, education, references, etc.

Retail—the sale of goods directly to the consumer

Retained earnings—the profits held in the business

Revenue—the gross increase in capital attributable to business activities

Review—a CPA's reexamination of a business's accounts and procedures based on the records supplied

Ring network—does not use a central computer or server, data passes around the ring through each node

Risk—the chance of injury, damage, or loss

Risk management—the planning for reducing the risk or transferring the loss through insurance

Read only memory (ROM)—memory which can be read, but not modified

Root directory—the base directory created when a disk is formatted

Sales forecast—an estimate of the sales that will result from a marketing plan during a specific future period

Sales manager—a person coordinating the work of sales people

Sales volume—the amount or value of sales made during a specific time period

Scalable font—each character is described as a mathematical formula

Scale—ratio between the dimensions of a representation and those of the object

Screenshow—a group of chart files on disk that have been specified for presentation as a group

Scrolling—allows the computer user to view the information ahead and back, as well as sideways

Search and replace—finding an equal condition and changing the data

Seasonal business—certain times of year when demand for products or services is much higher

Self-image—one's visual impression of himself or herself; self-concept

Semi-conductor—a substance used in transistors, rectifiers, etc.

Seniority—the status achieved by length of service in a given job

Server—a computer that provides disk space, printers, or other services to computers in a network

Severance pay—extra pay given to an employee who is dismissed through no fault of their own

Sexual harassment—the troubling, worrying, or tormenting of a person in a sexual manner

Shareholders—(see stockholder)

Silent partner—(see limited partner)

Skill—a great ability or proficiency

Small Business Administration (SBA)—a government agency whose purpose is to promote small business development

Software—the set of computer instructions that make the hardware perform tasks

Software piracy—software given to others without the permission of the copyright holder

Sole proprietorship—a single business owner responsible for management and policy with unlimited liability

Solvency—the ability to pay all one's debts or meet all financial responsibilities

Spin-off—the distribution to its shareholders by a parent corporation of the stock it holds in a subsidiary corporation

Spooling—temporary storage for information being output to a slower device

Spouse—one's husband or wife

Spreadsheet—a grid usually made up of 256 columns and 8,192 rows

Standard graphics file format—established formats developed for graphics files

Star network—a central computer with various personal computers and terminals attached

Statute of limitations—a law limiting the period within which a specific legal action may be taken

Stock—the proportionate share in the ownership of a corporation represented in the form of a stock certificate

Stockholder—one owning stock in a given company

Strategy—the skill in managing or planning

Structure—a manner of organizing

Subcontract—a secondary contract undertaking some or all of the obligations of a primary contract

Subdirectory—a group of files or lower child directories that contain related information

Subsidiary—a company controlled by another company which owns all or a majority of its stock

Suppliers—businesses furnishing a product or service to the business

Supply—the amount of goods or services offered for sale at a given time

Surveys—examines for some specific purpose

Switch—options as a part of a DOS command

System security—a procedure, usually through passwords, which limits access to computer applications

Target market—the most likely purchasers of a product or service

Taxation—the principle of levying taxes

Technology—a method, process, etc. for handling a specific technical problem

Template—a basic pattern for a spreadsheet

Terminal—the term used for a work station in a computer network

Terminal emulation—the imitation of all or part of one terminal by another so the mimicking device can accept the same data and perform the same functions as the actual device

Terminate-and-stay-resident (TSR)—application programs loaded into high memory at startup but not yet activated for use

Termination—the end of employment

Text features—commands that change the text from normal to text with special characteristics

Thesaurus—a list of synonyms and antonyms for a word

Time slices—period of time allocated by the operating system to each user

Trade association—an organization that serves the common interests of firms in the same business

Trade discount—a substantial reduction from the list price on the assumption the purchaser will perform part of the marketing function

Trademark—a distinguishing word, emblem, or symbol, or any combination used to identify a business

Traffic—the number of potential customers entering a business during a given period

Transactions—business deals or agreements

Transistor—a solid state, electronic device, composed of semiconductor material, that controls current flow without the use of a vacuum

Turnover—the number of times something is used during a specific time period

Twisted pair wire—a pair of copper wires, insulated, and twisted together, telephone line

Undelete—the ability to recall deleted information stored in a buffer in RAM

User-supported software—software that can be freely copied and distributed, but the user is expected to register with the author and pay a fee for using the software

User-friendly—the ease with which interaction takes place

Valuation—estimination of worth; appraisal

Variable costs—costs directly associated with production or service rendered

Variable interest rate—an interest rate that can change during a specified period

Vendors—businesses supplying a product or service to the business

Venture—a business enterprise where there is danger of loss as well as chance for profit

Venture capital—the funds invested or available for investment at considerable risk of loss in potentially highly profitable enterprises

Vertical integration—the performance of two or more of the marketing functions or steps in the marketing process by one business

Virtual memory management—the operating system increases available memory by allocating a portion of it to hard disk

Virus—a term for anything undesired that attaches to or corrupts files or programs in a personal computer

Virus protection—those utilities that scan disks for the presence of a virus

Warranty—a subsidiary promise or collateral agreement

Weighted average method—a method of costing inventory taking into consideration the number of units acquired and averaging the cost of each

Wholesaler—a business that specializes in assembly, breaking bulk, non-retail selling, etc.

Wide area network (WAN)—a series of personal computers spread out geographically and using telephone lines or satellite transmission to communicate between computers

Widow/orphan protection—elimination of the first line of a paragraph printed on the last line of a page or the last line of a paragraph printed on the first line of a new page

Wildcard—the asterisk (*) and question mark (?) when using DOS commands

Window—a rectangular area on a computer screen in which an application or document is viewed

Withholding taxes—earnings withheld from compensation and paid to governmental authorities

Workers' compensation—an insurance system covering employees for injury on the job

Work ethic—how an individual views work; usually viewed as honorable, necessary, and desirable

Working capital—the excess of current assets over current liabilities

Working conditions—those factors which have an impact on the attitudes, beliefs, ethics, health, and life style

Work in process—goods in the process of manufacture

Worksheet—an electronic spreadsheet grid usually made up of 256 columns and 8,192 rows in table format.

Value—a number entered into the cell of a worksheet

Zoning restriction—a section or district in a city restricted by law for a particular use

Bibliography

Agribusiness: An Entreprenurial Approach. William H. Hamilton, Donald F. Connelly and D. Howard Doster; Delmar Publishers, Inc., Albany, NY; 1992.

Agribusiness Finance. Gary T. Devino; Interstate Publishers, Inc., Danville, IL; 1981.

Agribusiness Management. W. David Downey and S. P. Erickson; McGraw-Hill, New York, NY; 1987.

Agricultural Marketing. Jasper S. Lee, James G. Leising and David Lawver; Interstate Publishers, Inc., Danville, IL; 1994.

AgriScience in Our Lives. Alfred H. Krebs, revised by Michael E. Newman; Interstate Publishers, Inc., Danville, IL; 1994.

Aquaculture: An Introduction. Jasper S. Lee and Michael E. Newman; Interstate Publishers, Inc., Danville, IL; 1992.

Biological Science Applications in Agriculture. Edward W. Osborne; Interstate Publishers, Inc., Danville, IL; 1994.

Careers in Agribusiness and Industry, 4th ed. Marcella Smith, Jean M. Underwood and Mark Bultmann; Interstate Publishers, Inc., Danville, IL; 1991.

Developing Computer Skills. Eric C. Egertson; Interstate Publishers, Inc., Danville, IL; 1989.

Economics: Applications to Agriculture and Agribusiness, 4th ed. Donald G. Chafin, Ewell P. Roy, Floyd L. Corty and Gene D. Sullivan; Interstate Publishers, Inc., Danville, IL; 1994.

Exploring Agribusiness, 3rd ed. Ewell Paul Roy; Interstate Publishers, Inc., Danville, IL; 1980.

Financial Management in Agriculture, 5th ed. Peter J. Barry, Paul N. Ellinger, John A. Hopkin and C. B. Baker; Interstate Publishers, Inc., Danville, IL; 1994.

Financial Management of Agribusiness Firms, Spec. Report No. 26. Frank J. Smith and Ken Cooper; Agricultural Extension Service, University of Minnesota, St. Paul; 1967.

Financial Planning in Agriculture. Kenneth C. Schneeberger and Donald D. Osburn; Interstate Publishers, Inc., Danville, IL; 1977.

Greenhouse Management for Flower and Plant Production, 2nd ed. Kennard S. Nelson; Interstate Publishers, Inc., Danville, IL; 1980.

Handbook of Agricultural Occupations, 4th ed. Norman K. Hoover; Interstate Publishers, Inc., Danville, IL; 1985.

Introduction to World AgriScience and Technology. Jasper S. Lee and Diana L. Turner; Interstate Publishers, Inc., Danville, IL; 1994.

Microcomputer Applications for Students of Agriculture. William G. Camp, Gary E. Moore, Richard M. Foster and Barbara Moore; Interstate Publishers, Inc., Danville, IL; 1988.

Nation's Business. U. S. Chamber of Commerce, Washington, D.C.; monthly.

The Retail Florist Business, 5th ed. Bridget K. Behe, Peter B. Pfahl and Charales E. Hofmann; Interstate Publishers, Inc., Danville, IL; 1994.

Index

A

Accounting software, 350-351
Advisory committee, 197-198
Aging accounts, 229-230
Agribusiness definition, 6
Approaches to management
    management by objectives, 37-38
    profit center management, 38-40
    SWOP management, 40-42
    SWOT management, 42
Audit
    financial, 57, 76-77
    management, 78-80
Availability of credit, 56-57

B

Balance sheet, 202, 204-205, 208-209
Binary logic, 244-245
Board of directors, 3-4, 30-31, 33
Bonds, 45, 53
Break-even analysis, 77-78
Budget projections, 202, 216-217
Bulk and packaged storage, 157-159
Business atmosphere, 10
Business graphics, 365-366
Business plan components, 92-93

C

Cash flow statement, 202, 215-216
Centralized control, 25-26
Characteristics
    of good directors, 30-31
    of good managers, 31-32
Commingling products, 171
Communications/networking, 274,
    383-397
    components, 384-385
    configurations, 393-394
    definition of, 383-384
    hardware, 387-388
    software, 388-390
    types of, 390-392
    UNIX operating system, 394-397
Competition, 92, 166, 184-185
Computer
    buying, 274-277
    defined, 234
    generations, 239-241
    history, 236-239, 242-243
    how computers work, 244-246
    memory, 245-246, 250, 282
        management, 310-311
        RAM, 245-246
        ROM, 245
    parts of, 246-268
        CD-ROM, 258-259
        expansion slots, 252-253
        floppy disk, 254-256
        hard disk, 256-257
        keyboard, 263-264
        microprocessor, 248-250,
          281-282
        monitor, 260-263
        motherboard, 248-250
        parallel port, 259
        power supply, 247-248
        printer, 264-268
        serial port, 259
        tape drive, 258
    start up, 288-290
Constraints to decision making, 10
Controlling, 14-15
Cooperative, 4-7
Coordinating, 14
Corporation, 3-4, 6-7
Cost of back order, 166
Cost of extending credit, 229
Cost of inventory, 165-167
Credit as a sales tool, 223-225
Credit cost, 57-58
Credit factors
    collateral, 226
    financial position, 225, 226